# Production & Consumption of Music

I0878403

This collection considers music within the spheres of production and consumption and pulls together an interdisciplinary collection of music studies from around the world, ranging from an ethnomusicological analysis of the condition of Tibetan music and its role within the Chinese state, the changing reception of anti-apartheid music by white musicians in South Africa according to new configurations of society and its memory of recent history, a lyrical exploration of jazz as a signifier of crime and other nefarious activities within film history, an analysis of how music charts and maps the social network and gender roles in Jamaica and a landmark commentary on how music consumption is framed by David Hemsondalgh. As opposed to other studies which explore music just in terms of its reception or its composition and distribution, this collection should make necessary reading for anybody interested in the wider nexus of music's existence and how it waxes and wanes with ideology, politics, gender, business and much more besides.

This book was previously published as a special issue of *Consumption, Markets and Culture.*

**Alan Bradshaw** is a Senior Lecturer in Marketing at Royal Holloway, University of London.

**Avi Shankar** is a Senior Lecturer in Marketing and Consumer Research at the University of Bath.

Previously, they were comrades at the University of Exeter from where this collection was hatched.

# Production & Consumption of Music

*Edited by*
**Alan Bradshaw and Avi Shankar**

Routledge
Taylor & Francis Group
LONDON AND NEW YORK

First published 2011
by Routledge
2 Park Square, Milton Park, Abingdon, Oxfordshire OX14 4RN

Simultaneously published in the USA and Canada
by Routledge
711 Third Avenue, New York, NY 10017

First issued in paperback 2014

*Routledge is an imprint of the Taylor and Francis Group, an informa business*

© 2011 Taylor & Francis

This book is a reproduction of *Consumption, Markets & Culture* 11.4. The Publisher requests to those authors who may be citing this book to state, also, the bibliographical details of the special issue on which the book was based

Typeset in Times New Roman by Taylor & Francis Books

All rights reserved. No part of this book may be reprinted or reproduced or utilised in any form or by any electronic, mechanical, or other means, now known or hereafter invented, including photocopying and recording, or in any information storage or retrieval system, without permission in writing from the publishers.

*British Library Cataloguing in Publication Data*
A catalogue record for this book is available from the British Library

ISBN 978-0-415-61206-7 (hbk)
ISBN 978-1-138-87046-8 (pbk)

**Disclaimer**
The publisher would like to make readers aware that the chapters in this book are referred to as articles as they had been in the special issue. The publisher accepts responsibility for any inconsistencies that may have arisen in the course of preparing this volume for print.

# Contents

# Introduction

Alan Bradshaw[a] and Avi Shankar[b]

[a]*School of Management, Royal Holloway, University of London, UK;* [b]*Department of Marketing, University of Bath, UK*

> Music is the water of life, whiskey of passion, it uplifts us, releases us, marks our joy and sadness, it is to live for and to die for, it caries the spirit of truth and freedom, it demands to be shared beyond the bounds of race and tradition.
>
> (Michael O Suilleabhain)

A principle agenda of *Consumption, Markets and Culture* relates to interrogating and collapsing distinctions between production and consumption. As previous Editor-in-Chief Fuat Firat passionately argued, the consumption–production nexus is a defining aspect of a modernity that alienates us from creative living and reduces art "into objects that acquire permanence to allow economic exchange and speculation toward monetary amassment" (1999, 289).

In such a context, the condition of music emerges as a sort of magical domain that can captivate audiences, provide cathartic and embodied experiences, and ground identities and communities, but also introduce us to rich exchanges between peoples while somehow both reifying and subverting power structures. Before the advent of recorded sound, music was the ultimate intangible experience rooted to time and place, simultaneously created and destroyed, produced and consumed. Even after the advent of recording technologies, Jacques Attali notes how music simultaneously exhibits three dimensions of human works: "joy for the creator, use-value for the consumer and exchange-value for the seller" (1985, 9); and as the musician may be creator, consumer and seller at once, music can be thought of as a social model in which consumption and production co-exist and are mutually constitutive. Beyond this nexus, Attali theorizes the interferences and dependencies between society and its music; music as ordering of noises is understood as a demonstration of the very possibility of society and as harbinger of future orders and a negotiation of power.

In agreement with Attali, the goal of this special issue is to locate music both within and beyond such consumption–production nexuses. The Attalian challenge is no less than mapping dependencies between societal power and its music and to understand the act of making and listening to music as a production and consumption of social meaning. We are delighted how the contributing authors have risen to the challenge and how the articles found in this special issue all locate music as a point through which ideology, state, crime and community values all intersect with personal identities, subversion and relationships. An important aspect of this journal relates to its inter-disciplinarity; hence herein we find ethnomusicology, film studies, sociology and consumer research studies. This is an issue that, we are confident, provides excellent documentation of the wider theoretical and methodological ramifications of music within consumption, markets and culture.

The special issue begins with a conceptualization of how music allows us situate relationships within Jamaica via Barbara Olsen and Stephen Gould's paper on lovemaps. Rather than freely floating texts, Jamaican dancehall is demonstrated as embedded within a rich fabric of sexual and romantic relationships that reveal a tapestry of Jamaican life. Following from this is the outcome of Anna Morcom's extensive travels through Tibet where she reminds us of the highly charged political nature of music and describes the problematic production of Tibetan music within a state-controlled market conscious of the subversive potential of music. From there, we move to South Africa and to Michael Drewitt's fascinating description of the attempts to create a retro-market for anti-apartheid music created by white musicians during apartheid. Just as the original subversive recordings were initially ignored by South African broadcasters, the attempts to re-launch the music are demonstrated to be almost as difficult because the role of white anti-apartheid movements jars with emerging dominant discourses of black resistance creating an unusual branding context.

The links between music and criminality are next explored via Morris Holbrook's description of how jazz is semiotically deployed in film soundtracks to advance plots in the crime film genre. Last, but certainly not least, David Hesmondhalgh draws upon empirical research to argue against what he takes to be the optimistic trend of positing a generally positive relationship between music, emotion and self-identity and calls for a more critically reflexive understanding.

The six papers that we are publishing were selected from the 22 that we received and that went into the review process. We would like to thank all the reviewers for their conscientious and considerate responses. Our selection of papers are exciting reviews of important conceptual issues relating to the production and consumption of music which, we hope, will contribute to wider discussions of music more generally within our field.

## References

Attali, Jacques. 1985. *Noise: The political economy of music.* Minneapolis: University of Minnesota Press.

Firat, Fuat A. 1999. Rethinking consumption. *Consumption, Markets and Culture* 3, no. 4: 283–95.

## Extra acknowledgements

We wish to acknowledge the support of Fuat Firat and Jonathan Schroeder. We also note the accompanying special session that was presented at the 2007 European Association for Consumer Research conference in Milan and included contributions by Taçli Yazicioglu, Linda Scott and Robin Canniford as well as the rocking sax jam of the great Dougie Brownlie.

# Revelations of cultural consumer lovemaps in Jamaican dancehall lyrics: An ethnomusicological ethnography

Barbara Olsen[a] and Stephen Gould[b]

[a]*School of Business, State University of New York at Old Westbury, New York, NY, USA;*
[b]*Department of Marketing, Baruch College, The City University of New York, New York, NY, USA*

We believe that dancehall music's more sexually explicit lyrics, labeled "slack" and maligned as evocatively misogynist, homophobic and xenophobic, mirror historically discordant social and economic tensions that entangle men and women in contested couplings, and thus render sexuality an instrument of socioeconomic power. Applying an ethnomusicological analysis, this paper fills a void by situating the slack Jamaican dancehall/ DJ lyrics within a revitalizing indigenization socialization perspective. By probing the cultural roots of this increasingly popular yet disparaged musical tradition that disturbs moral etiquette, we hear sexual bravado and counsel on love that betray important gender codes. For a particular social class, gender socialization nurtures a *cultural consumer lovemap* inscribed by a harsh economy during a particular point in time.

## Pre-mix

The quest to understand people's lived experiences through musical production and consumption is a recent, but under-explored, research pursuit. Frith suggests because "music is now the soundtrack of everyday life" (2003, 93), more research should be collected to understand why "particular music gets particular attention at particular moments, and how these moments are, in turn, imbricated in people's social networks" (101). Similarly, Negus, albeit working on the British music industry, asks that researchers question historically inscribed power dynamics exercised by cultural intermediaries acting as gatekeepers for entertainment production (2002, 512). At the individual level, music has become a means to interpret one's life experiences and validate "identity or sense of self" in a process Shankar calls "grounded aesthetics" (2000, 27–28). We also use popular music as our emotional jukebox accommodating transformations of self, while it also influences concomitant changes in social values. Toward this end, we apply an ethnomusicological analysis to extend earlier ethnographic research that situated dancehall/DJ music as a mirror of life experiences (Olsen and Gould 1999). We explore the multiple metaphorical meanings of this music as we understand them. Rice found a meaningful application for the metaphors "music as art, as entertainment, as emotional expression, as social behaviour, as commodity, as referential symbol and as text for interpretation" in his study of Bulgarian music (2001, 23). McClary, at the forefront of interpreting "gendered metaphors" in the "new musicology" claims that music is indispensably equipped to convey "the organization of sexuality, the construction of gender, the arousal and channeling of desire" because it communicates seemingly independent "of cultural mediation" (2002, x). She continues:

> It is often received (and not only by the musically untutored) as a mysterious medium within which we seem to encounter our "own" most private feelings. Thus music is able to contribute heavily (if surreptitiously) to the shaping of individual identities: along with other influential media such as film, music teaches us how to experience our own emotions, our own desires, and even (especially in dance) our own bodies. For better or for worse, it socializes us. (53)

We concur with Titon that "Ethnomusicologists … invoke a cultural relativism in which all musics have a legitimate claim to be understood: first in the terms that their own culture understands them, and then in terms of their contribution to our understanding of music as a worldwide phenomenon" (2003, 172). We probe DJ dancehall and slack genres for metaphors "music as art, as entertainment, as emotional expression, as social behaviour, as commodity, as referential symbol and as text for interpretation" as did Rice (2001, 23). We also explore socio-historical processes contributing to a blueprint (Holt 1995) for class-gender defined relationships heard in "slack" song lyrics. As slack means "vulgarity" (Francis-Jackson 1995, 48), we regard it sexually. The English-Jamaican definition of slack leans toward female moral degeneracy, that contests "conventional definitions of law and order; an undermining of consensual standards of decency…[and] …challenges the rigid status quo of social exclusivity and one-sided moral authority valorized by the Jamaican elite" Cooper (2004, 4). This has historical connections.

We find dancehall and its slack variant are part of the African continuum whereby people of the Diaspora celebrate communication in bouts of rhyme or in solo exhibiting brilliance, which Abrahams (1983) discovered in the "man-of-words" across the West Indies. In the process of creolization, local music combines multiple African tribal, European and other immigrant musical traditions originally brought together in the context of plantation slavery where music and dance were a means of preserving tradition as well as creating new forms of entertainment. Bilby says that musically:

> Not only the centrality of drumming and percussion, but also a number of stylistic features – such as the close interaction and communication between musicians and dancers, as well as the presence of a "metronome sense," overlapping call-and-response singing, off-beat phrasing of melodic accents, and occasionally polymeter – reveal the African origins of these traditions. (1985, 186)

Jamaican music then, is a most profound conversation with history. It incorporates, especially in slack lyrics, the playful articulation of an erotophilic culture reminiscent of the "…songs sung at slave dances" that were often "satirical vehicles, commenting on, and often ridiculing, the behavior of local personages" (185). Sex talk in lyrics reproduces authority and refines gendered metaphors over time.

Cross-cultural ethnological research with contemporary societies and inference from archaeological records, finds that "music and dance are inseparable" (Levitin 2006, 257). Historically, music has been a participatory event engaging the body with rhythm or added hand clapping and vocalizations as it encourages social bonding (258). Levitin claims scientific evidence corroborates "the evolutionary origins of music… developed through natural selection as part of human or paleohuman mating rituals" (246). Quoting Darwin in

*The Descent of Man*, "musical notes and rhythm were first acquired by the male and female progenitors of mankind for the sake of charming the opposite sex" (249), Levitin thus proposes that music's function is perhaps to attract a mate. His analysis of musicians' sexual proclivity leads to a love of sex. "The number of sexual partners for rock stars can be hundreds of times what a normal male has" (252). Musical ability and expression is one such way to advertise sexual availability, and mental and physical fitness.

Our theoretical analysis has been informed by years of fieldwork in Jamaica by the first author, a female anthropologist, who established a home there in 1970. She and her ex-husband lived near a newly emerging town where neighboring family networks became an extended family in the field. In the 1980s, she began collecting life histories. Regarding sex and love very little changed from one generation to the next. Love stories from respondents (renamed Clive, Duncan, Eunice, Gladstone, Glenda and Zoe), during fieldwork were influenced by a shared intergenerational experience (see Olsen 1995, 1997, 2003, 2005). Their retrospection illuminates music as metaphor for emotion, social behavior and interpretative text. Lyrics drive the heart of this paper because they resonate poignantly with the life histories captured in the field. Economic development was uneven, and it framed everyday life experiences. Few we knew would benefit from the wealth that tourism brought. For instance, on one visit:

> I wondered how tourism could survive at all in such a hostile psychological climate. I wondered why were the people so bitter? Amidst the economic depression, there was a party atmosphere always accompanied by music either from the radio or cassette deck playing traditional reggae or a new variant called DJ, named for a disc jockey talking over the music. After I actually listened to some of the lyrics, I realized another layer of consumption was going on. (Journal entry, July 1987)

While Jamaican DJ musicians (often used synonymously with dancehall) inscribe this socio-economic emic dissonance experienced within their own culture, Borgerson and Schroeder found a different situation in Hawaii:

> [Most Hawaiian] popular songs were written by white tunesmiths and were produced by mainlanders, though the liner notes attempt to represent the music as authentically Hawaiian by focusing on the use of Hawaiian instruments, musicians, and song lyrics that invoke the natural qualities of an island paradise. (2003, 226)

This packaging of a national "musical identity, provides a performative example of what has been called 'sonic branding'" (220). However, within this branding, the authors discovered sexist and racist stereotypes inscribed as national identity. Sonic branding is germane to the evolution of every country's national identity especially as musical genres are appropriated abroad. Jamaica is a case in point.

For our goals in this paper, we frame our ethnomusicological analysis by tracing DJ/dancehall and the slack tradition as a continuum within the evolution of Jamaican music. We consider the cultural role of music as a process of indigenization that embeds cultural codes in lyrics that facilitate a feedback loop for social reproduction. We continue with a probe of particular Jamaican socialization practices in an economic environment that produces and reproduces the material nexus for kin and gender relationships influencing a uniquely indigenous lovemap as a class and gender blueprint heard in the music lyrics. Throughout the paper we apply an indigenization perspective of socializing practices heard in the music lyrics that are elaborated by ethnographic reflection. Regarding globalization and world music, we suggest that future research incorporate ethnomusicological analysis with an indigenization perspective to interpret lovemaps where musical expression is localized in lyrical form.

## Riddim (rhythm)

"'The lyrics you can analyze – The riddim you must feel'" (Wayne in Chang and Chen 1998, dedication page). An indigenization approach interprets music as an evolutionary expression of everyday life informed by power dynamics in cultural history and consumed by local communities for whom its metaphors represent salient reflexive and projective experiences. Similar to finding the lived experience in music via "grounded aesthetics" (Shankar 2000), regarding indigenization, Gaunt demonstrates how hip-hop music is influenced by the sounds produced in young black girls' games such as double-Dutch jumping rope, cheering and call-and-response-rhymed verse. Her observations locate "the sexual politics of power and gender at work in musical performances" (Gaunt 2006, 11), where the music, beat and rhythm of the girls' games are appropriated by males for hip-hop (183), "initiating the textures that inspire the music" (2). She coined the formula that produced these sounds "oral-kinetic etudes." Such "etudes" emerge from Jamaica's musical history.

The primary ethnomusicological influence in Jamaica is its syncretic African-creole musical composition from multiple sources (Bilby 1985). Plantation work songs influenced the call-and-response style where a chorus responds to a leader. Bilby also found "some digging songs that sound predominantly African, with their short choral litanies and high syncopated melodies, and others whose melodic structure and use of part-singing based on European harmony attest to their European background" (1985, 196). African-influenced Kumina, Pocomania and Revival religious traditions combine African drumming with Christian church hymns and provided the sonic inspiration for the Rastafarian rhythm that informs contemporary reggae music (Simpson 1955). Chang and Chen claim "nearly all budding Jamaican singers got their start in the 'clap hand' churches," and when combined with Pocomania's "ecstatic exuberance," Jamaican music was able to evolve a very unique beat (1998, 27–8). The African percussion of "buru" (sometimes also associated with Kumina), with three drums, rattles and scrapers, emerges in slavery as work songs from the center of the island. By the twentieth century, as rural musicians moved to Kingston in the 1940s, buru evolves into a form called "nyabingi" played by Rastafarians (Bilby 1985, 188). At this time, the buru beat also combines with Trinidadian calypso and contributes to a new genre called mento. In the next decade, ska emerges as a totally new Jamaican sound borne from a blend of US rhythm and blues mixed with the Revival religion's more powerful beat. Ska contributes to rocksteady with a slower US "soul" tempo heard on radio carrying new sounds from the US – Sam Cooke, the Drifters, the Coasters, and Fats Domino – the music of rhythm and blues and early rock and roll. Then, by the late 1960s, reggae, also informed by its predecessors, emerges with distinct mento and Rasta nyabingi drum-beat – influenced by African buru drums and Kumina religious sounds (Bilby 1985, 206). Variations in tone and syncopation offer hypnotic background for the melody.

Sound systems since the late 1940s and 1950s accompanied dances and venues to hear music often too profane for radio. As electronic sophistication evolved, they later incorporated 300-watt amplifiers and between five and 10 speakers. Hebdige calls these systems "large mobile discotheques" (1994, 62). These sessions took place in halls and in back yards. Associated with the sound system style of presenting music to its listening and dancing audience was "talking over" the music provided by a DJ/disc jockey/master of ceremonies, who engineered the musical venue. DJ forerunners, Duke Reid and Prince Buster, also produced Jamaican artists on records for play on their own sound systems and would "talk over" that music into the microphone offering their own personal insights to heighten the message of the song (Hebdige 1994, 83). Francis-Jackson claims that dancehall music stems from the 1960s, but since the 1980s, it has been "usually referred to as 'Hardcore Reggae'" (1995, ii). This is due to a change in the newer sound produced by innovators using "new technology like drum machines, synthesizers, and samplers that allowed … more densely textured riddims" characteristic of 1970s dub sound. However, its songs also transformed:

> from a strict reliance on recycling classic reggae instrumental tracks – so called Studio One riddims – to ones that drew on the rhythms of Pocomania and Kumina, two Afro-Jamaican sacred forms, and musical forms such as mento and buru. The distinctive drum pattern, two-chord melodies, and electronic overdubs of these songs have become the distinguishing markers of what is referred to as 'hardcore dancehall,' as distinct from early dancehall-style musical arrangements that used live musicians in the studio. (Stolzoff 2000, 106)

In contemporary Jamaica, it is both the music and the words in combination that mediate the social metaphor. Sonic meaning is communicated by intonation using the voice as an instrument. "Deejays and rappers live or die by the timbre of their voice and the way their lyrics flow" (Walker 2005, 253), creating distinguishing effects. Walker credits Shabba Ranks for lowering "the pitch of deejaying to a gruff bassy standard" for contemporary DJ vocalization (248). Exceptions exist in the "singjoy style" of artists like Super Cat and U-Roy who use melody to carry their lyrics (253).

## Original cut

As Jamaican music evolved, the Rastafarian consciousness exemplified in reggae music expressed the need for social change, cooperation and a new world order based on brotherly love. This was the theme of British and American popular music culture in the 1960s (Platoff 2005) and of Bob Marley and the Wailers, especially in the 1970s. The source of inspiration for social change was a global youth-oriented transformation in consciousness. In Jamaica, while a conscious stream continues, other factors began to influence its sonic and lyrical sentiments. Hebdige reminds us:

> The older djs… talk over traditions had always been partly rooted in the church, where "speaking out" and "bearing witness" are part of normal worship. Slack style undermined these traditions. In Seaga's Jamaica Inc, sex, money, flash and nonsense have tended to become the new religion of the airwaves. (1994, 125)

During the 1980s, it was mean "slack" lyrics that seemed to slander women that intrigued the first author. In this paper, we answer lyricist Shabba Ranks's query in his song "Where Does Slackness Come From?" (1991) and venture beyond Lovindeer's answer in his song title "Man Shortage" (1999). Bilby proposes that while slack was popularized by calypso and mento earlier in the twentieth century, it is perhaps subject to a "generational amnesia" by those who discount its legacy in their own era when later songs are reworked by younger musicians. He says that those (middle-aged and older) who criticize

> the "slackness" and "indecency" of contemporary dancehall music, often conveniently "forget" how big a role slack/rude lyrics played in Jamaican popular music when they were young. In fact, it is also a big part of older folk traditions as well. (Bilby, personal communication)

The recent availability of the Trojan X-rated box sets reproduce many songs that tap into a very old folk culture, perhaps centuries old, and demonstrate that slack lyrics are not recent.

Although recorded in the 1960s, many are reworked songs from historical memory extending to the 1940s. As an expression of gendered power dynamics, most are egalitarian representations of playful, verbal jousts between a man and a woman boasting sexual capability, duration or stamina. Sometimes the woman is dominant, disparaging poor performance, criticizing lack of effort or even accusing him of drinking too much as Cock and Pussy sing in "Dead Buddy" ([1972] 2002). In other songs, the male counters with his own expert measures of sexual success. Sonic sexualized content leaves little to the imagination. Such sounds signify authority within the relationship by conveying pleasure or disappointment. However, while the attitude of earlier slack is mostly playful and fun representing an egalitarian, though competitive sexual co-existence, by the mid-1980s when the first author heard it, slack had already turned mean. We propose an economic causation, though later research may broaden this perspective. Slack performed during political unease and economic stress reveals subterfuge and scapegoat, which sounds different from its earlier more playful tone produced under less duress.

Stolzoff notes that over the 1980s, along with the changing sound of dancehall music, there was a concomitant change in women's dancehall fashion from a more modest Rasta style to one baring much more flesh. He says: "This change in dancehall convention coincided with slack lyrics which focused on women as sexual objects, and on men (the DJs themselves) as well-endowed lovers in both the financial and sexual senses". The triangulation of new lyrics with more revealing clothing ("puny printers" engraved the pubic area and "batty riders" revealed buttocks [Stolzoff 2000, 110]), and the dancehall as space for display with ever more erotic go-go type dance styles, exaggerated the historical cleavage embedded in gendered power relationships. As in our economic history, Stolzoff also contends: "The new prominence of women in the dancehall space was a reflection of women's greater economic power in the 1980s. Women gained on men, who lost secure union jobs under Seaga's policies" (111). Slack re-emerged with a meaner voice in the mid-1980s because the country's mood had changed along with the political administration in 1980. The proud poverty of Prime Minister Michael Manley's economic independence from international aid was replaced by the new Prime Minister Edward Seaga's involvement with President Reagan's Caribbean Basin Initiative, which further divided the rich from the poor. Poverty intensified since the 1980s, and targets of male frustration, we believe, became women.

The initial realization of multiple layers of meaning or metaphors in lyrics piqued an interest for the first author to hear more music. She went to Errol, a local entrepreneur, who advertized personalized cassettes for sale. In 1987 and 1988, she contracted for a fee to have four tapes made (Errol labeled them Reggae Mix, Revolution Reggae, Top Ten Party – The Best Mix, and Jamaican Girls' Best) before the fieldwork period ended. Several songs on the tapes fulfilled her request for gender-contentious lyrics. The tapes were taken home and transcribed for later research agendas. This method of "archiving," obtaining a set of songs by a researcher during one fieldwork visit for later analysis is a classic ethnomusicological technique (Armstrong 1986; Nettl 1964). The initial archive provided song names and in most cases also performers. On a return visit to fill in omissions, the store had closed. Subsequent musical choices were made from the purchase of CDs as well as from web sites that provided lyrics in print.

Turning to the lived experience of the lower classes, we find an erotophilic enculturation occurring in a society influenced by a more sexually repressive British elite that complicates the Jamaican cultural consumer lovemap. Erotophilia-erotophobia is a concept that reflects the idea that some people tend to respond more frequently and positively to sexual stimuli (erotophilia) than others who may be averse to sexuality (erotophobia) (Gould 1991, 1995).

Male peer reputation is assessed by having numerous lovers and the ability to father many children. From Errol's Reggae Mix tape we hear one male lovemap expressed in the slack lyrics of "Fat Ina Panty" by Jah Son (n.d.).

> To have sex, dat is my hobby
> Fit and me strong like a young donkey cubby
> Me as a youth lord me have sex daily
> Sex have me bred Panzy and de one Suzy.

Later expressions are heard from Beenie Man in "Stamina" (2006), "To sex every girl in this world is mi aim," while Dr. Evil in "More Punanny" (2006) says: "Each and every night I must get some punanny. Take a girl on the beach and create a tsunami." The male definition of slack is qualified by Stephen Nye, who quotes DJ artist Yellowman:

> "Slackness is we all make love and if the lady get pregnant it's baby. So slackness bring everybody here… I don't call it Slackness, I call it entertainment" and in response to the politicians protestations that music is crude and offensive, he argued "What I call slackness is like the road want fix, and they get the money to fix it and don't fix it!" (2007)

In Jamaica, while children are cherished and loved and often shifted among relatives to redistribute care taking, male desires for progeny complicate female ambitions. A female Jamaican journalist passes judgment on the consequences:

> Fathers are generally absent from the rearing nests of most Jamaican children. The male of the Jamaican species learnt generations ago that having several baby mothers was the cheapest way to have children. Each of the mothers can generally be counted upon to look after her own brood. This was always a fond hope, however, realized more often in the breach by granny in rural Jamaica. (Ritch 2002, 7)

Cross-cultural social investigation should always proceed cautiously, especially when researchers carry their own collectivity distinctions. Such cultural factors become exacerbated in the Caribbean when analysis involves a sexual component (Yelvington 1998) and as insider (native) – outsider (foreigner) status initiates debate (Cooper 2004; Walker 2005) over privilege to speak for another culture. Middleton claims:

> For "us" in "the West," the question arising then (a postcolonial question) is: who can, who *may,* speak from "over there"? Respect for cultural difference should not exclude the possibility that one might surprise "others" where they are with an excavation of what is hidden from their gaze. (2003, 261)

By concentrating on the cultural logic of slack content, we find lyrics inform on a wide range of behavioral choices to shape lovemaps and gender perception especially as experienced in the sexually charged dancehall. Francis-Jackson notes:

> Even the tone of the language is definitely pro hot-blooded male heterosexual, almost to the point where it is regressively anti female. … The actual Dancehall environment, despite its language which is often uncomplimentary to the female, is a highly sexual one where the female is definitely the queen, and it is she who rules. (1995, v)

While women may rule in the space of the hall, many male lyricists voice alarm. A 1980s Errol's Reggae Mix song, "Renking Meat" by Ninja Man (n.d.), betrays fear and disgust as it instructs:

Now all a de men dem
We a nyam [eat] de renking meat… [impertinent, smelly vagina]
Gal give me piece of de renking meat…
Nuff [many] man get nasty and eat under sheet
Me tell yuh de truth Ninja man naw [doesn't] go do it

*The Dictionary of Jamaican English* defines "Rengking," as "1. having an offensive smell… 2. Sour… 3. Impertinent" (Cassidy and le Page [1967] 1984, 380). Francis-Jackson defines "renking meat" simply as "vagina" (1995, 43). Gospel Fish also signals fear in his 1991 song "Punani Fi Smell," where the lyrics connect odor to disease. Vaginas are also dangerous places for producing blood and potentially harboring another man's polluting sperm. Thus, while we can read the lyrics as a gender metaphor representing sexual antagonism, "Renking Meat" is significant for revealing a strong cultural aversion (on the part of both genders) to oral sex. However, during the 1980s with presence of cocaine, local women told the first author that cunnilingus was often condoned particularly when cocaine caused impotence. In music venues, participants are often encouraged to put their hands in the air to signify disagreement with sexual and social acts. As with cunnilingus (and songs decrying homosexuality), one respondent advised that participants often sign according to pressure accommodating social norms, which contradict personal beliefs and behaviors. As Mr. Vegas's song "Nike Air: Hands in the Air" (1998a) suggests, the socialization effect in the dancehall helps reinforce particular behavioral norms. Bilby notes that "sung criticism functions as a means of social control" in "collective participation" of musical performance contexts where audience engagement contributes to success of the venue (1985, 201).

## Resonant indigenization

The indigenization model has come to be the dominant one, and particular genres are seen to articulate with local circumstances (Maxwell 2003). In this regard, Stoller (1989) notes that oral cultures transmit information and meaning heard through auditory channels, and therefore, sounds carry cultural resonance. De Certeau and Giard praise "orality [as] the essential space of community" (1998, 252). They elaborate that instead of becoming subsumed by the written, "the elements that were thought to have been eliminated (oral culture) continue to determine social exchanges and to organize the way of 'receiving' cultural messages, that is transforming them through the use made of them" (253). Our position follows the indigenization model because our ethnographic observation corroborates how one form of cultural music, Jamaican dancehall/DJ, expresses and reproduces socialization themes. When viewed post-structurally (Holt 1997), the role of music in the cultural consumer lovemap would be situated as a pattern of practices based in a particular localized site, as defined by various historical and social contexts and geographies (e.g., center–periphery and rural–urban). This is not to say that others, beyond the local context cannot appreciate Jamaican musical genres, much as Shankar (2000) used reggae to find comfort growing up as an outsider in England.

Moreover, as Frith suggests, the study of music not only involves how music reflects a people but also, and for him the more germane issue, concerns how it "creates and constructs an experience" (1996, 109), so people experience themselves in new or different ways. In a sexually charged example, Sherry (1980) analyzed "bawdy songs" of Midwestern rugby players whose lyrics provide endless options of sexuality while castigating fellow players' matching wit through metaphor in post-game bar-room performances that boost a singer's social status as well as group cohesion. Building on a theory of rhetoric in folklore, Sherry suggests,

> Expressive folklore is the "rhetoric of a community insofar as it embodies techniques of control and persuasion" – pleasure is provided, but persuasive intent is also executed. Performers not only instruct the young, but also seek to maintain their own positions of respect and authority. (1980, 140)

In most consumer research, papers focus on music as the background to commercials or shopping rather than as cultural product. However, following O'Donohoe, who in applying discourse analysis to advertising as a form of popular culture notes that its language is the "literature of consumption" (2000, 152), we similarly situate music lyrics as expressive of cultural consumer lovemaps. Especially informative for our work, Scott frames music in terms of culture, text, narrative and rhetoric, so it is "meaningful and language-like" (1990, 233). Others implicate music in constructing gender stereotypes (Blair and Hyatt 1997). Holbrook reviews the use of music in film by distinguishing between "diegetic music" and "non-diegetic" music (2003). His analysis of "ambi-diegetic" music (2005) is a combination of the previous two, whereby a song is produced by an actor in the movie as it also influences the story or has mood-inducing effects aligned with the film's theme. Grounding storied lyrics in context, both Branscomb (1993) and Rhodes (2004) find Bruce Springsteen's literary narratives linked to a working-class reality. Finally, with a cutting-edge audio-print compilation, Bradshaw et al. (2005) expose a dilemma for artists playing background music to a disinterested audience for income while trying to maintain healthy egos and artistic integrity.

Returning to the Caribbean, Fairley (2004) provides a similar indigenization perspective for an analysis of the new Cuban music and dance form called *timba*, which appeared during the 1990s economic downturn after the fall of the USSR. There are many parallels with Jamaican music. Fairley's analysis is also framed by an economic assessment of Cuba's new economy, which allowed tourism in the 1990s, creating income disparity, especially between the sexes. Women were often encouraged to generate cash from services provided to tourists. The new musical form, *timba* evolved from *son*, the syncretic blend of Afro-Spanish musical traditions created by slaves. *Timba*'s misogynist lyrics betray the current economic crisis while also laying the blame "at the feet of capricious women [who are] … simultaneously objects of desire and derided for their sexual availability." *Timba*'s dance form digressed from a couple embracing to women being the focus of attention while parodying sensual movements that "mirror coital narratives" (92).

### Dub version – music as cultural mediator

In Jamaica, the dub version evolved in the 1960s as a remix the DJs produced on an album's reverse side (often without vocals) to talk over the music and "toast" in "raps" without the original lyrics interfering with their version (Bilby 1985, 207).

Dancehall and slack are part of a stream of "social commentary" songs connecting to an historical tradition. Fairley (2004, 85) also notes that in Cuba's oral culture, *timba*'s lyrics report current events like an "oral newspaper" and can infer multiple meanings. "The topical song, [which relies] for its effect on such devices as double entendre, irony, and veiled allusions, is a Caribbean specialty that cuts across many musical genres" (Bilby 1985, 201). Recent reports prompt the deeper analysis of cultural codes embedded in the slack lyrics of the dancehall genre (Olsen and Gould 1997, 1999). While slack quite possibly is an older genre connecting to calypso and mento, its tone and content articulate differently across the centuries. We consider why this style reappears when it does, in a particular context, at a particular moment in time. While other researchers also attribute it to the deteriorating local economy (Cooper 2004; Stolzoff 2000; Walker 2005), this critique has become a debate over an insider versus outsider capability to speak on cultural matters that, we believe, obscures a truer understanding. By adding a socialization perspective (i.e., how children are enculturated to a social blueprint, particularly learning kinship, gender and status roles), we fill a void not adequately addressed in this research to date. Our indigenization contribution is germane to future research on globalization as transnational performers appropriate reggae patterns for rap, hip-hop (Erskine 2003) and *reggaeton.* Slack rhetorical style informs local cultural expressions, as for instance, heard in gangsta rap (Eckholm 2006, 14) and other diasporic and indigenous dancehall emerging around the world. Dyson connects hip-hop to its Jamaican and diasporic roots via DJ Kool Herc, who brought its sound to the Bronx in the 1970s transporting "rhetorical, rhythmic, percussive, tonal, and sonic structures" into its sound (2007, 46–7). He discusses the socio-political causes of a generational and conceptual divide between rap and hip-hop's two musical frames: conscious "Afristocracy" verses "Ghettocracy" about "broads, booze, and bling," representing the gangsta lifestyle and prison as second home security for those no longer able to live on the outside. Rap reflects these "prison narratives." For Dyson, songs that dehumanize and reduce women to male toys are not about the lyrics, but about patriarchal notions of masculinity and femininity, representative of "'femiphobia,' the sheer fear of women – in the rest of hip-hop" (22). In Jamaica, Cooper (2004) considers the slack tradition in dancehall as potentially empowering, while Stolzoff (2000) claims it maintains a sexual status quo.

Leppert speculates on Adorno's "new music sociology" saying popular music is regressive. "Commodified music works to define subjects as products of acoustical advertising" (Leppert 2002, 335–6). While music so "defines," it also suggests behaviors that reiterate said definition. As Attali notes:

> Music is inscribed between noise and silence, in the space of the social codification it reveals. Every code of music is rooted in the ideologies and technologies of its age, and at the same time produces them. ...What must be constructed, then, is more like a map, a structure of interferences and dependencies between society and its music. (2002, 19)

Attali's "understanding through music" relates to our examination of musical lyrics as cultural texts whereby lyrics do more than represent socio-political circumstances influencing cultural identity; they also help construct that identity (Leerssen 2000). The authors thus find a lovemap exists, albeit a malleable one, for the sexual and related gender relations that reflect dancehall culture. Looking at the emergence of reggae as a lower-class discourse on economic inequality, Prahlad considers, "In reggae, and particularly with proverbs that tend to recur within this discourse, proverb images tell stories that become symbolic markers for strategies for negotiation" (2001, 137). Within this discourse, a blueprint surfaces in the creation and consumption of dancehall lyrics that articulate an experiential lovemap as they resonate making sense of a lived reality for the many who define themselves as "ghetto youth" (Stolzoff 2000, 141–2). For them "music localizes and specifies power, because it marks and regiments the rare noises that cultures, in their normalization of behavior, see fit to authorize" (Attali 2002, 19–20).

Biddle claims: "[S]ound (and music in particular) has been made to take on many of the functions of discourse that language fails to enunciate" (2003, 216). Music in Jamaica evolved from the Diaspora, driven by the percussion of drums that originally "spoke" delivering a message telling a story transmitted over vast distances to an "oralic" community in need of information. Jamaican music thus, provides several layers of discourse. On one level as empowered expression of the disenfranchised, the evolution of the musical genre called ska in association with local back-yard "sound systems" emerges "in the mid-1950s as a reactionary response to the neocolonial control of Jamaican airways" that played primarily white American music (Prahlad 2001, 7). By the 1960s, with Rastafarian socially conscious reggae, Prahlad says its "reggae discourse, like other traditional narrative performances, *directs* the listener's interpretation. The discursive frame of reggae lyrics is encoded with certain values that are bound to influence the meanings attached to them by their audience" (137). Prahlad's "oralic discourse" analysis of Jamaican proverbs, finds "four levels of meaning that operate simultaneously when proverbs are used," and the *grammatical, social, situational* and *symbolic* levels locate meaning in personal experience and local knowledge (1–2). Similarly, in our indigenization perspective, lyrics express a discourse on gender socialization within a distressed economy, exacerbating fractious gender relationships.

To account for these indigenization and cultural phenomena in relation to sexuality, gender and music, we extend the individual consumer lovemap to a broader cultural level – i.e., the cultural consumer lovemap – situating sexual practices within a socialization experience and political economy at a certain point in time communicated in song. The individual consumer lovemap concerns how consumers map their sexuality in relation to consumption, reflecting, how they might express their sexual attractiveness and behavior practices through the personal choices, for instance, of clothing, music, home atmospherics and sexual accessories (Gould 1991, 1995). Individual differences might be found based on any number of variables, such as gender, age, social class and erotophilia-erotophobia (Gould 1991, 1995). Erotophilics may also tend to construct and erotocize meanings more generally in sexual terms than erotophobics.

This lovemap construct has its roots in the world of sex research and therapy. Originally, it was used by a sex therapist, Money (1986), to describe paraphilias or "non-normal" sexual functioning. In this sense, people tended to respond to their own sexuality and sexual situations in trait-like characteristic ways according to some early experience with sexuality in childhood. For example, a person with a shoe fetish may have walked in on his parents having sex and noticing shoes perhaps by looking at them instead of his parents in this awkward but arousing circumstance, focusing on them in relation to sex. However, some have commented that the paraphilia perspective is a rather limited way to conceive lovemaps and thus have focused on everyday sexuality and the way people express it (Lake 2006). Gould (1995) focused on consumer behavior in this regard and explored how people may use products and services in relation to it. It is useful to think of Foucault (1990) as well in this regard and consider the economy of pleasure and desire involved in the everyday consumer sexual and other linked practices. Thus consumers develop rituals, fetishistic behaviors and other sexual practices within culturally and personally prescribed patterns that can be recognized, both by the individual and outside observers of that individual though not necessarily with the same meanings or perspectives. In this regard and relevant to the music focus of this paper, Gould (1995) found that both stereo systems and the type of music listened to were marked by consumers as being related to both sexually attracting a mate and the sex act stage itself, with men and erotophilic consumers generally giving higher ratings to them than women and erotophobic consumers. In present contexts, music may interpenetrate individual and cultural consumer lovemaps in terms of lyrics, rhythms, timbres, instruments and occasions of use in sexual practices, ranging from dance to the sex act itself.

Gould (2003, 2006) further explored the consumer lovemap and its dynamics, not so much in terms of an unchanging or fixed expression on the part of the individual, but as being dynamic and responsive to social and cultural change. Indeed, he saw it as informed by postmodern and post-structural considerations, such that there is a constant hermeneutic circle involved in the shifting dynamics of the lovemap between cultural and individual.

Perhaps it is best to consider that various aspects of the individual, culture, music and sexual practices continually co-evolve and are co-produced. In that regard, a nuanced approach in which what is fixed and what is changing are both considered is perhaps best for applying this construct.

Here, we extend the lovemap idea to consider a broader cultural view. Our lovemap reconstruction is a culture-wide narrative reflecting three intersecting layers of identity construction: personal, social and cultural (Reid and Deaux 1996). As Gould (2003) points out, the lovemap construct in general is overdetermined, meaning its production is layered. These layers we theorize inform one another, as Wattanasuwan and Elliott (1999) suggest in finding an interaction between self and social symbolism in self-identity construction. In terms of personal identity, the individual lovemap within the cultural lovemap, embodies a particular socio-economic experience, influencing gender relationships and lifelong sexual development. The social layer as suggested by social identity theory (Tajfel 1982) involves consumers deriving aspects of their self-concept and norms for *appropriate* sexual behavior from collectivities they are associated with, such as gender, age and lifestyle groups. Thus, we find a Jamaican lovemap that within its own particular cultural milieu (i.e., reflecting cross-cultural differences, cf. Gould 2003; Nelson and Paek 2005) entangles men and women in contested couplings and renders sexuality an instrument of socioeconomic power (cf. Foucault 1990).

When music is viewed as a site of meaning within a cultural consumer lovemap, we need to consider that it has often been implicated in issues of representing and constructing national identities, and their contesting both within a particular society and the broader world (e.g., Araújo 2000). In general, ethnomusicological inquiry that studies such issues of national identity and music has been of two opposing minds, according to Maxwell (2003). One involves "cultural imperialism" where non-Western cultures opt to align their music with Western music either through substituting it for their own or at least imitating it by reproducing such music as their own. This we see in hip-hop, rap and *reggaeton*. A variant of this model might be seen in terms of the use of music to represent a colonized party by a colonizer that Schroeder and Borgerson (1999) suggest is the case for the US's appropriation and reconstitution of Hawaiian music. For example, Winders (1997) recognizes the value of a new global synthesis that blends musical genres. Alternatively, Stokes (2003) debunks imperialism theory in his discussion of rap carrying the indigenous lyric outcry of economically disenfranchised Turks in Germany. Implications of the cultural imperialism perspective might be found in more general views on the cultural production of music. Adorno believed most popular "light" music was commodified into a packaged formula for the masses, the effect of which was to remove the listener further from being in touch with reality (Leppert 2002). Perhaps dancehall has now standardized gangsta and slack misogynistic themes that desensitize the mind by their ubiquity over time in the Jamaican context.

Contemporary slack resonates earlier eras. Bilby played songs for the first author from his collection of old 45s that demonstrate the historical continuum of this tradition and its connection to mento from the 1950s. From the mid 1970s, Lynthia Cooper sings in mento-reggae style about the "Three Minute Man" saying, "I don't like to do things in a hurry… to me it don't matter what kind of man; baldhead [conventional], soul-head [US values and afro hair style], or dreadlocks man [Rasta]; one-eye, one-foot, or one-hand man as long as him can stay de long". What matters is her satisfaction. Again, this song represents the two sides of sexual egalitarianism we hear in this cultural expression.

When women like Lady Saw in "Do Me Better" (2004) and Lady P in "Wuck Me Tender" (1994) assume a dominant role by expressing their own desires, they resonate earlier mento 1950s and 1960s egalitarian and female lovemaps. Vybz Kartel and female artist Delicious sing about "Rough Sex" (2006), which also resonates earlier slack from the 1950s equally expressing sexual preferences for lovemaking, i.e., the woman wants it slower, also inferred by her sound effects, while the man wants it faster and more forceful. The gender dynamic is a contest for control. In this gender match, Erskine (2003, 82) perceives the dilemma of US female rap singers struggling to express sexual empowerment in a genre where male lyricists address them as "hos and bitches." Johnson, writing about female musicians in the US, highlights "a new group of black feminist critics who…argue that hip-hop can also be seen as a place where black women oppose and take power away from men" (2003, 154). Thompson and Holt's (2004) "crisis-of-masculinity thesis" relates to our ethnomusicological discourse of slack by considering the "phallic masculinity" heard in lyrics communicating sexual exploits as a power struggle over male-to-male (not female) dominance. As they note, "While the societal articulation of 'male trouble' may change and its ideals of authentic manhood may shift, masculinity-in-crisis may be an enduring cultural frame through which prevailing socio-economic conditions (and their implications for manhood) are understood" (315).

As we turn to the context of cultural meaning inherent in the lyrics of dancehall/DJ music in Jamaica ("meanings" defined as "endlessly referring symbolic chains… or discourses" [Holt 1997, 329]), we are constantly reminded of the powerful historical forces that shaped the social relationships we hear spun in song. Cultural meanings "are always constructed – through a process known as intertextuality – by metaphoric, imagistic, and narrative association with other cultural objects and practices that are part of the historically accumulated cultural resources of a collectivity" (Holt 1997, 329).

## Club mix: the cultural-historical thread of gender perception

We preface this section with a reflection on fieldwork within the community and this project's emergent design. At the onset of involvement in 1970, the first author moved into a rural area of farmers, fishermen and small shopkeepers. A divorce three years after building a home resulted in an outpouring of empathy from several matriarchs, most importantly Eunice and Zoe, who shared their own similar encounter with love lost. The relationships formed first, and then immersion in the literature on the region presented an opportunity for exploration that, when integrated with the life stories, substantiated discoveries found in song lyrics that reflected observations of actual socialization practices. Jamaican music is the historical legacy of a sonic culture encapsulated in characteristic sounds that carry survival stories and strategies embedded in its music. Lyrics represent articulated emotions and interpretive texts. Finnegan maintains that emotions are not "universal facts of nature but [are] differently formulated in different times and places. We *learn* how to feel, and how to deploy emotions in ways and contexts appropriate to our situation" (2003, 183).

It is possible that contemporary lovemaps and gender perceptions have their roots in West African cultures and transformation in their diasporic communities. We ground our analysis of gender relationships in Jamaican socialization and material culture, which continue to inform lower-class family survival and healing practices. However, Douglass's (1992) study of the Jamaican elite reveals that men of all classes in all manners of domestic relationships (married or visiting) expect the woman to be subordinate, and most do act accordingly. Interpretation of causality, however, remains controversial. Broadly speaking, the West Indies Diaspora has retained many vestiges of African influence. On the other hand, it is possible that the historical experience of slavery also significantly had its influence on gender perceptions. Regarding mating patterns and the family in particular, its matrifocal formation and marginalized males link to a West African model of polygyny and polyandry permitting several wives and lovers (Herskovits 1941; Patterson 1967). Marriage between slaves was prohibited (Sherlock and Bennett 1998), removing the male from the household (Frazier 1966). This perhaps contributes to what Clarke calls a "denuded family household" (1979, 100). Consequently, as Alleyne (1988) notes, freed slaves evolved a collectivist lifestyle that broke down when vast numbers of the population moved into towns after 1930.

The Caribbean family is connected to a particular contextual development where the male–female relationship evolved in a developmental sequence based on economic need (Smith 1988). In the Jamaican experience, Moses (1977) connects matrilocal land transfer to the assurance that daughters have a house site while sons, raised as "guests" in the home, are destined at maturity to find a lover to care for them. The degree of community cohesiveness also influenced mating patterns. Family instability is connected to conditions where men are unable to fulfill their roles as husbands, fathers and sons. The strongest tie is to the mother. A man often replaces his mother with a wife or girlfriend in whom he places complete trust. Throughout a man's life, he never completely leaves the mother and, in fact, is expected to keep contributing to her welfare, or to both parents' if need be. Thus, the responsibilities on men are heavy. Clarke notes:

> A mother impresses upon her sons that it is their duty to make up for the hardships she has endured as the sole or principle support of her children. When the boy begins to earn money he is expected to give her part at least of his earnings and while he is in the home this is the usual practice. In return she continues to cook and wash for him. When he sets up on his own he still feels that he is under an obligation to contribute to her support. (1979, 163)

This is heard in "Remember When" (1998), sung by the group Dance Hall Divas:

> You cyan't [can't] leave out your modda and your fadda. Not even a letta, cho!
> Remember when! Remember who used to wash your clothes for you,
> who used to change your diaper, who used to prepare your food for you,
> who used to make your suppa, who used to hug and kiss you.
> Your modda and your fadda.

Staying in touch implies maintaining a relationship, and is often accompanied by asking for or giving money. These contacts and gifts are also deeper metaphors for friendship and caring (Horst and Miller 2006, 100). The notion that remembrance is due in remittances is a strong tug on family heartstrings and pocket book throughout the lifetime, especially for males. "Not even a letta, Cho!"

Many Jamaicans have large families and grandparents and other good souls – such as Eunice and Zoe, who both raised several besides their own – often raise extra children. Eunice regretted that a "son," whom she adopted at age nine, became successful but never visited or looked after her since working for a rich American only seven miles away (Olsen 2005). The introduction of affordable cell phones to Jamaica in the 1990s facilitates such connections in "linking-up," especially where land lines are unavailable or geographic separation makes costs prohibitive. Horst and Miller (2006) relate the benefits of cell phone usage from enabling love trysts to greater contact between baby fathers and baby mothers and their children, who often live with relatives in "child-shifting" relationships. The cell phone secures relationships in Jamaica's gregariously social culture. It also enables social banking, ensuring timely exchanges of needed resources. However, they say: "if there were a single most common form of extensive networking in Jamaica, it revolves around the potential of sexual liaisons" (93). Thus, Vybz Kartel's message on "U Nuh Have a Phone

(Hello Moto)" (2006) describes the necessity of a cell phone to make a link-up when he asks a woman to call him:

> Call me Cingular – Can you hear me now?
> The time is modern. Mi I use my cellular. Get girls regular.
> Vodaphone for one of your British friends…
> Check mi number, but you have no phone

As we hear in Bounty Killer's "Cellular Phone" (1998), his phone is used for "romance" to make his house a "love zone," boasting "phallic masculinity" (Thompson and Holt 2004).

Listening to women's stories about love and marriage during ethnographic research in 1987 and 1988, we learned that male pressure for sex and their disdain for birth control complicated delaying pregnancy. It has been reported that one of the strongest factors influencing female cultural lovemaps informing love, marriage and children includes early pregnancy from premarital sex, usually in their teens, that establishes a pattern for future pregnancies (Blake 1961). This initiates serial monogamy and having several "baby fathers," which hopefully increases income from the father of each additional child (Brown 1975). Men fear girlfriends cheating on them. If a different lover gets the woman pregnant, the main boyfriend can be tricked into being the father to another's baby. This is called, "cutting a jacket," as Mr. Vegas says on "Jacket" (1998b):

> Caw some gal a raffle up an a dip
> Me dem wah fi gi di jacket
> [a girl names him out of the group of lovers as father to her child]
> But mi nah go mine no pickney if me know a nuh me mek it
> [but he refuses to support it since he is not the father]
> Drop back dat an mek another pick
> Smaddie else dat might a fit [she should name another for the paternity]

Bilby (personal communication) provides a male perspective saying that what outsiders hear as "misogynistic ranting" is part of a sexually egalitarian culture in which sexual antagonism is heard from both sides of the contested lovemap. Gender tensions have a time depth exacerbated by the economy and Protestantism in an "eros culture." Jamaican women are "psychically strong" but dependent economically on men, so men are in a difficult situation with many expectations placed on them. Bilby related hearing this tension in very early "jacket genre" songs like "Maintenance," a mento song by Cobra Man from the 1950s later reworked in the 1970s under a different title by Count Lasher as a reggae song. Cobra Man applies humor to being sued for support as a baby father:

> A girl decide to make a baby for me; Well let me tell you, I black, you just think; And she, I know closely related to ink; But when the baby born, it was white as snow; So the reason for that I wanted to know; Her mother told me why it born that way; The girl was drinking milk of magnesia everyday; That's why I ain't paying, I ain't paying

Although women prefer marriage in later years to secure the fortunes of their children, Curtin found that many women view marriage as slavery (1968, 25). The wife cooks and cleans for the family, and the husband supports them. Marital satisfaction is based on economic remuneration. A man's reputation is built on his ability to contribute to a household, especially when he has children; however, most men will wait for marriage until they can afford to build or buy a house first. Until then, many couples live in visiting unions, with the male dropping in to eat and sleep and get clean clothes. Such visiting relationships are commonplace and acceptable. Eunice, near age 85, said she felt like a sister to the first author because of our similar history. After bearing a daughter with a lover in a visiting relationship whom she wanted to marry, he convinced her to help him build his house on his land. On completion, he found a new girlfriend who moved into the house. When he told Eunice he no longer loved her, Eunice and her daughter moved to her family's land inherited since emancipation (Olsen 2003).

Men often play the field while promising fidelity, so females fear sexually transmitted diseases. Women also resent diverted resources to support other baby mothers. One female respondent reported asking her lover to use a condom to protect against pregnancy and disease to no avail (Olsen 1995). Lady Saw addresses this in her song "Condoms" (1996a) urging protection, "No girl don't play shy, No bareback ride, AIDS will take your life, When having sex use protection." Sobo found that men can "trick" women into pregnancy by piercing holes in condoms (1993, 212). Women also try to trick men into getting them pregnant to try to get childcare and further assistance from the baby father. As a postscript in the present time of AIDS, we are hearing a more responsible approach to male sexuality from Frisco Kid's advice in "Rubbers" (1996).

Girls learn from an early age to want children as insurance because children care for elders in old age. They also learn that they can trade sex for material comforts (cf. the film *Dancehall Queen*); however, accepting money equates with prostitution and forfeits social responsibility for progeny or bodily harm that may result from sex (Sobo 1993, 129, 182–3). Sobo noticed that "Some girls are encouraged by their caretakers to 'look men.' Their caretakers cannot afford school fees and see 'outside help' as a solution. Girls get lunch money, bus fare, tuition, and clothing in trade for sexual favors" (168). Some women choose to trade sex for money, and a man becomes her "patron." Women who engage in these long-term profitable relationships call their benefactor a "Boops." The Boops is usually a man of means who gives money and gifts in exchange for sex with his favored women heard in "Boops" by Super Cat (1986):

> See Boops there, him have a bag a money, yes,…
> She affi [has to] find the Boops mi say pon a Friday.
> And when you check it out mi say Friday a pay day,
> Him carry her round the lane and give her dollar pon away.
> [the woman is only interested in seeing her Boops on Friday, pay day, when he has the money to give her and take her out]
> And every where him go, him just a run up him mouth, yes,…
> [the Boops talks too much bragging about his prowess]
> Him walk and tell the world him have a dozen gal friend,
> But just thru [because] him no know a this ya money wha him spend
> [the Boops doesn't know that the only reason he has girls is because of the money he spends on them]

Sometimes women protest and want their man to settle down, as we hear Lady Saw singing about a man's duplicitous wandering ways in "Over and Over" (1996d):

> You've been playing me for the clown, baby
> I'm tired of hanging around
> I do understand you've got your women
> But you told me in time I'd be the only one
> My time is running out, I need my answers now.
> Should I leave or are you coming home?

One such woman was Glenda, who managed a hotel with her husband. After learning the first author's introduction to the community, she volunteered her story of betrayal to the women's life history archives. Glenda said she felt like a prisoner because her husband was cheating on her with the female staff, and although she wanted a divorce, she believed the judges in the courts always support the husband (Olsen 1997, 2005). Many Jamaican women believe it is in the male "nature" to have extra sexual relationships, and these are often tolerated to keep his economic support. Women, however, are expected to be faithful and tolerate philandering. Again, Lady Saw seeks logical answers in "Give Me the Reason" (1996c):

Is there a reason you fall for the other girls?
Tell me the reason why you tour around the world
And why you make me into your clown
When I thought I was the number one lady in your world
Why in the world did I build my world around you?
When all you do is make me blue.

A man is often reluctant to marry or move into a house when the woman owns it because she can curtail his abilities for affairs, and he could be evicted if caught. Zoe's grandson Clive said he learned from the lyrics in "Why Me Lord," sung by Shaggy, not to wear white and bathe before returning home (Olsen 2005).

Early Sunday morning in the spring of '96
Chilling on the couch, watching the bulls against the knicks,
My honey marches in and ask if I think I'm slick
It seems she found my shirt with lipstick
I thought I could explain but then my story wouldn't stick
Incriminating pictures show me some other chicks
It happened once before and she was tired of the tricks
She ask me if I can spell the word evict.
(http://www.afunk.com/shaggy/)

It was found that female-headed households also influence the frequency of extra-residential mating (Otterbein 1965). When the man owns the house, the double standard is effectively carried on with the wife as subordinate (77).

Jamaica's African-inspired legacy also surfaces in the practice of Obeah (and in songs about it), which is used for healing and to obtain protection from evil (Handler and Bilby 2001). Many lower-class Jamaicans have a significant fear of being poisoned and getting ill. These beliefs stem from African beliefs in benevolent and malevolent supernatural forces and a fear of those who obtain potions for harm (Sobo 1993). In particular, this can occur through eating tainted food, through sex and by rubbing potions on the skin. Traditional belief maintains that women can pollute the food they prepare with their own sweat and blood; therefore, men are careful to accept food only from trusted lovers and close family members. In 1987, the first author arranged with Gladstone, the first Rastafarian she met in 1971, to obtain his life story (Olsen 1995). On one occasion, I brought a cake from the local bakery for his son's birthday. He refused to eat it because he did not know the baker. After eating our meal, he sent his son away on an errand and said, "If it is your desire we could share our pleasure." He interpreted my overture with the cake as something entirely more intimate. Eating a woman's food carries overtures of sex. It means placing one's life in her hands (Sobo 1993). When a woman "ties" a man to her, he is controlled by her (229). We hear this fear in the song lyrics of "Nuh Tie Me" (1988) by Yellowman. However, in 1987 the first author found "Can't Tie Me" (Barker B 1987) on *Errol's Top Ten Party: The Best Mix* tape. Vocal distribution is in call-and-response style between a man and woman. Since song lyrics are borrowed and reworked by multiple performers, this theme could be calypso or mento. The food message on "Can't Tie Me" further illuminates Gladstone's lovemap:

(Male) Lucky ting [thing] seh me grow wid me granny
[He's lucky he was raised by his grandmother]
An granny used to tell me seh nuh beggy beggy
Bwoy [boy] you nuh fe nyam [not eat] from any body
[Granny told him not to accept food from strangers or those he can't trust]
(transcription by Ken Bilby)

This condition became clear when Duncan, the uncle of Clive, reported being "tied" by his live-in girlfriend. He later died from complications (Olsen 2005). Duncan said:

*Q* What if a woman doesn't like a man and wants to hurt him? Can she do that in his food too?

*Duncan* Yes. She use other stuff. She look like she use Compellance Powder. Black powder. The Science Woman [Obeah woman] call it Compellance powder. From the drug store she can do anything she wanna do. She can compel him to go over the cliff. And can compel him to stay at home and don't come out. A lot a ting. And [want] her alone.

Compelling Powder is defined as "A cant term (OIL OF COMPELLANCE): a powder supposed to be able to compel someone to love another. …*Compellin-powder*, Tempting-powder or 'stay-home.' An obeah charm to secure somebody's love" (Cassidy and LePage [1967] 1984, 117). To carry this fear is terrifying for males who are raised to be dependent on women. During our last conversation, Duncan expressed this well:

*Duncan* So, you know really, the woman in Jamaica don't have no relationship anymore. Is just, ah um, what you call it, money for love. OK. There's no relationship, … like take my woman here. She gone here and gone to her mom. … And within myself, now, my self-conscious self now, I don't like it. Cause I don't know what she's doing when she's out there.

Herein lies another double-bind of the Jamaican lovemap. Duncan wanted his girlfriend and daughter to leave, yet he was worried she had other lovers while away. He tried several times to break up with her, but after two weeks they returned to his care. Duncan's fear turned to suspicion of her using Obeah to tie him when he said,

*Duncan* Cause like this time it looks like she's got control of me. And she going to trick me. Cause in this relationship, they come from, she come from a poor, a poverty family. So, I want to kick them out now, but I wonder if I'm tied up and can't kick her out. Because this time around now she control my head. I wonder if they give her something to put in my food and I ate it.

Listen again to the woman (F) spar with her male (M) counterpart in *Can't Tie Me* (Barker B 1987):

(F) Hey Barker B, you think you caan lef me?
[Woman saying "You think you can't leave me?]
You think sey me ah mek nuh [no] girl get me out?
[Do you think I'd let any girl replace me?]
(M) You think you going tie me ina you rice and peas, an it go suh, nuh!
[The man thinks the woman is going to put a potion of poison in his food so he'll never want or be able to be with another woman]

(F) But Barker, you know seh me luv you an me nuh do you nuttin
[Woman saying "I will never harm you"] (transcription by Ken Bilby)

Duncan expressed that his relationship with this girlfriend was more involved than being a "Boops," which would have been easier if he had more money.

Jamaican music as an eloquent voice of gender socialization is best understood through an indigenization perspective. Thus, music becomes an excellent textual (Scott 1990) site for revealing consumers' lovemap discourses and related lived experiences in song. Indeed, Stolzoff (2000) warns against a singularly hermeneutic focus of individual targets of analysis such as music lyrics, without understanding the context of their production and relationship to an entire cultural genre (i.e., holistic indigenization).

## Roots: the evolution of Jamaican music as a site of cultural meaning

The discovery of the roots – or social origins, as Chang and Chen (1998) use the term to connect the "Kumina, Quadrille, Mento, Blues and Jazz" musical forms – is applied to our probe of how Jamaican music and meaning emanates from the past.

Over the 1950s and 1960s, as noted earlier, musical genres evolved, influencing each other. By the late 1960s, with reggae a newer beat is heard based on the old mento style, carrying a theme of reggae conscious roots lyrics. An underlying concern influencing early reggae music was the "rude bwoy," about whom many of the songs were written. Ivanhoe Martin, the main character in Perry Henzell's film *The Harder They Come* (1972), typifies the survival story of a rural "rude bwoy" who becomes a gangster in urban Kingston (cf. Cooper 1995). White (1967, 39) describes rudies as Jamaican urban, lower-class youth between 14 and 25 years old who target the middle class. The rude boy of Kingston's slums was legitimated by the Wailers's song "Rude Boy" (1966), but by 1968, Bob Marley and the Wailers began following the tenets of Rastafari, singing about social reform and racial equality, though the rude boy theme remained an appendage to reggae.

Politics and popular culture usurped the transformative power of reggae especially after the election of 1980, when the music scene was drastically altered by Prime Minister Seaga's economic agendas (Waters 1985). The sentiment of reggae music, mirroring the socialism of Prime Minister Michael Manley, and the Rastafarian creed of social redemption, morphed into its Dancehall/DJ analogue expressive of the rude boys' anger over economic disenfranchisement expressed in gangsta lifestyle. Stolzoff says that in dancehall culture the "need to eliminate one's rivals is worked out symbolically in song and performance, especially in duels known as clashes" (2000, 10). This is reminiscent of the West Indian man-of-words rhyming contests in nineteenth-century tea meetings (Abrahams 1983; Keith 1992). Reflexivity between gender tensions and DJ music mirrors Stolzoff's analysis of the hermeneutic circle of the gangster lifestyle and dancehall themes. "Thus, DJs and singers give expression to the gangster lifestyle through performance, which the gangsters in reciprocal fashion enact the scripts performed by these entertainers in their real lives". However, "some youths fortified with inspiration from 'reality' songs and Rasta-influenced 'culture' lyrics resist the lure of the gangs and criticize the use of the gun" (Stolzoff 2000, 11).

Jamaican music since the 1950s has had a powerful influence as an entertainment medium in Jamaica and increasingly around the world, where lyricists voice the inversion of historical power relationships (Cooper 1995; Stolzoff 2000). As Manuel, Bilby and Largey (2006, 206) and Cooper (2004, 76–7) note, there is also a continuous uneasy refrain of distrust toward women even in the lyrics of musicians like Marley. As popular music evolved in the 1980s with dancehall/DJ, the tone of frustration becomes apparent in mean slack sexual and often violent lyrics. Perhaps in a culture that has historically recognized black women as male property for sex, reproduction and care-taking (Patterson 1967, 159–64), contemporary violent, homophobic and sexist slack lyrics represent the displacement of frustration with the political and economic structure (Stolzoff 2000, 225). Dollard et al. note: "*[A]ggression is always a consequence of frustration*... the proposition is that the occurrence of aggressive behavior always presupposes the existence of frustration and contrariwise, that the existence of frustration always leads to some form of aggression" (1967, 1, italics in the original). We believe Jamaican women are not only a most vulnerable target but metaphorically represent the rival and power of authority; in times of economic frustration, the blueprint for gender socialization expressed in slack dancehall exposes a culturally embedded dimension. Dancehall music continues toward the violent extreme with "gun lyrics," sonic gunshots and ricochets. The first author knew another youth who grew up near a local nightclub where he learned worldly ways. During a visit he said he wanted to be a DJ and was writing songs about being wrongfully charged for a shooting and got a life sentence. He played guitar while singing about finding "deliverance" through the Bible while in jail (Olsen 2005). Similarly, many older DJ performers of the late 1980s who specialized in gangsta and sexual slack lyrics returned to conscious lyrics in the late 1990s due in part to the former's designation as "not fit for air play." By 2004, local corporations like Pepsi-Cola Jamaica, among others, chose not to sponsor events for "artists who continue to incite violence through their lyrics and performance" (Campbell-Livingstone and Lindsay 2004). News reporting (Henry 2006) violent and sexually explicit lyrics are equally lamented by early DJs like Burru Banton, who fears for his own children socialized to violence through lyrics: "The amount of gun songs out there, telling kids you can kill people and is nothing … [d]em tings must clean up."

## Sound clash: the economics of frustration

Our study of Jamaican music in relation to socialization and socio-economic history is similar to Fairley's (2004) research on three music traditions in Cuba. She found the *son* genre connects Cuban-African tradition with its Spanish influence. She found communication through metaphor in *nueva trova*, and *timba* is reflective of ideological changes intersecting with transformation in Cuba's political economy. Those who control the cultural capital of a nation usually write its history inscribed in state policy and producing (though not performing) culture's artistic representations. This has been characterized as a top-down flow of influence on the rest of society. However, the source of the creative imaginary written in stories and sung in song more often percolates from the grass roots of its folk culture; it is more attuned to the nuances of political/economic oppression and expresses this first-hand experience within the dynamic of their creative productions, which ultimately flavor many artistic achievements giving character to national art in all media. Thus, folk art as an expression of felt history equally impacts on a nation's cultural capital. During the 1970s, Michael Manley as Prime Minister nationalized industries and avoided borrowing from the IMF in an attempt to keep Jamaica out of debt. Fearing Cuban-style socialism, corporate and personal fortunes relocated to other countries. Edward Seaga, the new Prime Minister in 1980, built a strong relationship with the IMF and World Bank to fulfill his campaign pledge to "make money jingle" in Jamaican pockets (Sunshine 1985, 118).

An irreversible trend began with the importation of agricultural produce that directly competed with Jamaican products – i.e., potatoes, onions, red beans and other vegetables – causing an 18% decline in agricultural production by 1982. In manufacturing, Jamaican-produced clothing and shoes competed unfavorably with foreign-made items, forcing the closure of domestically owned companies. Instead of reinvesting or saving what foreign exchange was earned, the money was spent on luxury imports (153–4). Michael Manley assessed the consequences:

> When the foreign capital comes pouring in, that enables your middle class to buy Cadillacs and Mercedes Benz and whatever they like – a spectacular level of living – because the foreign exchange which comes with foreign capital creates an artificial capacity to import ...[and] in the end, that you really create two societies (Johnson and Rankin 1982, 29).

The 1980s saw certain sectors of Jamaican society benefit from the flow of foreign capital, while others at the bottom remained untouched, hurting rural communities the most. Many public-sector laborers were fired. Jamaica's dollar was devalued from J$1.77 to J$3.25 for a US$1.00 in 1982. By 2006, it was US$1.00 to J$63 (dates represent fieldwork visits). This escalating devaluation pushed prices beyond many laboring families' ability to buy basics like rice, beans, tinned milk and corned beef. Jamaicans nicknamed it the "'paralyzed market'" (Sunshine 1985, 154). While the Jamaican economy has been struggling since 1980, the strongest sector remains tourism. Along with the demand for lower-priced goods and cheaper imported agricultural produce, local farmers and marginal Jamaican entrepreneurs are still competitively disadvantaged. Miller (1995) mentions similar conditions for Trinidad, and indeed, this situation is replicated throughout the developing world where the IMF and World Bank restructure local economies to accommodate foreign debt (Stiglitz 2002).

Since the period we covered in-depth, from a bottom-up perspective, the urban and rural poor have been affected the hardest. The mean turn in dancehall and slack since the 1980s has particularly become the expression of the disenfranchised, echoed through lyrics contoured by an economy that textures the lived experience on back roads and urban ghettoes that only complicates a distrusting lovemap.

### Rub-a-dub

Rub-a-dub performances or dances were the venues where the DJs spoke over a record's (dub) music version of the reverse side with lyrics. Like the heavy instrumentation of rub-a-dub style music, our paper reaches its crescendo. Applying a critical ethnomusicological analysis to indigenous Jamaican cultural consumer lovemaps expressed through music lyrics requires interpreting the lived emotional, social, economic and political experiences. Singers share joy and angst while listeners identify and learn. Music, in human terms, has long been a folk idiom communicating public and personal histories, both real and conjectural, but always contributing to the collective historical collaborative imaginary of a populace. Music reifies history, and it is reflexive of that history. The Jamaican musical stream that we have presented here in its multiple manifestations is influenced by a fecund socio-economic cultural experience, from religion and kinship to culinary practices, all of which inform musical expression.

The themes we found in this process inscribed in song were heard also in the lived experiences of respondents'. Regarding gender socialization of boys within the lower class segment of our analysis, they are initially raised as guests in the primary household. Males evolve in a double bind of dependency on females without building requisite skills of self-sufficiency. As they age, male reputations evolve among peers increasingly based on success as romancers, often demonstrated by the progeny they produce with several women. A depressed economy rules against easy provision for the families that they create. These diametrically conflicting conditions contribute to the sexual tension we hear in the song lyrics. In Jamaica, once boys leave their yard for the street and begin the search for building a reputation that their peer status depends on, it may be gained by having "numerous and productive sexual exploits and for having the money to 'keep' many women" (Sobo 1993). The reputation for the "phallic masculinity" of lower-class Jamaican males is similar to that which Freilich (1968) found in Trinidad's "sex-fame game." Freilich found that men try to impress each other by bragging about the amount and frequency of sexual conquests in "breed" or "brush" relationships. The object of the game for the male is: "1. To have sexual escapades widely known. 2. To get lovers pregnant – for greater fame. 3. To keep few promises. 4. To have many outside women and a common-law wife" (57). We see similar conflicts in female gender socialization. Girls are raised in a blatantly erotophylic, sexually expressive culture that also has a very British Protestant, sexually repressive historical legacy. Lower-class girls are in a double-bind, expected to protect family respectability preserving virginity until marriage, while simultaneously pressured to be a sexual player often by families needing support from the men they attract. While males pressure girls to become sexually active to boost their reputations, it is also reported that girls like to prove they are fertile to negate the stigma of being called a sterile "mule." Experience tells lower-class girls not to rely on male support after babies arrive, so the hope is that with each new pregnancy a new baby father will provide for all the children.

Thus, the construction of the cultural consumer lovemap is fraught with contradictions and contraindications of trust and love. Females fear being tricked into pregnancy to boost male ego and reputation, often done with males purposively "cutting a jacket" by piercing a hole in a condom. However, for a pregnant female or one who already has several children, another baby father represents additional monetary income. Thus, males fear being "tied" to a woman for economic support, especially from poisoning by her blood or oils purchased from an Obeah woman or pharmacy, as Lovindeer sings "Give me the oily, give me the oily" in his song, "The Oil" (n.d.). After discussing "Can't Tie Me" with three of Zoe's teenage grandchildren, they confirmed that Oil of Hold Me, Oil of Come With Me, Oil of Rich, Oil of Get Money, and Oil of Find Me a Job could be procured from the local pharmacy (fieldwork notes 1999).

With respect to masculinity and self-identity and the similarities between dancehall and hip-hop, we consider Arthur's (2006) contention that disenfranchised male identities are rebuilt with more sexualized and aggressive projections of the self. In this scenario, women are objectified, and the male ego obtains from power-profiling for respect. Arthur notes that, "[marriage] in some cases is even viewed as emasculating" (109) and promiscuity is preferred to monogamy. In Jamaica, promiscuity that begets pregnancy and progeny is cushioned by a traditional culture prepared to accommodate a plethora of love children. Though some might argue to the contrary. Unwanted youth are more prone toward violence and a life of crime heard in "gun lyrics." When male promiscuity and female objectification diffuses to other global contexts, each receiving culture may not have traditional supports to absorb the consequences. The diffusion of entertainment is problematic when the entertainment form acts as a transformative cultural intermediary. As an element of consumer behavior, music embodies the evolving dynamics of a cultural consumer lovemap as it both mirrors and commodifies cultural production. Consumers listen to and hear justification for observations in family and peer settings; music sanctions reality as it makes it real in future behaviors. Thus, they construct the lyrics in their own personal ways, at once embodying, transmitting and constructing culture even as they contest and redirect it.

Music may be viewed as an ever-re-schematizing instrument guiding individual practices that problematizes pleasures and especially erotics in seemingly historically and culturally deterministic ways, although paradoxically full of the individual consumer's desire to comply or not comply with these strictures (Foucault 1990). We find that music is a meaning carrier that bubbles up from the consumers' everyday experience as much as it produces it, often in new directions. Thus we find that the data problematize any simple conclusions. There seem to be at once affirmations of certain cultural roots, long-standing in Jamaican culture, as well as various evolving changes, some subtle and transient, others more long-lasting, if not permanent. Clearly, as our longitudinal perspective demonstrates, the socio-cultural history of Jamaica provides a stage and event chain that interacts with lived experience and music. This hermeneutic is dynamically semiotic (evoking, transforming and [de]constructing signs) and deconstructive (playing with and shifting cultural categories, personal identities and practices; cf., Oswald 1999). To some degree, cross-cultural influences seep into this hermeneutic equation (e.g., the changing dynamics of women's roles), but for the most part, they may be read as insinuating themselves into Jamaica's general cultural history.

Alternatively, reggae spread from Jamaica to influence the American genres of rap and hip-hop primarily because many early musicians had Jamaican roots. Erskine makes the connection with "Kool Herc, a Jamaican immigrant to New York City… credited with playing an instrumental role in the development of rap as a segment of hip-hop culture. …Kool Herc provided rhythmic patterns that would define the genre of rap as he created a new art form infused with energy of reggae" that emerged in New York's South Bronx in the 1970s. As the African American church lost its influence on youth, Erskine says hip-hop provided a new focus for "identity formation and social standing in the community" (2003, 73). Indeed, while the play between Jamaican and world culture itself constitutes an interesting hermeneutic and is itself two-way (e.g., the spread of Jamaican music, the movement of Jamaicans to other countries and tourism in Jamaica), there remain clearly visible Jamaican elements that at least for the present allow us to focus on the distinctive Jamaican cultural consumer lovemap. In this regard, we expect that extensions of this lovemap perspective to other countries will provide heterogeneous conclusions regarding cross-cultural lovemap differences and the role of music in shaping and embodying them, albeit that they may appear to converge and diverge in various aspects. Thus, we find that the Jamaican case exemplifies how a cultural consumer lovemap manifests and functions in constructing erotic thought and behavior, serves as a tool of both cultural and individual identity production, and relates to the simultaneous formation of individual consumer lovemaps.

## Wine-up and wine-down

In Jamaica, to "wine" is to move sensuously to the sounds of music that impels the body to be carried away by the rhythm. Lest we get too carried away with our theme, we should consider future research. Expansion will greatly benefit from a global study on the aspect of diffusion of music genres as metaphors for the disenfranchised. Rather than disparage artistic creations, they should be interpreted emically for meaning derived in situ by producers and consumers, not with the value judgments of bystanders. Cross-cultural research on gender construction could reveal how attitudes are informed by political economies and folk beliefs and are expressed in cultural commercial commodities including forms of entertainment. Particular attention should also be given to the pervasive homophobic culture (Cooper 2004 extends it to heterophobic) recently reviled by global human rights organizations. Moreover, while music remains a keen object of lovemap embodiment since it so explicitly and affectively lays out the lyrics of sexual and related behavior, other products and services and their roles in the lovemaps might be investigated (cf. Bounty Killer's song "Benz and the Bimma" [1996]). Finally, while we stress the existence of cultural consumer lovemaps, we also need to emphasize the need not to be wedded to one conceptualization of them. Historical change, the dynamics of postmodern globalization and fragmentation, and cross-cultural differences all suggest that perhaps the greatest potential contribution of the cultural lovemap concept to consumption research may lie in its capacity to accommodate comparative narratives. A global database of ethnographic investigations and narratives would do much to inform such research on the production of meaning embodied in cultural consumer lovemaps, not to mention the very construction of culture itself. For example, our comparisons and links to Cuban parallels are instructive, even as particular differences of site and meaning are also apparent. In this regard, we must also add a cautionary note: music is glocalized, such that comparisons involve interpreting embedded interlinkages in the construction of lovemaps among nations, cultures and increasingly tribes of tastes and lifestyles (Maffesoli 1995), which render borders porous. Cultural ideology takes material form in the artifacts used to negotiate our everyday reality – e.g., food, adornment and entertainment. The values we ascribe to these artifacts and the ways in which they are used often reveal the inner logic of a culture's moral code and ideology, including in our case, the relations between genders. Using a mirror metaphor, we considered the links between music as mirror and everyday gendered and sexual behavior in constructing cultural consumer lovemaps (Gould 1995). Using only Jamaica, and particular classes within that country, we find from the literature, lyrics and fieldwork that gender relations are characterized by a hostile tension. This tension, reflected in its lovemaps, is steeped in Jamaican socio-economic history and reproduced in succeeding generations through folklore, oral and scribal traditions (Alleyne 1988).

From our vantage points as Americans, and although we did not explicitly compare Jamaican music with that of other countries, we can safely say that the cultural consumer lovemaps of various places and their expression could vary quite a bit across cultures, and even by genre within those cultures. In this regard, we suggest that understanding these lovemaps as fully as possible requires the illumination of cross-cultural research. This is neither to rule out similarities nor the fact that various cultural crossings, intertextual encounters and hybridization might not occur. For instance, the music of the US and Jamaica do meet with a cross-fertilization occurring among hip-hop, rap and DJ. And we find that the Jamaican musical genre, diasporic reggae, characterized by "its ability to convey the struggles and aspirations of Caribbean people in their specific diasporic environments" (Walker 2005, 162), is increasingly transforming into "higher consciousness" lyrics.

Jamaican authors Chang and Chen (1998) hail the culture of sexuality expressed in song and consider the freedom of speech that nurtures such expression. Without judgment, they note how the "double standard for men and women" is extant. Since women cheer for and sing along with lyrics promoting male promiscuity, Chang and Chen conclude: "Polygamy seems to be officially accepted in Jamaica" (1998, 214). They conclude their grand tour of Jamaican music with a lament on the negative mediation of entertainment for Jamaica's musical future:

> Ineluctably, the mores of youth in Jamaica are being shaped by channels like Black Entertainment Television [from the U.S.]. In ten or 20 years time, although rap may have originally

> evolved from dancehall, given rap's far larger market, artist population base and media exposure, it's difficult not to see dancehall eventually being devoured by its offspring, becoming just another branch of the rap tree, differing from hip hop in a similar way as say East Coast rap differs from West Coast rap. (219)

We considered the source of the journey, from its ancient yearning for love, if Darwin was correct, to the drum that gave it rhythm, and the man- (and now woman-) of-words. As Jamaican musicians are inspired by a need for discourse that also moves the body to motion, we can only hope they retain their unique creativity in future generations.

## Acknowledgments

The authors most importantly thank the respondents who provided their stories for this paper, as well as SUNY Old Westbury for a 1999 fieldwork grant, the editors and reviewers who inspired greater depth, and Ken Bilby for his invaluable guidance and lyric transcriptions.

## References

Abrahams, Roger. 1983. *The man of words in the West Indies.* Baltimore, MD: John Hopkins.

Alleyne, Mervyn C. 1988. *Roots of Jamaican culture.* London: Pluto Press.

Araújo, Samuel. 2000. Brazilian identities and musical performances. *Diogenes* 48, no. 3: 115–27.

Armstrong, Edward G. 1986. Country music sex songs: An ethnomusicological account. *Journal of Sex Research* 22, no. 3: 370–8.

Arthur, Damien. 2006. Hip hop consumption and masculinity. In *Gender and consumer behavior,* vol. 8, ed. Lorna Stevens and Janet Borgerson, 105–16. Edenburgh: Association for Consumer Research.

Attali, Jacques. 2002. *Noise: The political economy of music.* Minneapolis, MN: University of Minnesota Press.

Biddle, Ian. 2003. Of mice and dogs: Music, gender, and sexuality at the long fin de siecle. In *The cultural study of music: A critical introduction,* ed. M. Clayton, T. Herbert and R. Middleton, 215–26. New York: Routledge.

Bilby, Kenneth M. 1985. The Caribbean as a musical region. In *Caribbean contours,* ed. S.W. Mintz and S. Price, 181–218. Baltimore, MD: John Hopkins University Press.

Blair, M. Elizabeth, and Eva M. Hyatt. 1997. Meanings of the home in popular song lyrics: A feminist critique examining rock and country music. *Consumption, Markets and Culture* 1, no. 3: 271–96.

Blake, Judith. 1961. *Family structure in Jamaica: The social context of reproduction.* New York: Free Press.

Borgerson, Janet, and Jonathan Schroeder. 2003. The lure of paradise: Marketing the retro-escape of Hawaii. In *Time, space, and the market: Retroscapes rising,* ed. S. Brown and J.F. Sherry Jr., 219–337. Armonk, NY: Sharpe.

Bradshaw, Alan, Pierre McDonagh, David Marshall, and Harry Bradshaw. 2005. Exiled music herself, pushed to the edge of existence: The experience of musicians who perform background music. *Consumption, Markets and Culture* 8, no. 3: 219–40.

Branscomb, H. Eric. 1993. Literacy and a popular medium: The lyrics of Bruce Springsteen. *Journal of Popular Culture* 27, no. 1: 29–42.

Brown, Susan E. 1975. Love unites them and hunger separates them: Poor women in the Dominican Republic. In *Toward an anthropology of women,* ed. R.R. Reiter, 322–31. New York: Monthly Review Press.

Campbell-Livingstone, Cecelia, and Clinton Lindsay. 2004. Corporate Jamaica takes a stand regarding dancehall lyrics. *Jahworks.org,* 6 October. http://www.jahworks.org/music/features/corp_Jamaica.htm

Cassidy, Frederic Gomes, and Robert B. LePage, eds. [1967] 1984. *Dictionary of Jamaican English.* New York: Cambridge University Press.

Chang, Kevin O'Brien, and Wayne Chen. 1998. Reggae routes: The story of Jamaican music. Philadelphia, PA: Temple University Press.

Clarke, Edith. 1979. *My mother who fathered me.* London: George Allen and Unwin.

Cooper, Carolyn. 1995. *Noises in the blood: Orality, gender, and the "vulgar" body of Jamaican popular culture.* Durham, NC: Duke University Press.

———. 2004. *Sound clash: Jamaican dancehall culture at large.* New York: Palgrave Macmillan.

Curtin, Philip D. 1968. *Two Jamaicas.* Westport, CT: Greenwood Press.

*Dancehall Queen.* Directed by Rick Elgood and Don Letts. Kingston, Jamaica: Palm Pictures, 1997.

De Certeau, Michel, and Luce Giard. 1998. A practical science of the singular. In *The practice of everyday life,* vol. 2, ed. M. de Certeau, L. Giard, and P. Mayol, trans. T.J. Tomasik, 251–6. Minneapolis: University of Minnesota Press.

Dollard, John, Leonard W. Doob, Neal E. Miller, O.H. Mowrer, and Robert R. Sears. 1967. *Frustration and aggression.* New Haven, CT: Yale University.

Douglass, Lisa. 1992. *The power of sentiment: Love, hierarchy, and the Jamaican family elite.* Boulder, CO: Westview Press.

Dyson, Michael Eric. 2007. *Know what I mean? Reflections on hip hop.* New York: Basic Books.

Eckholm, Erik. 2006. Rap fan asks hard questions about the music he loves. *The New York Times,* December 24.

Erskine, Noel Leo. 2003. Rap, reggae, and religion: sounds of cultural dissonance. In *Noise and spirit: The religious and spiritual sensibilities of rap music,* ed. A.B. Pinn, 71–84. New York: New York University Press.

Fairley, Jan. 2004. "*Ay Díos, Ampárame*" (O God, protect me): Music in Cuba during the 1990s, the "special period." In *Island musics,* ed. Kevin Dawe, 77–98. Oxford, UK: Berg.

Finnegan, Ruth. 2003. Music, experience, and the anthropology of emotion. In *The cultural study of music: A critical introduction,* ed. M. Clayton, T. Herbert, and R. Middleton, 181–92. New York: Routledge.

Foucault, Michel. 1990. *The use of pleasure: The history of sexuality,* vol. 2. New York: Vintage Books.

Frazier, Franklin E. 1966. *The Negro family in the United States.* Chicago: University of Chicago Press.

Freilich, Morris. 1968. Sex, secrets and systems. In *The family in the Caribbean,* ed. S.N. Gerber, 47–62. Río Piedras, PR: Institute of Caribbean Studies, University of Puerto Rico.

Francis-Jackson, Chester. 1995. *The official dancehall dictionary: A guide to Jamaican dialect and dancehall slang.* Kingston: Kingston Publishers.

Frith, Simon. 1996. Music and identity. In *Questions of cultural identity,* ed. S. Hall and P. du Guy, 108–27. London: Sage.

———. 2003. Music and everyday life. In *The cultural study of music: A critical introduction,* ed. M. Clayton, T. Herbert, and R. Middleton, 92–101. New York: Routledge.

Gaunt, Kyra D. 2006. The games black girls play: learning the ropes from double-Dutch to hip-hop. NY: New York University Press.

Gould, Stephen J. 1991. Toward a theory of sexuality and consumption: consumer lovemaps. In *Advances in consumer research,* vol. 18, ed. R.H. Holman and M.R. Solomon, 381–3. Provo, UT: Association for Consumer Research.

———. 1995. Sexualized aspects of consumer behavior: An empirical investigation of consumer lovemaps. *Psychology and Marketing* 12, no. 5: 305–413.

———. 2003. Toward a theory of advertising lovemaps in marketing communications: Overdetermination, postmodern thought and the advertising hermeneutic circle. In *Sex in advertising,* ed. T. Reichert and J. Lambiase, 151–70. Mahwah, NJ: Lawrence Erlbaum.

———. 2006. The fetishization of people and their objects: Using lovemaps to view "style" from the *New York Times Magazine.* In *Sex in consumer culture: The erotic content of media and marketing,* 263–80. Philadelphia: Lawrence Erlbaum Associates.

Handler, Jerome S., and Kenneth M. Bilby. 2001. On the early use and origin of the term "Obeah" in Barbados and the anglophone Caribbean. *Slavery and Abolition* 22, no. 2: 87–100.

Hebdige, Dick. 1994. *Cut 'n' mix: Culture, identity and caribbean music.* New York: Routledge.

Henry, Krista. 2006. Dancehall grows away from roots. *Jamaica Gleaner,* 24 September. http://www. jamaica-gleaner.com/gleaner/20060924/ent/ent1.html

Herskovits, Melville J. 1941. *The myth of the Negro past.* Boston: Beacon Press.

Holbrook, Morris. 2003. A book-review essay on the role of ambi-digetic film music in the product design of Hollywood movies: Macromarketing in La-La-Land. *Consumption, Markets and Culture* 6, no. 3: 207–30.

———. 2005. Ambi-digetic music in the movies: The Crosby duets in High Society. *Consumption, Markets and Culture* 8, no. 2: 153–82.
Holt, Douglas B. 1995. How consumers consume: A typology of consumption practices. *Journal of Consumer Research* 22, no. 1: 1–16.
———. 1997. Poststructuralist lifestyle analysis: Conceptualizing the social patterning of consumption in postmodernity. *Journal of Consumer Research* 23, no. 4: 326–50.
Horst, Heather A., and Daniel Miller. 2006. *The cell phone: An anthropology of communication.* Oxford: Berg.
Johnson, Leola A. 2003. The spirit is willing and so is the flesh: The queen in hip-hop culture. In *Noise and spirit: The religious and spiritual sensibilities of rap music,* ed. A. B. Pinn, 154–72. New York: New York University Press.
Johnson, Janis, and Robert A. Rankin. 1982. Interviewing Michael Manley: The role of the opposition in Jamaica. *Caribbean Review* 11, no. 3: 26–9.
Keith, Nelson W. 1992. Nonnibutibus: The sociocultural messages of the Jamaican tea meeting. *Anthropology and Humanism Quarterly* 17, no. 1: 2–8.
Lake, Tracy Melanie. 2006. *Investigating radical contradictions of original lovemaps: Therapeutic implications.* PhD dissertation, University of South Africa.
Leerssen, Joep. 2000. The rhetoric of national character: A programmatic survey. *Poetics Today* 21, no. 2: 267–92.
Leppert, Richard. 2002. *Essays on music: Theodor Adorno.* Berkeley: University of California Press.
Levitin, Daniel J. 2006. *This is your brain on music: The science of a human obsession.* New York: Plume, Penguin Group.
Maffesoli, Michel. 1995. *The time of tribes.* London: Sage.
Manuel, Peter, with Kenneth Bilby, and Michael Largey. 2006. *Caribbean currents: Caribbean music from rumba to reggae.* Philadelphia: Temple University Press.
Maxwell, Heather A. 2003. Divas of the Wassoulou sound: Transformations in the matrix of cultural production, globalization, and identity. *Consumption, Markets and Culture* 6, no. 1: 43–63.
McClary, Susan. 2002. *Feminine endings: Music, gender, and sexuality.* Minneapolis: University of Minnesota Press.
Middleton, Richard. 2003. Locating the people. In *The cultural study of music: A critical introduction,* ed. M. Clayton, T. Herbert, and R. Middleton. New York: Routledge.
Miller, Daniel. 1995. Consumption as the vanguard of history. In *Acknowledging consumption,* ed. D. Miller, 1–55. New York: Routledge.
Money, John. 1986. *Lovemaps: Clinical concepts of sexual/erotoci health and pathology, paraphilia, and gender transposition in childhood, adolescence and maturity.* New York: Lexington.
Moses, Yolanda. 1977. Female status, the family and male dominance in a West Indian community. *Signs* 3, no. 1: 142–51.
Negus, Keith. 2002. The work of cultural intermediaries and the enduring distance between production and consumption. *Cultural Studies* 16, no. 4: 501–15.
Nelson, Michelle R., and Hye-Jin Paek. 2005. Cross-cultural differences in sexual advertising content in a transnational women's magazine. *Sex Roles* 53, nos. 5–6: 371–83.
Nettl, Bruno. 1964. *Theory and method in ethnomusicology.* New York: The Free Press.
Nye, Stephen. 2007. Liner notes to disc three. In *Censored!* Trojan slack reggae box set. Sanctuary Records Group.
O'Donohoe, Stephanie. 2000. Reading advertising texts, understanding advertising consumption. In *Interpretive consumer research*, ed. Suzanne C. Beckmann and Richard H. Elliott, 151–75. Copenhagen: Copenhagen Business School.
Olsen, Barbara. 1995. Consuming Rastafari: Ethnographic research in context and meaning. In *Advances in consumer research,* vol. 22, ed. F.R. Kardes and M. Sujan, 481–5. Provo, UT: Association for Consumer Research.
———. 1997. Environmentally sustainable development and tourism: Lessons from Negril, Jamaica. *Human Organization* 56, no. 3: 285–93.
———. 2003. Reflexive introspection: The participant in the observation. Abstract. In *European advances in consumer research,* vol. 6, ed. D. Turley and S. Brown, 74. Valdosta, GA: Association for Consumer Research.

———. 2005. Empathetic ethnography: The reflexive lens on fieldwork in Jamaica. Paper presented at the N.E. Anthropological Association Conference.

Olsen, Barbara, and Stephen J. Gould. 1997. The construction of cultural consumer lovemaps: An ethnographic study of the creative roots, consumption and mirroring effects of DJ music in Jamaica. Abstract. In *The sixth symposium on cross-cultural consumer and business studies proceedings,* ed. S.M. Smith, 165–6. Provo, UT: Brigham Young University.

———. 1999. Jamaican DJ lyrics and postmodern consumption: Liberatory for whom? In *Advances in consumer research,* vol. 26, ed. E.J. Arnould and L.M. Scott, 44. Provo, UT: Association for Consumer Research.

Oswald, Laura R. 1999. Culture swapping: Consumption and the ethnogenesis of middle-class Haitian immigrants. *Journal of Consumer Research* 25, no. 1: 303–18.

Otterbein, Keith F. 1965. Caribbean family organization: A comparative analysis. *American Anthropologist* 67, no. 1: 66–79.

Patterson, Orlando. 1967. *The sociology of slavery.* London: MacGibbon and Kee.

Platoff, John. 2005. John Lennon, "revolution," and the politics of musical reception. *The Journal of Musicology* 22, no. 2: 241–67.

Prahlad, Sw. Anand. 2001. *Reggae wisdom: Proverbs in Jamaican music.* Jackson: University of Mississippi Press.

Reid, Anne, and Kay Deaux. 1996. Relationship between personal and social identities: Segregation and integration. *Journal of Personality and Social Psychology* 71: 1084–91.

Rhodes, Carl. 2004. Utopia in popular management writing and the music of Bruce Springsteen: Do you believe in the promised land? *Consumption, Markets and Culture* 7, no. 1: 1–20.

Rice, Timothy. 2001. Reflections on music and meaning: Metaphor, signification and control in the Bulgarian case. *British Journal of Ethnomusicology* 10, no. 1: 19–38.

Ritch, Dawn. 2002. Testosterone poisoning. *Weekly Gleaner,* Februay 3.

Schroeder, Jonathan E., and Janet L. Borgerson. 1999. Packaging paradise: Consuming Hawaiian music. In *Advances in consumer research,* vol. 26, ed. E.J. Arnould and L.M. Scott, 46–50. Provo, UT: Association for Consumer Research.

Scott, Linda M. 1990. Understanding jingles and needledrop: A rhetorical approach to music in advertising. *Journal of Consumer Research* 17, no. 2: 223–36.

Shankar, Avi. 2000. Lost in music? Subjective personal introspection and popular music consumption. *Qualitative Market Research* 3, no. 1: 27–38.

Sherlock, Philip, and Hazel Bennett. 1998. *The story of the Jamaican people.* Kingston, Jamaica: Ian Randle Publishers.

Sherry, Jr., John F. 1980. Verbal aggression in rugby ritual. In *Play and culture,* ed. H.B. Schwartzman, 139–50. West Point, NY: Leisure Press.

Simpson, George. 1955. The Ras Tafari movement in Jamaica. *Social Forces* 34, no. 2: 167–70.

Smith, Raymond T. 1988. *Kinship and class in the West Indies.* Cambridge: Cambridge University Press.

Sobo, Elisa Janine. 1993. *One blood: The Jamaican body.* Albany: State University of New York Press.

Stiglitz, Joseph E. 2002. *Globalization and its discontents.* New York: W.W. Norton.

Stokes, Martin. 2003. Globalization and the politics of world music. In *The cultural study of music,* ed. M. Clayton, T. Herbert and R. Middleton, 297–308. New York: Taylor and Francis.

Stoller, Paul. 1989. *The taste of ethnographic things: The senses in anthropology.* Philadelphia: University of Pennsylvania Press.

Stolzoff, Norman C. 2000. *Wake the town and tell the people: Dancehall culture in Jamaica.* Durham, NC: Duke University Press.

Sunshine, Catherine A. 1985. *The Caribbean: Survival, struggle and sovereignty.* Boston: EPICA.

Tajfel, Henry. 1982. Social psychology of intergroup relations. *Annual Review of Psychology* 33: 1–39.

*The Harder They Come.* Directed by Perry Henzell. Jamaica: International Films, 1972.

Thompson, Craig J., and Douglas B. Holt. 2004. How do men grab the phallus? Gender tourism in everyday consumption. *Journal of Consumer Culture* 4, no. 3: 313–38.

Titon, Jeff Todd. 2003. Textual analysis or thick description? In *The cultural study of music,* ed. M. Clayton, T. Herbert, and R. Middleton, 171–80. New York: Taylor and Francis.

Walker, Klive. 2005. *Dubwise: Reasoning from the reggae underground.* Toronto: Insomniac Press.

Waters, Anita. 1985. *Race, class and political symbols.* Piscataway, NJ: Transaction Books.

Wattanasuwan, Kritsadarat, and Richard Elliott. 1999. The Buddhist self and symbolic consumption: the consumption experience of teenage Dhammakaya Buddhists in Thailand. In *Advances in consumer research,* vol. 26, ed. E.J. Arnould and L.M. Scott, 150–5. Provo, UT: Association for Consumer Research.

White, Garth. 1967. Rudie, oh rudie! *Caribbean Quarterly* 13, no. 3: 39–44.

Winders, James A. 1997. Genre, gender, and the postmodern blues. *Consumption, Markets and Culture* 1, no. 1: 31–44.

Yelvington, Kevin A. 1998. Public sex culture in the Caribbean: play, performance, power. Paper presented at the 97th Annual Meeting of the American Anthropological Association, Philadelphia.

## Discography

Barker B. 1987. "Can't Tie Me." *Errol's Top Ten Party: The Best Mix.*

Bennie Man. 2006. "Stamina." *Ragga Ragga Ragga!* Greensleeves Records.

Bob Marley and the Wailers. 1966. "Rude Boy." *One Love.* Studio One Productions.

Bounty Killer. 1996. "Benz and the Bimma." *My Xperience.* TVT Records.

———. 1998. "Cellular Phone." *The Best of Bounty Killer.* Artists Only! Records.

Cobra Man (Joseph Clemendore). 1950s. "Maintenance." MRS.

Cock and Pussy. [1972] 2002. "Dead Buddy." *Trojan X-Rated Box Set,* disc one. Sanctuary Records.

Dance Hall Divas. 1998. "Remember When." *Conspiracy.* Mesa/Bluemoon Recordings.

Dr. Evil. 2006. "More Punanny." *Ragga Ragga Ragga!* Greensleeves Records.

Frisco Kid. 1996. "Rubbers." *Joy Ride.* Mad House Productions. Lyrics from http://www.dancehall-reggae.com/

Gospel Fish. [1991] 2007. "Punani Fi Smell." *Censored!* Disc two, Trojan slack Reggae Box Set. Sanctuary Records.

Jah Son. n.d. "Fat Ina Panty." Errol's Reggae Mix.

Lady P. [1994] 2007. "Wuck Me Tender." *Censored!* Disc three, Trojan slack Reggae Box Set. Sanctuary Records Group.

Lady Saw. 1996a. "Condom." *Give Me The Reason.* VP Records.

———. 1996c. "Give Me The Reason." *Give Me The Reason.* VP Records.

———. 1996d. "Over and Over." *Give Me The Reason.* VP Records.

———. 2004. "Do Me Better." *Strip Tease.* VP Records.

Lovindeer. 1999. "Man Shortage." *Lovindeer Supersize It. Caribbean Party Mix.* Prolific Productions.

——— n.d. "The Oil." *The Best of Lovindeer.* Prolific Productions, the Sound of Jamaica and Brown Sugar Productions.

Lynthia Cooper. 1975. "Three Minute Man." Jigsaw.

Mr. Vegas. 1998a. "Jacket." *Heads High.* Greensleeves Records.

———. 1998b. "Nike Air: Hands in the Air." *Heads High.* Greensleeves Records.

Ninja Man. n.d. "Renking Meat." Errol's Reggae Mix.

Shabba Ranks. 1991. "Where Does Slackness Come From?" *Raw As Ever.* Sony.

Shaggy. 2000. "Why Me Lord?" *Hot Shot.* MCA Records. Lyrics from http://www.afunk.com/shaggy/run.html.

Super Cat. [1986] 1993. "Boops." *On The Story of Jamaican Music,* CD #4. Produced by Winston Riley. Westbury Music/Prophecy Music.

Vybz Kartel. 2006. "U Nuh Have a Phone (Hello Moto)." *J.M.T.* Greensleeves Records.

Vybz Kartel and Delicious. 2006. "Rough Sex." *J.M.T.* Greensleeves Records.

Yellowman. 1988. "Nuh Tie Me." *Don't Burn It Down.* Sanachie Records.

# Getting heard in Tibet[1]: Music, media and markets

Anna Morcom

*Department of Music, Royal Holloway, University of London, Egham, Surrey, UK*

This article is an ethnographic study of the production of recorded music and popular music culture in Tibet, examining who gets their voice heard and how, and the roles played by the state, the independent realm that has emerged since the late 1980s, and the illegal/pirate sphere that has also resulted from economic liberalisation. While the question of IPR violations in China has become a global issue, it is largely discussed in the context of big, multi-national business. This article examines the little known implications of China's IPR and piracy issues for the production of minority culture.

Since the 1950s, the debate on Tibetan culture has centred on issues of political repression. This article aims to open up socio-economic factors and international legal and trade issues as crucial to the question of cultural expression and identity in Tibet, now China is connected to global capitalism.

## Introduction

The idea that the people are best served by culture produced entirely by the state began to be discredited in the People's Republic of China (PRC) following the death of Mao in 1976 and the end of the Cultural Revolution, one of the most creatively desolate eras in history. Whereas during the Cultural Revolution, the dictum that all art must serve socialism was taken to its logical extreme with only revolutionary songs and a handful of model operas permitted, after the end of the Cultural Revolution, the only art that was *not* permitted was that which questioned the state or the Party or their versions of history, or was, on the other hand, pornographic.

In addition to this change in cultural policy, a process of market reforms begun by Deng Xiaoping in 1978 took the whole of the PRC from a planned economy with restrictions on any private commerce to what is now in many ways a capitalist market economy. While the broadcast media remains entirely owned and controlled by the state, there has been considerable de facto deregulation of the market of recorded music with regard to domestic production.[2] Although a large part of production still takes place under the umbrella of state institutions and state personnel, a music business in the sense of a market-oriented cultural industry has therefore been able to emerge not just in mainland China, but also in politically sensitive and poor minority regions, including Xinjiang and Tibet.[3]

Few would now advocate a controlled economy model for cultural production, especially a Maoist one. However, ever since Adorno's ([1938] 1978) and Adorno and Horkheimer's (1979) searing critiques of capitalist industrial cultural production as fundamentally unhealthy for individuals and society, it continues to be argued strongly, though less polemically, that the public sphere this mode of production gives rise to is far from fair and representative of people and cultural diversity.[4] Despite varying amounts of regulation of markets and subsidies of the arts and cultural production that aim to avert an Adornian scenario of mass culture, uncomfortable facts about the culture industries worldwide remain: most famously, that five multinational conglomerates dominate global production and US/English language pop acts as a powerfully hegemonic force on musical cultures across the world, the majority of which are totally or largely unknown to the average member of the English-speaking world.[5]

On the other end of the scale from such global network capitalism (Louw 2001), however, the very existence of a music industry of the 5.4 million Tibetans in China would appear to speak for the potential of deregulation and supply-and-demand-based production to "democratise" the cultural domain.[6] As with the whole of post–Cultural Revolution China, "new voices" are very much being heard in Tibetan musical culture (Baranovitch 2003). However, that there are Tibetans (including those not directly related to the government sphere) who have access to the production of mass-mediated culture should not be assumed to unproblematically indicate the existence of cultural diversity and representation. As Sreberny-Mohammadi has pointed out, global diversity as disproving cultural imperialism is too easily seen in terms of national cultures (1996, 189). Similarly, it would be simplistic to take the mere presence of a Tibetan minority voice as definitively proving national diversity in China, or indeed the success of deregulation and a market economy in cultural production.

Rather, a close examination of Tibet's new music business is necessary to understand clearly the possibilities and problems of cultural production in the configuration of state ownership and control, private production, and "grey" and illegal zones that exists in Tibet, with its unique demography, economy, culture and politics. In Tibet, given the still extensive state control and ownership of even non-broadcast media, crucial questions must be asked relating to how state production serves the people, who gains access to the state sphere, and how the state sphere interacts with the private and, indeed, pirate spheres. However, now capitalist logic is at work in cultural production in Tibet, questions relating to socio-economic factors and profitability must also be asked in order to understand how China's "socialist market economy" mode of production affects cultural participation, representation and diversity. While anyone is allowed to produce music as long as it is not anti-state/Party, is it actually possible to do so in socio-economic terms for ordinary Tibetans? How financially viable is the production of albums now, and how does this affect participation and representation? How easy is it for different voices to *emerge* in Tibet, for people to *access* the field of cultural production? Does talent and determination alone get you where you need to go? How far does the advent of free market aspects of cultural production in Tibet actually give rise to opportunity for all kinds of people to get their voices (musically) heard?

That a music business exists in Tibet is a direct result of China's post-Cultural Revolution economic policy of "opening up." However, as the process of connecting to global capitalism continues, there will be further implications for cultural production inside China, potentially including remote areas like Tibet. At present, China is highly protectionist about its cultural markets. Only a limited number of cultural goods that have been checked and passed by the Ministry of Culture are legally imported into China (Wang 2003, 66–7). However, following accession to the World Trade Organisation (WTO) in 2001 in particular, there is increased pressure on China to abide by global trade rules such as access to markets, including those for cultural goods.

Ironically, while China cites "cultural-imperialism" type arguments for protection of its cultural markets, foreign cultural goods are in fact abundant in China, produced and circulated in violation of the Intellectual Property Rights (IPR) laws, which were worked, or rather, battled out with the US in the 1990s (Mertha 2005). While the restriction on the legal importation of American cultural goods into China (in particular, films) has been a sticking point between China and the US, the cause of far more bad blood between the two countries has been the *unrestricted* way that US cultural and other goods have been and continue to be counterfeited and pirated in China. The rampant nature of IPR violations as well as the general poor standards of quality control and safety in production in China somewhat luridly reached the consciousness of "ordinary" suburban, Western consumers during 2007 with the toxic pet food scam. More alarmingly, in 2006, diethylene glycol imported from China had been labelled as glycerine and mixed into a cough mixture, killing hundreds of people in Panama.[7] With membership of the WTO, as well as political pressures on governments fuelled by public outrage from such scams, demands on China to abide by IPR laws will continue. How China works out the IPR "problem" could have very important implications on China's domestic cultural industries, including questions of profitability, viability and cultural diversity in places such as Tibet, where piracy is presently responsible for the vast majority of both foreign musical products (mostly Bollywood and exile Tibetan) and sales of locally produced music.

This article is an ethnographic study of the music business of twenty-first century Tibet based in Lhasa, Amdo (northeastern Tibet, in Qinghai and Gansu provinces) and Chengdu (serving all the Tibetan areas, but in particular eastern Tibet or Kham, which lies largely in Sichuan).[8] It is based chiefly on fieldwork in a range of Tibetan regions over 15 months between 2004 and 2007, where I formally and informally met a variety of famous and not famous singers as well as members of state and private institutions and establishments related to the music industry, including bars, recording studios and retail outlets. My insights into the viability of making albums in economic and social terms is supported in particular by my own experience of making a VCD of Amdo (northeast Tibetan) songs, *Trin Gyi Metok* ("Cloud Flowers"), released in February 2006, which I produced and sang with Tanzin Gyatso.[9] Based on this fieldwork, this article seeks to address fundamental issues regarding Tibet's new public sphere through a detailed, "bottom-up" account of the complex workings of state and private institutions, legal and pirate markets, and social, economic, and cultural capital that characterise the early twenty-first century music business. It attempts to give, however, not just a detailed account of local production, but to place this production of minority culture in national and global contexts. In particular, it examines the possibilities, potentials and present actualities of China's increasing interaction with global capitalism and emergence as a global economic superpower on the vast, yet poor, sparsely populated and politically highly sensitive minority region of Tibet. With China's membership in the WTO, the global and the local should be meeting in the cultural industries of Tibet. This article examines how much this is the case and considers what might be the implications for a greater implementation of in particular IPR laws.

A substantial body of work has been carried out on the global entertainment majors (for example, Negus 1997, 1999; Peterson and Berger [1975] 1990), and work is also emerging on Bollywood, the major non-English language (or Spanish) hegemonic global music industry (Manuel 1993; Morcom 2007a). A number of small music industries have been examined in Wallis and Malm's classic studies (Wallis and Malm 1984; Malm and Wallis 1992), and non-Hindi, regional industries in India by Manuel (1993). The new music businesses of China's minorities, however, present very different scenarios of cultural production to these case studies, with their combination of small populations (5.4 million Tibetans in the PRC), a low involvement with the global media industries and the ideologically challenging mix of a socialist legacy of heavy (though in many ways sporadic) state control and rampant capitalism.[10] Harris, in her study of the Uyghur music industry in Xinjiang, has presented the first analysis of one of these industries and the ensuing new popular music culture (2002).[11] This article takes a more political economy style approach focussed on production itself and participation.[12] These (de facto) semi-deregulated centres of music production are in many ways surprising spaces in the PRC, especially given the continuing state control of broadcast media and the Internet. In the case of Tibet and Xinjiang, both of which have active independence movements and are hence subject to especially heavy state control, they are particularly surprising, and an understanding of them offers new perspectives on the positions of minorities in China. This study of the Tibetan music business examines, therefore, the production of a remarkable kind of "public sphere" in a region famous outside China for repression rather than expression.[13]

## Background to the twenty-first century music industry in Tibet

Tibet's current music business emerged entirely from the state realm in a slow process that saw both laws and the mindset of people change after the end of the Cultural Revolution. The first Tibetan albums were released in Amdo and Lhasa by government offices in 1983–4 and 1985 respectively.[14] Private albums were first produced in the late 1980s and 1990 in Amdo and Lhasa respectively. However, both cases involved artistes with existing links to state cultural production.[15] Officially speaking, all albums had to be, and indeed still have to be, produced by the state. Furthermore, given that the first private recording studio was only set up in 1994 in Lhasa,[16] private production for those with no connection to the government realm was not feasible. In the mid-1990s, access to cultural production began to spread more significantly beyond the narrow circle of government personnel and close contacts as it became possible to effectively buy the International Standard Recording Code (ISRC) that is compulsory for legal production in China from government offices and to produce private albums using government facilities. However, some kind of connection with the government realm was necessary to buy the ISRC. The option of producing and selling albums illegally – i.e., without the ISRC, under the counter – does not appear to have been a highly significant phenomenon in Tibet.[17] This is in sharp contrast to much of the world where "cassette revolutions" transformed local industries in the 1980s with "backyard" production (Harris 2002; Manuel 1993; Wallis and Malm 1984). It seems that government control, extreme poverty and an apparent lack of enterprise hindered this potential of cassettes in Tibet.

By the late 1990s, and in particular the early years of the twenty-first century, a more genuine private sphere of production can be seen as having emerged in Tibet. A number of private studios had been set up in Lhasa (serving central Tibet), in Chengdu (which lies just to the east of Tibet and serves the whole of Tibet, especially the east), and also in Xining (serving largely northeast Tibet or Amdo).[18] Within reason, depending on the prestige of the studio, if an artiste has the money, these studios will arrange the production of an album, including the purchase of an ISRC. This realm of private production was enhanced in particular by the emergence of what are known as *nangma* bars in Lhasa in the late 1990s. These are Tibetan nightclubs or drinking houses where live music is performed, initially traditional styles from the Lhasa area.[19] However, they rapidly became commercialised and a key venue for popular music performance, and are now found in prefecture and province capitals as well as some county towns across the Tibetan areas (Figure 1; Morcom 2007b).

*Nangma* bars have become a highly dynamic nexus point in the music industry, constituting the main arena for exposure of new artistes who do not have existing contacts to the mostly government-based institutions and personnel of the music industry, and

Figure 1. Performance by a "girl band" in a *nangma* bar in Lhasa, 2006. Photograph by Anna Morcom.

some are also involved directly in music production. The late 1990s also saw the move to the digitalisation of musical production in Tibet, with Video CD (VCD) technology. The first Tibetan VCD was released in 1998, and it is now the preferred recording media.[20] However, cassettes still constitute 50% or more of sales in nomadic areas where electricity is limited, being available only from portable solar panels in many remote areas.

An account of the emergence of the music business in post-Cultural Revolution Tibet is beyond the scope of this article. However, it can be stated that in the 1980s and early 1990s in particular, but also up to the present day, the music industry as a phenomena sharply challenges commonly held views of what government controlled and owned cultural production consists of, particularly in a region such as Tibet, which is a minority of a vast country whose political system consists of one-party rule. Tibet's first megastar, Dadon, was a singer from the Tibet Song and Dance Troupe.[21] Her albums, produced by the Tibet Audio Publishing House, consisted of songs composed by government personnel and checked by government censors (Henrion-Dourcy 2005, 241).[22] These songs were based on a style of popular singing that originated from Taiwan, a radical change from the Cultural Revolution era, and the lyrics are widely recognised as some of the most poetic and potent expressions of not just Tibetan identity, but a collective sadness of the Tibetan people. As Henrion-Dourcy writes, Dadon's songs "gave voice, for the first time since the 1950s, to a feeling of grief amongst Tibetans, emerging after the hardships of the previous twenty years" (237). Some of these songs have in fact been banned (246, footnote 120).[23] Similarly, from the early 1980s, Amdo *dunglen* was nurtured and heavily disseminated on radio and later cassettes by the radio offices in Gannan, Gansu Province, and Xining,

Qinghai Province. Extremely powerful in its expression of grass-roots Tibetan identity in its vocal, musical and lyrical style, *dunglen* remains *the* style of Amdo and the nomadic areas of Tibet, and is to this day closely tied to a number of government institutions in Amdo for its production and also distribution, as is discussed below. While until the late 1990s in particular there was very little freedom for those outside the government realm to access musical production, rather than producing an oppressive musical culture, the government's monopoly on production can be seen as having genuinely catered for unsated public demand.[24] A proliferation of styles certainly occurred in Tibet in the 1980s and 1990s. However, this was due to the relaxation of the extreme censorship on style and content of the Cultural Revolution rather than a rise in grass-roots cultural production due to the "democratic-participant" nature of cassettes, as happened across much of the rest of the world.[25]

This article now turns to an ethnography of the music business of Tibet in the form it took from the late 1990s. It begins with a description of practical considerations in making an album, including costs, and then moves to an account of distributing and selling albums in legal and pirate markets in Tibet. It then focuses on the question of access to or participation in the music industry and cultural production.

## The music business from the late 1990s: making an album

### *Legal permission*

The only bodies officially allowed to release albums in China are the Audio Publishing Houses that exist in each province. The Audio Publishing Houses are the repository of the ISRCs, which are the licenses for legitimate production in the PRC, but they pass some on to other government offices. Strictly speaking, ISRCs are not supposed to be sold to private producers since all production in China is officially by the state, either by state artistes or artistes commissioned specially by the government offices. However, from the mid 1990s, ISRCs started to be sold to members of the public via contacts from the government. This hardly secret, though not strictly legal, practice continues today and is fundamental to the existence of private cultural production in Tibet. The private recording studios that have emerged since the early years of the new century have greatly improved access for outsiders by obtaining the ISRC for albums from government contacts for a fee. Thus, participation in the recording industry has become connected more directly with factors of financial capital than with "social capital" (Bourdieu 1986), in particular, being connected with the government realm. However, the ease with which you get your ISRC will depend on the quality of your relationship with the studio and the quality of their relationship with the audio publishing house, so the element of "social capital" is still very significant. This is especially important since ISRCs are scarce, and albums of even established singers may be delayed for a considerable length of time, even years, due to not being able to obtain an ISRC. Hence, a considerable level of state control is kept on (unofficial) private production in this way.

The other legal issue in production is censorship. This takes place largely through self-censorship, but lyrics also have to be formally checked by government offices before an ISRC can be issued. Despite this, very surprising things slip through the net, and some singers have got into significant trouble as a result. Again, while censorship in China and Tibet is commonly seen as absolute, the repressive hand of the all-powerful state, the reality is in fact much more complex and also haphazard. The process of clamping down on transgressive lyrics is also made far more complicated by the fact that Tibetan song lyrics tend to work through highly symbolic language, and hence rely on the unpredictable role of interpretation at the reception stage for their meaning.[26]

It must be emphasised how important "grey" areas are to production at the most fundamental level. Private production only exists at all through a lack of implementation of actual policy with the sale of ISRCs. Furthermore, most of the new private studios so crucial to the existence of an active private sphere in fact do not have the official papers necessary for production of music. The new public sphere of Tibet in relation to cultural production can therefore be seen to exist in a precarious space, which it would be easy to clamp down on if it was so decided by the state.

### *Costs*

With a capitalist mode of production albeit unofficially in operation in Tibet, costs are crucial to questions of participation on socio-economic grounds. While cassette technology has been seen across the world to have radically improved access to production due to low costs (Munuel 1993; Wallis and Malm 1984, 1990), digital technology and the VCD can be seen as a considerable backtrack, with not just high expenditure on capital and production costs, but a large amount of educational capital also necessary.

- Video as well as sound recording is necessary, which means that video has to be either shot or lent/loaned from a government office or private entrepreneurs.
- A greater capital investment in equipment is necessary, with a video camera, digital recording equipment, a computer, and editing software all necessary – in fact, a basic audio-visual studio.
- Far greater investment in training is necessary, with persons skilled in the use of computers and sophisticated software, recording, filming and editing.

The level of financial and educational capital necessary for production is a particularly marked issue in Tibet, which is, except for a small minority, very poor and minimally educated. In Lhasa, a good salary is ¥2,000–¥3,000 (£132.19–£198.28 or $261.44–$392.17), and in places like Gannan or Qinghai, you are looking more at ¥500–¥1,000, or at the most ¥1,500. Nomads may have considerable amounts of wealth tied up in their livestock and jewellery, but this is not liquid capital. When you consider, in this context of ordinary wealth and capital, that to produce just the master for a decent quality commercial album usually costs ¥60,000–¥100,000, it is clear how far the picture is from the "democratic-participant" ideal of cheap cassette technology, which in the context of Tibet was limited anyway as discussed above. For the production standards of a high range album, as produced by Tibet's top singers (such as Yadong, Yungdrung Gyal, Chungshol Dolma), the costs are more like ¥200,000 for the master.[27] The costs per song of a decent but not high-end pop (not *dunglen*) album would break down something like as follows:[28]

- ¥1,000 composing of lyrics
- ¥2,500 composing of melody
- ¥1,200 composing of MIDI
- ¥400 recording
- ¥1,500 shooting video

The total cost per song would be ¥6,600, and the total cost of 13 songs typical of an album, ¥85,800. *Dunglen* is generally cheaper per song, with lower costs for lyrics and melody;

there are many lyricists in Amdo who will give lyrics free to singers they know and/or want to support, and quite a number of singers compose their own melodies. *Dunglen* is often sung without MIDI accompaniment, just a small acoustic ensemble, which also makes it cheaper than pop. However, *dunglen* albums contain more like 20 songs, since they are shorter than pop songs, and so the difference in song costs for an average *dunglen* and pop album is not very considerable.

The above per song costs may be less if the singer/producer knows the lyricist and songwriter well. Filming costs are also considerably cut in cheaper albums with the use of less locations, no background dancers, less variety of clothes (and borrowed clothes), lower-quality equipment and less-skilled personnel. In the case of many *dunglen* albums, on-location shooting costs are eliminated by filming the singer lip-syncing the songs in a studio and then superimposing this over film of scenery, etc., acquired from government offices or private film banks. The above per song costs can also be considerably higher if top-end lyricists and composers are employed, with the top composers taking over ¥5,000 per song, maybe ¥10,000. The cost of the ISRC is also extra, ¥1,500 as the official fee, with probably ¥1,000–3,000 as an (unofficial) fee to an appropriate government official to obtain it.

Once the master has been made, the album has to be duplicated, which costs in the range of ¥2.2 to nearer ¥4 depending on the size of the print run and the quality of box, leaflet, etc., chosen. One of the biggest problems in Tibet is that the still substantial state control over the cultural market means that VCDs and cassettes must be duplicated in a state factory, so it is impossible to do it really cheaply, and certainly not for the "back-yard" prices of the pirates, which are probably less than ¥1 per copy. Despite the fact that our VCD involved unusually low costs for the master (¥8,000[29]), the total cost – including reproduction, the ISRC and transport costs for sending 10,000 VCDs from Chengdu to Xining, where they were distributed from – was about ¥50,000. Even on this small budget project, we have not made a profit.[30]

The emergence of private studios has increased professionalism, public access and brought about more of a production-line ethos. Money is never everything, however, since to get good songs/lyrics and be taken seriously will always require good relationships with composers and singers, as well as talent. The best are very difficult to contact, especially for uneducated Tibetans new from the countryside, since they form largely an elite intelligentsia.[31] At the moment, owning a studio provides a very good income, so more are likely to emerge since, despite the difficulty of making a profit or even breaking even, it seems that more and more Tibetans want to make albums, subsidising production in various ways.

## Production, distribution and sales: official and pirate markets across Tibetan regions

### *Legitimate industry*

As shown in Figure 2, the Tibetan areas of the PRC are spread across five provinces (Tibet Autonomous Region [TAR], Qinghai, Gansu, Sichuan and Yunnan), and there is no one major city that is home to any overarching Tibetan music industry.

Chengdu (capital of Sichuan Province, not shown on the map, situated just east of Kardze Tibetan Autonomous Prefecture [TAP], i.e., not in a traditional Tibetan area) has become the Tibetan music centre with the greatest pan-Tibetan reach and is the focal point of the production of the highest quality albums and those in the newest styles from China and the international arena (big vocal rock, disco, and more recently R&B and girl and boy bands, though all centres now produce the latter). It is also the main centre for Khampa albums, though some are also produced in Lhasa (since part of Kham falls inside the TAR).

Figure 2. Map of the Tibetan areas of China: the Tibetan Autonomous Region (TAR), Tibetan Autonomous Prefectures (TAP), and a Tibetan Autonomous County (TAC) – © Tibetinfonet. Used by permission.

Chengdu has become particularly important as a leader of Tibetan pop styles since the *nangma* bar/nightclub Thangula started producing albums and the first VCD in 1998.[32] Chengdu has the best studio facilities, and top or well-funded and ambitious artistes from across the Tibetan areas will generally produce their albums in Chengdu or Beijing (though Lhasa is catching up somewhat). It also offers the best distribution channels. In addition, Chengdu is the place nearest the Tibetan areas where there are facilities for the legal duplication of VCDs or cassettes; there are no facilities in the TAR or Qinghai. Hence, most Tibetan albums are printed in Chengdu, though some are printed in Guangdong and Beijing.

In addition to Thangula, several other Tibetan well-equipped production houses have emerged in Chengdu since around the year 2000. These offices (and the government offices) have by far the best distribution networks of the Tibetan areas, being able to distribute across the Tibetan areas and to connect with nation-wide distribution networks and mainstream (as opposed to Tibetan specialty) music shops for certain artistes with nationwide appeal. They hence offer good distribution for albums aimed just at the Amdo or Khampa market, though they only handle the glossier end.

The (relatively) effective distribution networks emanating from Chengdu make sales more reliable than in Amdo, and piracy is controlled to some degree in Chengdu. I did not see any pirate VCDs or cassettes for sale in the Tibetan quarter of Chengdu. Furthermore, in Kardze, one of the TAP of Sichuan, while there were pirate albums to be seen, there were just as many legitimate albums for sale, even in small county towns like Lithang and Dao Chen. In Dartsedo, the capital of Kardze, I saw almost no pirate albums for sale. While there is no enforcement of piracy in Kardze (unlike Chengdu), there is a demand for legitimate sales as well as pirate (possibly due to greater wealth in the whole of Sichuan), plus a distribution system that provides shops with legitimate copies.

However, to put this in context, sales are still limited. Currently, the top sale for a Tibetan album is 70,000 copies (VCDs and cassettes), but this level of sales is firstly exceptional and secondly only possible if a substantial number of the songs on the album are sung in Chinese, which appeals to all regions of Tibet as well as some Chinese people.[33] Many such Chinese-language or largely Chinese-language Tibetan pop albums may not manage to sell even 1,000, which on an investment of ¥100,000 or more results in significant financial loss. While such VCDs retail at ¥12–18, the producer will only receive ¥5–¥8 per VCD,[34] so a sale of 10,000 gives ¥50,000–¥80,000 which does not even cover the capital. The break-even point would be 16,667–12,500 copies, which is difficult to achieve. Albums entirely in Tibetan language are harder to sell, and there are very few made in Chengdu that are not *dunglen*. The top sale I have heard of for a *dunglen* album sold from Chengdu is 20,000, which is exceptional.[35]

The music industry in Amdo (Qinghai and Gansu) presents a much bleaker picture for singers than that of the glossy, largely Chinese-language Tibetan productions aimed at the pan-Tibetan market through Chengdu or the new Tibetan-language productions of Lhasa, described below. The facilities in Amdo are not nearly as good as Chengdu, and the market is overwhelmed with piracy. However, Amdo is still probably the most prolific area of musical production in Tibet, and it is undeniably the biggest centre of Tibetan-language production, though Lhasa has also become important since the early years of the twenty-first century.

The Xining Radio Office, via its shop in Xining (capital of Qinghai Province, not shown on the map, but situated towards the east of the province near Gansu Province), provides the only legitimate distribution channels in Amdo and helps many singers sell their albums. However, despite clear good will, distribution is very limited and is in no way able to keep up with the pirate networks. Albums are sold in just a handful of government shops in some (not all) areas of Amdo and are also distributed to some private shops, which sell originals as well as fakes, via private businessmen. The Radio Office has as yet no means of distribution in Kardze, which has valuable markets for *dunglen*,[36] due to the lack of reliable contacts, i.e., people who would send money back from sales of VCDs. However, these links may be established in the near future and could improve things considerably.[37] The highest selling albums are those of the big festivals and the *dunglen* open competition organised by the Xining Radio Office, of which 10,000 copies are printed. The 2005 Amdo festival in Machu, for example, has so far sold 4,000 copies, and 2,500 were taken by Machu County for promotional purposes. Most Amdo albums, however, now struggle to sell a few thousand copies, some not even 1,000 (our album has sold so far a bit short of 3,000 copies in Amdo). At ¥6–¥8 per copy this results in receipts of ¥18,000–¥40,000 (for 3,000 copies) or ¥6,000–¥8,000 (for 1,000 copies), which generally does not cover the capital expenditure. The government productions, or those produced privately but via government personnel, are certainly privileged by the fact that in addition to these individuals having greater experience in production and knowing which albums are likely to sell well, their production costs will be lower (due to availability of equipment, good contacts with composers, lyricists, technicians, etc.), and distribution is also likely to be a bit more efficient.

Amdo albums are also distributed by small private businessmen buying a few hundred at a time from the singer and selling them on to shops in places like Lhasa and Nagchu, and perhaps Chengdu. Tanzin Gyatso distributed our album in this way, painstakingly selling about 3,000 in Lhasa and Nagchu for ¥10 at the most, and finally offloading a few hundred for ¥4 each. It is these (and other) additional sales which have brought us to a more or less break-even point. The album, as with many *dunglen* albums, was popular, but this popularity was expressed overwhelmingly in the sale of pirate copies. Self-distribution is not just time-consuming, exhausting and, due to piracy, soul destroying, but it is also practically speaking impossible due to the sheer size of the Tibetan areas. This is particularly the case with Amdo music, which caters to the nomadic audience, spread across an immense, remote landmass. Furthermore, even when legitimate copies can be sold, getting money back from shop owners and middlemen is notoriously difficult, which can reduce the projected income of ¥6–¥8 per copy considerably.

Quite a lot of Amdo singers are now distributing their albums through Chengdu, in addition to selling them in the government shops in Qinghai and Gannan and to various "middlemen." However, the Chengdu companies would only distribute glossier albums, leaving no options for the more grass-roots albums.

In the mid 1990s in Amdo, the "heyday" of cassettes, it cost generally around ¥35,000 to make the master of an album and print 10,000 copies, and if the album was reasonably good, it was possible to sell all these copies and make a sure profit therefore of around ¥6,000.[38] This financial viability certainly supported the prolific Amdo industry in the early era. However, the infrastructure has not kept up with the development of the pirate industry. The Tibetan music market has boomed following the (uneven) state-sponsored economic development of the Tibetan areas from around 2000, but the expansion of sales is almost entirely from the pirate market. While the pirate market is driven by profit, it is clear that the legitimate Amdo market is not.

In Lhasa, the recording industry has really blossomed in the last couple of years with the setting up of several private recording studios. These private studios produce Tibetan-language albums, are strongly supportive of Tibetan culture and cater for many singers who would not have access to the government Audio Publishing House which aims its releases at nationwide distribution, often with more Chinese language, and largely uses artistes from state song and dance troupes. The Lhasa studios will handle the entire production process for you, down to providing backing dancers if you so desire. The greatest advantage, however, is that they will handle distribution for you to various places of the TAR where they have good contacts (Nagchu, Lhokha, Shigatse) and will take care of piracy to some extent, although it still remains a significant problem. The control of piracy is essentially unofficial, involving, as I was told, a fee of ¥10,000 to groups of individuals who will beat up anyone they find producing or selling pirate copies for two months. After two months, it is then de facto all right for the pirates to sell copies (many still produce copies before the two month deadline). Piracy is also addressed in smaller and often messier confrontations with pirate sellers. There is no other way of controlling piracy, since either the government largely takes care of only their own productions in Lhasa or the pirates leave the government productions alone.[39] Control of piracy is slightly easier in Lhasa than say Amdo, since the market is very much concentrated in Lhasa itself.[40]

The other advantage of the Lhasa market, in addition to the curbing (though certainly not controlling) of piracy, is the fact that albums sell for much higher prices than in other Tibetan areas, initially for ¥25 or even ¥30, dipping later to ¥20 or ¥15 minimum, compared with Chengdu sales, where ¥15–18 is the norm, and Amdo sales, where the absolute maximum is ¥15 and the norm for new albums is ¥10–¥12, sometimes less if they are not doing well. This means that it is easier to make a profit from distributing through Lhasa. With a successful album, it should be possible to sell 10,000 copies, which for ¥20 per album gives a gross income of ¥200,000 which covers your costs and leaves some profit.[41] In Amdo, even a successful album is unlikely to give profit, or if so, very little. However, most albums are not profitable, with some, as in Amdo, struggling to sell 1,000 copies.

The willingness to pay high costs in Lhasa reflects the fact that salaries are far higher there due to heavy state subsidies. However, there is also far less of a culture of piracy there, at least of the Lhasa produced albums, perhaps because distribution channels have been made anew rather than relying on effectively obsolete networks, as is the case with Amdo. The majority of pirate albums sold in Lhasa are of Amdo music and foreign music, and are sold to the Amdo or poorer rural migrant community. With at least some hope of financial viability (unlike Amdo), albeit with high capital costs, a large number of Tibetan-language albums are being produced and a lot of new singers are emerging in Lhasa. Chinese-language Tibetan songs were going somewhat out of fashion in Lhasa in 2006 and 2007, though they were still dominating in Chengdu and Kham.

### *The pirate industry*

The most efficient production and distribution networks are undoubtedly those of the pirates. As pointed out by Wang (2003, 13), effective distribution has become far harder in the digital era due to the speed of disseminating information and of duplication, which helps piracy. Furthermore, markets are bigger and more diffuse. While reasonably effective distribution existed in the cassette era when the pirate industry was not developed and when costs were lower, the digital era has not kept up, particularly in Amdo. The biggest advantages the pirates have, however, are of course no production costs, very low reproduction costs, a public with a negligible concept of intellectual property and the fact that there is virtually no enforcement of the laws.

There are two main pirate networks that operate in/affect Tibet. The less harmful of the industries to the Tibetan music business is based in Guangdong, where high-quality, large print-run copies of albums are produced that are sold in all the provinces I visited (Gansu, Sichuan, Qinghai and TAR) and possibly across the whole of China. Similar pirate copies are also said to originate from Chengdu. These are pirate copies of Chinese pop music, pan-China Tibetan pop, Western pop, and Bollywood, all of which have a wide market, so mass-produced, high-quality copies are viable, which are difficult to distinguish from pirate copies.[42] Given that only limited foreign music is legally distributed in China, this pirate network greatly increases musical diversity in Tibet.[43]

The other pirate industry is run by Chinese Muslims and began in Amdo but now spans most if not all the Tibetan areas. It is apparently a network of interlocking producers with their own territories. They have their own illegal CD manufacturing and duplication factories that enable them to dramatically undercut the costs of production of legitimate producers who must use state duplication facilities. The CD manufacturing takes place in Qinghai and Gansu, just on the doorstep of the Amdo industry, and duplication facilities exist in Amdo as well as Lhasa (and possibly other Tibetan areas). I have seen copies from this network in Kardze in Sichuan, brought by drivers from Qinghai and Gansu, and Nagchu, brought presumably from Lhasa. Many other Tibetan areas are presumably served by these networks. Needless to say, these pirate producers have excellent relationships with local officials in the Cultural Bureau and are able to continue their activities virtually unchecked. They are extremely efficient. While originals may sell out, pirate copies rarely sell out and reach areas where originals do not. These pirates produce mostly Amdo music (and the industry certainly began there), but also other Tibetan music. In Lhasa, they also produce cheap Bollywood music imported from Nepal rather than China as well as exile Tibetan music. While the illegal importation and duplication of Bollywood and exile Tibetan music increases cultural diversity, the pirate industry as a whole causes severe damage to the profitability and viability of making music in Tibet, particularly in Amdo, where the ratio of pirate to original copies is, in general opinion, something like 10:1. The copies this network produces are very cheap, selling for as little as ¥4 or ¥5, or for a new, popular album, ¥8 or ¥10. This undercuts the unit cost of many albums.

The lack of control of piracy is staggering. On the whole, pirate copies of albums are sold in broad daylight, with maximum caution consisting of under-the-counter sales, which everyone anyway knows about. The copies produced by these Muslim networks are very bad quality and do not attempt to pass for originals (Figure 3).

Shops often stock only one or two original copies for appearances sake, with the bulk sales consisting of pirate copies, which people request. There is no conception that selling or buying pirate copies is a bad thing. I walked into several shops in Amdo and Kardze where shop owners showed me a pirate copy of our album in a friendly manner and asked "is that you?" I photographed several shops, one with the owner's explicit consent, showing the stocks of real versus pirate copies.

There are a number of reasons behind this frustrating situation.[44] China is on the whole new to the concept of copyright: work only began on a law in 1979, and it was only after a long and drawn-out process led overwhelmingly by foreign pressure that the Copyright

Figure 3. Low-quality pirate VCD of Tibetan songs from Tibetan exiles in India using images of Indian film stars on the cover. Collection of author.

Law was passed in 1990 (Mertha 2005, 119–26). The major problem with copyright and other Intellectual Property breaches in China, however, is not the absence of legislation, but a persistent lack of enforcement. As Mertha states: "All of the pressure that the USTR [US Trade Representative] has brought to bear on China from 1991 up through the present day has translated to an astonishingly low degree of copyright enforcement" (15). The reason for this is bureaucracy: "The layout of the administrative infrastructure for copyright management and enforcement in China is such that the Copyright Law and related laws and regulations cannot be effectively enforced" (133). Two problems are understaffing and, similarly, the under-funding of copyright enforcement. An official of the National Copyright Administration is quoted as stating: "There are only 200 people in all of China engaged in full-time copyright management work" (137).

This lack of resources is related to the problem of "embeddedness," which reveals a more fundamental conflict in the management of the cultural market in China. The National Copyright Bureau is subordinate to the National Press and Publications Bureau (PPB), and on the provincial level, the copyright departments are contained within the PPBs. The PPB, however, "is concerned mainly with censorship and has no interest in promoting the rights of authors or creating a free market in publishing," so copyright retains a low priority.[45] On the lower administrative levels of prefecture and county, there are no separate copyright offices; copyright enforcement is just one of the responsibilities of the Cultural Bureau, which supervises the cultural market. "Where priorities and scarce resources earmarked for the supervision of the 'cultural market' conflict with or supersede those of local copyright enforcement, the latter is often sacrificed to the former," which usually means that "copyrighted products that do not have a pornographic or antigovernment or anti-Party orientation" are not a priority (Mertha 2005, 149–50). In Lhasa in 2006, for example, the Muslim traders, who do not know the Tibetan language, pirated and sold an album from exile that contained the political song "*Jetsun Pema la*," unaware of its meaning. The sale of this album was clamped down upon very rapidly, and some of these traders got into trouble. That this album was clamped down on was clearly because of its political nature, not because of its lack of copyright in China, since pirate copies of non-political music continue to sell unchecked in Lhasa. In addition to the problems of understaffing and the conflicting priorities of the bureaucracy, corruption is also a major problem in piracy enforcement.

If one looks at the bigger picture, this inadequate administrative apparatus is itself a symptom of the fact that copyright and other intellectual property rights (IPR) protection is not a political or national priority for China. When something really needs to happen in China, politically speaking, it happens, and with immense efficiency, as was seen in the handling of the SARS crisis, for example (Mertha 2005, 225–6). Intellectual property rights have only gained any importance in China due to pressure from foreign governments and big companies who lose large amounts of revenue due to a lack of laws initially, and subsequently their enforcement. The tiny population of Tibet and the level of poverty there, however, mean that there is no infringement of IPR worth the attention of such foreign companies. Furthermore, the political problems Tibet raises for the Chinese state dwarf all other social and cultural issues, leaving not just IPR neglected to the detriment of local people and culture, but also a range of other issues.[46] All but a few pictures of the Dalai Lama have been eliminated from Lhasa through consistent campaigns, searches and punitive measures, while pirate copies and counterfeit goods literally line the streets. Furthermore, while pirate or unlicensed *production* was effectively clamped down on in the mid 1990s,[47] pirate distribution and sales continue largely unabated.

## Participation in the Tibetan music industry

While it is possible now to make private albums without close direct contacts to the government following the establishment of private studios in Chengdu, Lhasa and Amdo since around the turn of the millennium, it is not the case that all types of Tibetans are making recordings and all types of Tibetan music are represented. This section examines the key issues that govern what facilitates people getting their voices heard and what impedes them.

### *Socio-economic issues*

The most obvious factor inhibiting access to the music industry is the high production costs. Most albums are privately funded, yet only a very small number of Tibetans can raise the capital needed to make a VCD, immediately stacking the odds against poor Tibetans, who are in fact the majority. Furthermore, the fact that profit is so difficult to secure due to the small market size, but particularly because of piracy, means that it is not just a question of raising the capital for production, but of being prepared for the high possibility that a substantial amount of the capital will be lost, although singers who became famous from their albums may then gain good fees from singing in nightclubs and summer festivals, or singing songs in compilation albums, in which case an album becomes (with hindsight) an investment.[48] As stated, the situation with cassettes was much better at least in Amdo, and a certain class of reasonably well-off and well-connected Tibetans could make their own albums, perhaps by borrowing money from family and friends or raising capital from livestock and jewellery. Furthermore, it was easier to find people to sponsor albums since it was good cultural work, plus there was sure, though modest, profit. The picture is not black and white, since there are routes of access for poorer Tibetans now, as described below, but money is a big issue.

If wealth were equal, access to the music industry on the grounds of money would not privilege some over others, but since economic disparity in Tibet is acute, production is in the hands of only an elite minority. It is perhaps no coincidence that the more capital-intensive VCD production really took off from 2000 as the state-subsidised economic boom began to take hold in Tibet, which, as is now known, has made a small minority rich and the rest comparatively poorer.[49] The problem extends further than money to social capital (Bourdieu 1986), since a degree of social status and familiarity with the urban environment are necessary to "fit in" to popular culture venues, not to mention microphone skills, etc., which Tibetans from deep in the rural areas do not possess (Morcom 2007b). Amdo music is slightly more accessible, since it is a rural genre as a whole, and the vocal skills of nomads are well recognised and to a certain extent sought after. However, it is still controlled by a government and social elite. In this way, it can be seen how the economic boom and the resulting increasingly intensive capitalisation of culture has led to the exclusion of socio-economically disadvantaged Tibetans (who are the majority) from the new public sphere. This problem is set to increase as the industry becomes more highly capitalised, unless the disparity lessens.[50]

This situation is further compounded by the fact that it is becoming harder for cheaply made albums to compete with glossier ones since the audience (even at the poorer end) is becoming increasingly discerning, which makes participation harder for average (i.e., poor) Tibetans and new singers who cannot afford to make glossy productions. The commercial viability of cheaper albums is also disproportionately compromised by piracy. The glossier albums are able to get better distribution, and furthermore, since they appeal to urban (as well as some rural) Tibetans who are more likely to look for quality, it is possible to sell more original copies. In this way the Amdo market, which is also the bulk of the Tibetan-language market, is hardest hit, since the audience is generally poor and prefers to buy cheap, low-quality, pirate albums rather than originals. The commercial success of VCDs reflects in particular the buying power and hence the tastes of the rich, with the majority (possibly as much as 90%) of the buying power of average (poor) Tibetans, which is also the bulk of the Tibetan-language market, masked by the pirate industry. This is particularly detrimental to the representation of the preferences of the Tibetan majority, since the pirate industry is controlled by non-Tibetans and does not produce any new Tibetan music. In other words, the profits supported by the majority of Tibetans does not feed back into new production of Tibetan music, which could certainly threaten the long-term viability of Tibetan-language production in particular. This contrasts with a country like India, for instance, where legitimate companies also engage in "back door" pirate production, which means that the profits can feed back into cultural production.

### *Institutional/professional issues: song and dance troupes and nangma bars*

While money is an increasingly important factor in participation, there are two main ways of gaining exposure and opportunities on talent alone (though those with good contacts are still privileged). The first and older route is that of joining a government song and dance troupe, though they normally recruit people in their mid or early teens or even earlier. There are open auditions for at least some dance troupes, with publicity reaching into rural areas (though I doubt very remote areas), but there are stipulations on literacy, which excludes a great many of the most talented singers in the rural areas.[51] Exceptions to age and literacy requirements can be made for outstanding singers, but dancers have to enter while young.[52]

However, even for a talented member of a dance troupe, a chance to sing on an album is by no means assured. Some dance troupes are well funded (such as prefecture- or province-level ones, and certain counties with leaders sympathetic to cultural life), but most county troupes do not have the funds to make albums. However, being in a troupe does increase a singer's general level of exposure, especially since many county troupes have the chance to perform at prefecture-level festivals, where people with money and/or contacts will be present. A range of singing competitions also exists, which it will be easier to enter for members even of county troupes who have at least some stage/presentation experience and familiarity with officialdom. Virtually all the early Tibetan singing stars were launched through song and dance troupes, and this is still the case. Providing a stable, though modest, livelihood for singers and dancers plus the benefits of contact with the state sphere, the dance troupes are extremely important in the new mass-mediated cultural sphere and have strongly influenced popular culture. Equally important are the wider state training institutions where individuals can take degrees in singing and dancing. These graduates are stylistically marked by state aesthetic preferences, though the state preferences have themselves changed radically in response to the private sphere of production that emerged after the Cultural Revolution (Baranovitch 2003), and as the case of Dadon and Amdo *dunglen* show, state institutions can produce radical styles.

For those who miss the chance to audition for a song and dance troupe, or are excluded on literacy grounds, there is another route of entry to the music business that has emerged in the late 1990s, coinciding with (and contributing to) the expanding private and commercial sphere of the music business. This route is through *nangma* bars, nightclubs with live music and dance, which began in Lhasa around 1997, and have since spread across the Tibetan areas. *Nangma* bars help singers in three ways: exposure and experience, money, and direct recording opportunities.

Singing in *nangma* bars in Lhasa was extremely well paid until 2005–6, with the best singers earning over ¥5,000 in a month, when, as stated above, ¥2,000 was a good salary. With this kind of a salary, plus loans from friends and relatives, it was possible for highly paid singers to gradually build up a master. Wages elsewhere were much less, but were still reasonable or good by local standards, though of course varying according to the size and prestige of the *nangma* bar. However, wages in *nangma* bars in Lhasa have greatly reduced from 2005–6, and in 2007, it was difficult for singers to earn more than ¥2,500 per month, with typical salaries more like ¥1,800 per month. This is a respectable wage, but not the kind of money needed to support the production of an album. This drop in wages is partly due to greatly increased competition, with singers from Amdo, who are content to sing for lower wages, having entered the field. It is also because the overall business of *nangma* bars in Lhasa has reduced markedly: in 2007, there were five or six *nangma* bars in Lhasa, whereas in 2005, there were 10 to 15. Other parts of Tibet do not seem to be affected. This decline in the Lhasa *nangma* bars reflects a certain snobbery of the richer class of Lhasa Tibetans who now see *nangma* bars as places where rural Tibetans go and get drunk and fight, and prefer to visit the many new bars that are appearing in the city (many of which are sponsored and prominently decked out by Budweiser). Previously, *nangma* bars were frequented by rich businessmen.[53]

In addition to exposure and salary, some *nangma* bars also have a more direct connection to the music business. Thangula, set up in 1998 in Chengdu, was the first *nangma* bar that produced albums, with the best of its contract singers getting a chance to sing on Thangula's disco VCDs and possibly to be launched as solo artistes. Until 2006, when the independent studios and the Lhasa market gained ground, Thangula was the place to head to for an ambitious singer. A number of *nangma* bars are also owned by singers or people in the music business, giving new singers instant access to the right people. *Nangma* bars are also places where people come to scout talent for new albums. Singers also come into contact with people in *nangma*s who may, in a more emotional or spontaneous way, want to help them in their career.

In theory, anyone can approach the management of a *nangma* bar for an audition, though in practice it is not so simple to get heard. Contacts, persistence, plus the actual need for singers are all significant factors, and there may be pressure for or at least advantage from sexual favours from female singers. However, *nangma* bars are still much more widely accessible than the dance troupes. Nevertheless, certain styles and types of singer are definitely preferred. While *nangma*s started off with folk music performance, they rapidly moved towards pop, and now, unmodified traditional music is virtually unheard of. A slick performance style is essential, with singers that look cool (in the urban sense) and can sing pop songs and sing well in Chinese. Hence rural singers, even if they have excellent voices (which many do), have little hope of getting work in *nangma* bars until they have spent at least some time getting acculturated to (sinicised) Tibetan cities, and even then, it is hard for them (Morcom 2007b). This is thus another crucial factor in the issue of socio-economic access to the music business. The competition is such that many *nangma* bars in the big cities are now populated with singers who already have their own album; an album can now be a means to getting work in a *nangma* bar as much as the other way round. *Nangma* bars compete for audiences by inviting famous singers. In the case of a big *nangma* bar like Thangula's new branch in Lhasa, this is a big, ticketed event (Figure 4).

The downturn in *nangma* bars will have implications for the Tibetan music business, especially if it spreads to places outside Lhasa, though to a certain extent, the new private

Figure 4. Ticket for Tibetan popstar Chungshol Dolma at Thangula *nangma* bar, Lhasa, June 2006. Collection of author.

Figure 5. "Khampa Shepherdess" Diva Yangchen Lhamo performs at Nagchu horse race festival, August 2004. Photograph by Anna Morcom.

studios are providing alternative access points, which are based more on money than talent. However, as one singer in Lhasa said, if singers' wages go down, singers will become less prestigious members of society, which will affect the degree of sacrifice people are prepared to make for music. Furthermore, if there is little scope for exposure and a financially rewarding career following an album, people may not wish to make an album. Other forms of live performance exist, in particular festivals in the summer, where famous singers are invited (see Figure 5), plus performances on state television (which may be unpaid). However, this will cater to only a small percentage of the top singers.

## The music business and a Tibetan public sphere

Although there are many aspects of the entertainment business that this article has barely touched on (the broadcast media and their relation to the recording industry, the wider arena of live popular concerts and state-funded competitions), it is possible to draw some preliminary conclusions on who gets their voices heard in Tibet in the mass-mediated musical culture of the twenty-first century and how this relates to state, private and illegal spheres of cultural production.

The emergence of private production in Tibet has certainly improved access to recording for the general public, in particular through the advent of private recording studios in the twenty-first century. However, it is a long way from reaching into really grass-roots, rural communities due to issues of wealth and social status. In the post-2000 era, very large amounts of money are needed to produce an album, and in addition, a significant degree of social capital is also necessary to gain access to private studios and *nangma* bars. In addition to social capital, proficiency with the styles that now carry cultural capital (Bourdieu 1986) (i.e., almost anything but unmodified traditional music) is also necessary to enter this new public sphere, and in many cases, the ability to sing in Chinese. While currently issues of social and economic capital are key to participation, in the 1980s and 1990s, the main criteria for getting recorded was belonging to the government cultural realm or having good access to it (friends, family, etc.). Therefore, the recording industry in fact remains in many ways restricted in access to an *elite*, but the difference is that this elite is now defined in socio-economic as well as political terms.[54] In fact, it can be argued that because the opening up of the recording industry through the advent of private production has coincided with the (subsidised) economic development of Tibet and subsequent growing disparity and social exclusion, relatively speaking, there has been little widening of access as compared to the 1980s and early to mid 1990s.

In terms of diversity and representation, little difference can be seen between state and private production in Tibet, and the state and independent spheres in fact overlap considerably. The most radical music in the last 30 years certainly came from the state domain, though there was no private domain to compare with in the (relatively) politically relaxed 1980s. The major musical force that is heavily excluded from Tibet's new mass-mediated public sphere is without a doubt unmodified traditional music. This is not due to it being banned by the government (the TAR Audio Publishing House has in fact produced several traditional albums). It is more to do with questions of taste and ideas of modernity that were created by the state in the socialist period and now, in a slightly modified form, have gained consensus with urban elite classes even outside of the government realm and act hegemonically on the wider Tibetan society (Morcom 2007b). These new notions of taste, of course, translate into markets and profitability. Traditional music also suffers from being unable to benefit from the economies of scale crucial to mass production, being generally associated with and hence bound to local dialects and stylistic identities. However, as *dunglen* shows, there is also a potential to muster large, pan-Tibetan audiences due to the many similarities in style and identity that local "folk" music from different areas in fact share. In many ways, *dunglen* can be seen as a new meta-tradition, a kind of "Ur-folk," powerfully linked to people, place and traditional styles, yet also owing its existence to the mass media.

Although the state can be seen as active in contributing to the new public sphere through the production of various forms of popular music (in addition to propaganda songs which still continue), it significantly fails the people through the lack of control of piracy, which heavily undermines the viability of local production. However, as discussed, the "state" that can be seen to be creating and supporting styles of music that are genuinely meaningful to Tibetans has negligible *practical* relationship to the "state" that is failing to control piracy or indeed that which crushes protests. However, the fact of the control of unauthorised production on the one hand and lack of control of piracy of legitimate products on the other does illustrate the overall political priorities of the state.

This article has highlighted the prohibitive costs of the production of VCDs in Tibet, arguing that it is a technology significantly less "democratic-participant" than cassettes. However, the VCD is the only medium where an albeit largely elite Tibetan public are able to represent themselves visually as well as aurally with a significant degree of autonomy, and with a reach as wide as television.[55] For the visual style of pop (and to a much lesser extent *dunglen*), VCDs certainly draw on hegemonic modes of representation. However, the contrast with the propagandic, dubbed or happy/glossy fare of Chinese state television is marked.

One of the most striking features of the Tibetan music industry is the small degree to which production is driven by profit. The only area that is entirely profit-driven is the pirate industry. Several writers have seen culture as potentially operating outside the logic of a capitalist market system due to its special value (Laing 2003, 319). Bourdieu draws a comparison between "large-scale cultural production, which submits to the laws of competition for the conquest of the largest possible market," and "the field of restricted production [which] tends to develop its own criteria for the evaluation of its products, thus achieving the truly cultural recognition accorded by the peer group whose members are both privileged clients and competitors" (1993, 115). Toynbee similarly states: "In order for culture to be sold it must be shown to be (partially) external to the economic system" (quoted in Laing 2003, 319). Although the current Tibetan music business certainly exists solely due to the entry of free-market forces in China and the relaxing of government control in many areas, it does not function as a purely capitalist industry. Like much official production in China, it runs effectively through subsidies and is largely overshadowed by the primordial, "Manchester" capitalism of the unofficial economy.[56] Rather than being subsidised by the government, however, the official music business of Tibet is "subsidised" or patronised by the money generated by peoples' desires to express and support Tibetan identity and to promote and develop Tibetan culture, which most Tibetans are aware is crucial to their survival as a small minority in a vast nation state with a very dominating, ethnocentric majority. In fact, most production is funded by private individuals rather than corporations, even some of the state productions, which may be funded by rich business contacts. The "subsidising" or patronage of music production is also driven by personal ambition, which people are now prepared to pay large amounts of money to fund. Although it is possible to see Tibetan popular music as influenced by global "commercial" styles such as rock and pop, it is not possible to see the industry overall as commercial.

In the early years of the twenty-first century, globalisation is visible in the music industry of Tibet largely in the form of pirated foreign cultural products. Global pressure on IPR enforcement relating to China's increasing connectivity to global capitalism leaves Tibet, and indeed much of the rest of China, largely untouched.[57] In other words, it is the lack of IPR enforcement that characterises the Tibetan music industry at present. If China did begin to prioritise IPR enforcement, it would have an immense impact on the economy. In Tibet, it could make the production of music financially viable. Global interest in Tibet's culture has typically been approached with charges of political repression and cultural genocide, and more recently with arguments about cultural heritage (UNESCO, etc.). With the move to the market system, however, it is possible to see how economically motivated attention to IPR enforcement could have a substantial though unintended effect on Tibetan cultural identity.[58]

However, to speculate further, if music production in Tibet became a solidly profitable business, it would attract the attention of bigger capitalists, inevitably corporations and entrepreneurs from China, as has been the case with retail ownership in Lhasa for instance. This would make access even harder for ordinary Tibetans who do not speak Chinese well. Indeed, this can be seen to be the case to a certain extent with the studios in Chengdu.[59] The especially unprofitable or unreliably profitable nature of the Tibetan music business means that it is of no interest to anyone apart from the Tibetans themselves. While top-end production, particularly that involving multinationals, is gaining some level of IPR enforcement in China due to financial and political clout (Mertha 2005), the Tibet music business end of the scale is not. In other words, rather than IPR enforcement reaching grass-roots production, it is quite possible that grass-roots production and globally linked production could remain in increasingly separate spheres, with the latter functioning increasingly in an official sphere and the former in tandem with the unofficial sphere. It is well known that it is the poor who are most involved with the unofficial sphere of the world economy, including its considerable dangers in the case of counterfeit medicines and food products. Similarly, it is low-end (which is also Tibetan-language) production that is particularly hard hit by piracy in Tibet in the realm of cultural production. However, it is also possible to see that the undermining of the profitability of the Tibetan music business by piracy in fact protects its autonomy, while at the same time making its very viability precarious.

## Notes

1. There are Tibetan indigenous areas spread across five provinces of China, the Tibet Autonomous Region (TAR) (Ch: *Xizang*) and the provinces of Qinghai, Gansu, Sichuan and Yunnan. In the interests of brevity, all the Tibetan areas of China will be referred to as "Tibet" in this article.
2. While private albums have been produced with the full knowledge of and often collaboration with government offices since in particular the mid 1990s, the private purchase of the International Standard Recording Code (ISRC) that makes production legally licensed in China is strictly speaking not allowed. The other de facto deregulation of the recording industry has been through piracy. These aspects of production are discussed in more detail below.
3. See Harris (2002) regarding Xinjiang.
4. Recent writers that have critiqued the culture industries include Stokes (2003), Negus (1999, 1997), Golding and Murdock (1996), Sreberny-Mohammadi (1996), Garnham (1990), Peterson and Berger ([1975] 1990) and Laing (1986). Concerns with unequal control over the power of the mass media led to UNESCO's special study (UNESCO 1982).
5. Wallis and Malm ([1984] 1990) discuss globalisation and the idea of cultural imperialism in the context of global musical products and local markets and production. See Negus (1999, 35–45) for a brief description and history of the five major record companies.
6. Curran (1996) and Manuel (1993) both discuss issues of the media and democratisation. Manuel argues that it is the cheap and "two-way" nature of cassette technology that is key to its ability to democratise production, essentially forcing deregulation or at least decentralisation through piracy (1993, 1–20). It must be emphasised that in China and Tibet, the deregulation and opening up to private production, or moves towards "democratisation" of the non-broadcast media, are restricted only to the cultural world and not in any way paralleled in the political arena. Broadcast media and the Internet remain entirely under government control, and as seen in the suppression of protests in Tibet in March 2008, there remains zero tolerance for a plurality of political voices.
7. An article in the *New York Times* reports that possibly thousands of people in China and other countries have been killed by products made from counterfeit glycerine made in China (Bogdanich and Hooker 2007).
8. A small part of the Tibetan areas of the PRC is incorporated in Yunnan province, and production of Tibetan music presumably takes place there. However, it was not included in my fieldwork.
9. I would like to thank the Leverhulme Trust for the Study Abroad Studentship 2004–5 during which I undertook the bulk of fieldwork for this article, including the recording and filming of songs for the VCD. I would also like to thank the British Academy for the Larger Research Grant 2006–7 during which I conducted further fieldwork on the Tibetan music business in the context of research on Bollywood in Tibet. Personal thanks in particular go to Tanzin, my co-singer of *Trin Gyi Metok*, *dunglen* teacher and source of endless information of grass-roots music-making in Tibet, plus all those who helped us with the VCD, most notably Pema Khar, our first link to the music business and long-suffering editor of our amateur filming and sound recording. Immense thanks go to my friend Rinchen Dolma, an outstandingly talented and versatile singer who also coached me hard in *dunglen*, put me in touch with many worlds of Tibetan singing and was on occasion a formal research assistant too. I would also like to thank warmly my supportive colleagues Thierry Dodin, Isabelle Henrion-Dourcy and Holly Gayley for their invaluable feedback on drafts of this article.
10. See also Baranovitch (2003), who discusses post-Mao popular music in mainland China. Tibet Information (TIN 2000a) offers a broad overview of the broadcast and print media in Tibet,

though does not discuss the music industry. TIN (2004, 62–4) provides a brief overview of the non-broadcast music industry in Tibet.

11. See also Harris (2005a), focussing on globalisation in markets of recorded music in Xinjiang, largely through (illegal/pirate) import, copy and distribution of foreign musical products.
12. See Garnham (1990) and Golding and Murdock (1996) for political economy approaches to the media.
13. This article was researched and written prior to the widespread protests in Tibet during March 2008 and is based on fieldwork between 2004 and 2007. The political suppression of protests by the military and police has been immediate. However, it is not yet known as to whether this will affect cultural production and the (de facto) space for independent production, whether there will be shifts in the degree of government control over the music business and popular culture.
14. Pema Khar (composer, lyricist and recording engineer, Gannan Radio Office, Gansu Province), interview with the author, 15 July 2005 and 25 May 2007; Tenzin Penor (composer, lyricist and recording engineer, Tibet Song and Dance Troupe, and private studio owner, Lhasa), personal communication, October 2006 and May 2007.
15. Palgon in Amdo and Jampa Tsering in Lhasa (Pema Khar, interview with the author, 15 July 2005 and 25 May 2007; Tenzin Penor, personal communication, October 2006 and May 2007).
16. By Tenzin Penor, from the Tibet Song and Dance Troupe. Hence, access to even this private sphere of production involved the same social contacts as for the government realm.
17. Henrion-Dourcy notes that there are some unlicensed cassettes sold in Lhasa (2005, 241, footnote 108). This domination of licensed production is contrary to the situation described by Harris in the 1990s in Xinjiang, which was clamped down on in 1995–6 (2002, 279).
18. For example, the well known singers Karma and Gyalpo have both set up private production houses in Lhasa since 2000, and Yadong set up a state of the art recording studio and production company in Chengdu in 2005–6. Since May 2007, Yadong's company has started distributing music too. Other smaller private businesses that undertake sound recording, filming, editing and full production have also been set up since 2000, particularly since 2005. As stated above, far and away the first private studio was Tenzin Penor's studio in Lhasa, which was set up in 1994.
19. See TIN (2004, 78–81) and Morcom (2007b) for details of the emergence of *nangma* bars and implications for popular dance culture respectively. See Adams (1996) on Karaoke and *nangma* bars in Lhasa in the late 1990s. Karaoke bars also provided local exposure and experience for singers, such as Dadon and Jampa Tsering, in Lhasa in the 1980s and early 1990s. However, in those days, as explained above, production was controlled by the government almost entirely, so singing in Karaoke bars never directly facilitated access to the recording industry.
20. See Wang (2003, 49–52) for an account of VCD technology and its popularity in China.
21. See Henrion-Dourcy (2005, 234–46) for the most detailed biography of Dadon.
22. Henrion-Dourcy reports that Dadon's album in fact caught the censors "off-guard," and it was only with subsequent albums that the practice of checking lyrics began (2005, 239). However, I was assured that the lyrics of this album were indeed checked like all the others.
23. Although the lyrics of these songs are extremely powerful, it must be emphasised that much of the controversy of Dadon's songs emerged *after* she left Tibet for exile in 1992. More importantly, the relatively relaxed political climate of the early 1980s rapidly changed following riots in Tibet in 1987.
24. The government institutions still continued, and indeed continue, to produce political propaganda-style performing arts while producing more entertainment-oriented popular songs not explicitly related to politics.
25. However, as argued below, the cassette era in Tibet in many ways still offered more access than the VCD technology that has largely taken over.
26. See TIN (2004, chapter 5) for a discussion of the expression of protest in Tibetan song lyrics and the role of interpretation; see Henrion-Dourcy (2005, 234–46) for a discussion of the lyrics of a selection of Dadon songs. The subtlety of Tibetan lyrics, the key role of interpretation and the (relatively) liberal political climate of the time are revealed in the following comment by Dadon: "By then I had no idea that what I was doing was political. I was just doing things spontaneously, without asking myself many questions. If you want to move other people, you have to sing from your heart. Express the feelings and speak the truth. I always say that I don't know anything about politics. I say things as I feel, like any regular Tibetan" (quoted in Henrion-Dourcy, 241–2).
27. Tsewang (one of the owners of Thangula), interview with the author, Chengdu, 8 June 2005.

28. These costs were given to me as a guideline by a singer in Lhasa who owns his own studio and produces albums for singers, and were also corroborated by conversations with other singers and studio owners.
29. This was only possible through filming and recording done ourselves and/or by friends, and a significant capital expenditure on a portable solid-state recorder, a microphone and a three-chip video camera, around £2,000 worth of equipment (¥30,260), which I had purchased (with part-support from the Leverhulme Trust) for my fieldwork. We also sang old or traditional songs apart from one composed by Tanzin and a friend, which we got away with due to the novelty value of my being a foreigner. The sound and video editing was also done for a minimal cost by a friend in a government office, who also very generously composed MIDI accompaniment and re-recorded some songs for free.
30. This was partly because, out of lack of experience and available advice, we printed too many VCDs (7,000 or 5,000 would have been plenty, given the level of piracy) and did not print cassettes, which would have sold well in the nomadic areas. However, VCDs, especially of *dunglen*, are generally not financially viable.
31. Many government personnel are involved in private album production (song and lyrics composing, private funding of albums, etc.). To get an album produced by the government office itself is very difficult, as they are careful to only support projects likely to make money.
32. Tsewang (one of the owners of Thangula), interview with the author, 8 June 2005. Before this, there were very important releases from Chengdu, such as Yadong's first album in 1990. However, this did not constitute a large-scale industry that set trends for all the Tibetan areas.
33. Manager, Golden Eagle music company, interview with the author, Chengdu, 10 August 2006; Tsewang of Thangula quoted 100,000 as a top sale (interview with the author, 8 June 2005).
34. Manager, Golden Eagle music company, interview with the author, Chengdu, 10 August 2006.
35. This was for *Lhamo Lhatso* (Manager, Golden Eagle music company, interview with the author, Chengdu, 10 August 2006).
36. The demand in Kardze is largely due to the nomad population there. I would also expect a favourable situation in (Amdo) Ngaba TAP also in Sichuan but have not visited there. There is immense demand for *dunglen* in Nagchu, the nomadic area north of Lhasa, but due to extreme poverty, sales of original copies are minimal.
37. Aten Kyab, Xining Radio Office, personal communication, May 2007.
38. Tanzin Gyatso, personal communication, 2006.
39. I am not sure which is more the case.
40. The small, condensed nature of the Tibetan exile market in Delhi and Dharamsala certainly helps the sale of legitimate copies through community support and contrasts with the smaller, more remote Tibetan settlements. Pirate copies of two albums released by singers from Lithang were also not sold in Lithang itself by local agreement. However, given that the greatest value of the mass media is to transcend the local, having to rely on sales in such condensed areas is frustrating.
41. The boss of the Audio Publishing House in Lhasa stated to me that (with a well-produced, good album) you should be able to make a profit of at least ¥100,000 (interview with the author, July 2006).
42. These VCDs appear to be genuine, especially in the Tibetan context where most of the fakes make no attempt to pass off as real, since they have high-quality print, the image on the disc is printed rather than just a sticker, and the box is good quality with leaflets front and back. See Wang (2003, 199–200) for a VCD/DVD "examination sheet" used in Hong Kong by the Motion Picture Association indicating a range of more subtle ways of identifying fakes. In the case of Bollywood music, there is no legal distribution in China, so all copies are fakes.
43. Harris (2002) argues such a case for Xinjiang in the 1990s. The sale of cheap Chinese pop music and albums of the few big nationwide Tibetan singers may well undercut sales of Tibetan music, particularly on the more grass-root level.
44. This is a summary of the major and relevant points from Mertha (2005), in particular chapter 4. See also Rees (2003) and Harris (2005b), who discuss the issue of ownership and commodification of traditional music in China.
45. Economic Intelligence Unit (1999), quoted in Mertha (2005, 139–40).
46. See for example TIN (2007), which addresses some of these issues.
47. Harris (2002, 279) describes the impact of the "strike-hard" anti-dissidence campaign in Xinjiang on the independent production of music.
48. Compilation albums also represent a safe bet for producers using mostly well-known singers. Such albums were dominating production in 2006 and 2007, illustrating the high-risk nature of the music business.

49. See TIN (2000b) on the early Western Development Drive. See Fischer (2005) for analysis on the winners and losers of the state-subsidised economic boom that has ensued from the Western Development Drive.
50. One factor that complicates this analysis somewhat is the fact of the widespread tendency for Tibetans to put resources into educating just one or two children in a family, leaving others to look after the herds and fields. It is not uncommon to have uneducated nomads and masters graduates in prestigious government jobs as brothers and sisters. This makes the question of social class based on family circumstances a particularly subtle one.
51. Some of the most powerful Tibetan voices are those of nomads, and in many cases, the ones who have spent their lives herding and singing outdoors rather than going to school have the best voices.
52. Dore (singer, Machu County Song and Dance Troupe), interview with the author, 14 July 2005, and Rinko (singer and official, Gannan Prefecture Song and Dance Troupe), interview with the author, 15 July 2005.
53. This seems to be another layer in the processes of "distinction" in the ethnic and socio-economic hierarchies of Tibet's post (state-sponsored) economic boom society (Morcom 2007b). In Amdo, Xining, there are still some bars frequented by rich businessmen, and wages, which were never as high as Lhasa, do not seem to have suffered a comparable crash.
54. The socio-economic and political elite converge heavily due to the need for contacts with government officials to carry out business. This is the case in the recording industry, and furthermore, many singers also have associations with government institutions.
55. Private film and documentary production is beginning to open up in Tibet, apparently on the back of VCD production.
56. I am grateful to Thierry Dodin for this observation. The strictly government productions, however, are on the whole more profit driven than private ones, as the government offices now will only produce very selected products that they are sure will be profitable.
57. There are occasional CD and DVD burning sessions and sometimes raids on pirates, but little has changed. Some people reported to me pirate discs being confiscated only to be returned a few days later to the pirates.
58. This would include aspects religious culture, the main subject of charges of cultural genocide from Tibetan exiles and the West and unrest in Tibet itself, since there is a sizeable circulation of mass-mediated religious products, including VCDs of songs in praise of Lamas and of religious teachings. See Gayley (forthcoming) for a discussion of the multimedia dissemination of the messages of Jigme Phuntsog Rinpoche of Amdo. It is also worth noting that many *dunglen* albums are funded by monks and lamas.
59. Two Tibetan singers expressed anxieties of how difficult it would be for them to operate in such environments due to the very high level of Chinese spoken there. One of these singers' Chinese is in fact good, including a certain degree of reading skills, but she still felt it would be very difficult for her to manage in Chengdu. Similarly, all the printing of VCDs takes place in China proper, normally Chengdu, Beijing or Guangdong, also making it a difficult or impossible for most Tibetans to organise this aspect of production for themselves, hence the need for intermediaries in the form of studios.

## References

Adams, Vincanne. 1996. Karaoke as modern Lhasa, Tibet: Western encounters with cultural politics. *Cultural Anthropology* 11, no. 4: 510–46.

Adorno, Theodor W. [1938] 1978. On the fetish-character in music and the regression of listening. In *The essential Frankfurt school reader,* ed. A. Arato and E. Gebhardt, 270–99. Oxford: Oxford University Press.

Adorno, Theodor W., and Max Horkheimer. 1979. The culture industry: Enlightenment as mass deception. In *Dialectic of enlightenment,* trans. J. Cumming, 120–67. London: Verso. Originally published as *Dialektik der aufklärung* (Amsterdam: Querido, 1947).

Baranovitch, Nimrod. 2003. *China's new voices: Popular music, ethnicity, gender and politics, 1978–1997.* Berkeley: University of California Press.

Bogdanich, Walt, and Jane Hooker. 2007. From China to Panama, a trail of poisoned medicines. *New York Times,* 6 May. http://www.nytimes.com/2007/05/06/world/americas/06poison.html [Accessed 4 February 2008].

Bourdieu, Pierre. 1986. *Distinction: A social critique of the judgement of taste.* London: Routledge.
———. 1993. *The field of cultural production.* Cambridge: Polity Press.
Clayton, Martin, Trevor Herbert, and Richard Middleton, eds. 2003. *The cultural study of music: A critical introduction.* New York: Routledge.
Craig, Timothy J., and Richard King, eds. 2002. *Global goes local: Popular culture in Asia.* Vancouver: University of British Columbia Press.
Curran, James. 1996. Mass media and democracy revisited. In *Mass media and society,* 2nd ed., ed. J. Curran and M. Gurevitch, 81–119. London: Arnold.
Curran, James, and Michael Gurevitch, eds. 1996. *Mass media and society.* 2nd ed. London: Arnold.
du Gay, Paul, ed. 1997. *Production of culture/cultures of production.* Milton Keynes: Open University Press.
Economic Intelligence Unit. 1999. *China hand: The complete guide to doing business in China.* Hong Kong: Economic Intelligence Unit.
Fischer, Andrew Martin. 2005. *State growth and social exclusion in Tibet: Challenges of recent economic growth.* Copenhagen: NIAS Press.
Frith, Simon, and Andrew Goodwin, eds. 1990. *On record: Rock, pop and the written word.* London: Routledge.
Garnham, Nicholas. 1990. *Capitalism and communication: Global culture and the economics of information.* London: Sage.
Gayley, Holly. Forthcoming. The ethics of cultural survival: A Buddhist vision of progress in Mkhan Po 'jigs Phun's *Heart Advice to Tibetans for the 21st Century.* In *PIATS 2006: Tibetan Studies: Proceedings of the 11th Seminar of the International Association of Tibetan Studies, Königswinter 2006.* Halle: International Institute for Tibetan and Buddhist Studies.
Golding, Peter and Graham Murdock. 1996. Culture, communications, and political economy. In *Mass media and society.* 2nd ed., ed. J. Curran and M. Gurevitch, 11–30. London: Arnold.
Gyatso, Janet, and Hanna Havnevik, eds. 2005. *Women in Tibet, past and present.* London: C. Hurst.
Harris, Rachel. 2002. Cassettes, bazaars, and saving the nation: the Uyghur music industry in Xinjiang, China. In *Global goes local: Popular culture in Asia,* ed. T. Craig and R. King, 265–83. Vancouver: University of British Columbia Press.
———. 2005a. Reggae on the silk road: The globalization of Uyghur pop. *China Quarterly* 183: 627–43.
———. 2005b. Wang Luobin: Folk song king of the northwest of song thief? *Modern China* 31, no. 3: 381–408.
Henrion-Dourcy, Isabelle. 2005. Women in the performing arts: Portraits of six contemporary singers. In *Women in Tibet, past and present,* ed. J. Gyatso and H. Havnevik, 195–258. London: Hurst.
Laing, D. 2003. Music and the market: The economics of music in the modern world. In *The cultural study of music: a critical introduction,* ed. M. Clayton, T. Herbert and R. Middleton 309–20. New York: Routledge.
Louw, Eric. 2001. *The media and cultural production.* London: Sage.
Malm, Krister, and Roger Wallis. 1992. *Media policy and music activity.* London: Routledge.
Manuel, Peter. 1993. *Cassette culture: Popular music and technology in north India.* Chicago: University of Chicago Press.
Mertha, Andrew. 2005. *The politics of piracy: Intellectual property in contemporary China.* Ithaca, NY: Cornell University Press.
Morcom, Anna. 2007a. *Hindi film songs and the cinema.* SOAS Musicology Series. Aldershot: Ashgate.
———. 2007b. Modernity, power and the reconstruction of dance in post-1950s Tibet. *The Journal of the International Association of Tibetan Studies* 3. http://www.thdl.org/collections/journal/jiats/index.php?doc=jiats03morcom.xml.
Negus, Keith. 1997. The production of culture. In *Production of culture/Cultures of production,* ed. P. du Gay, 67–118. Milton Keynes: Open University Press.
———. 1999. *Music genres and corporate cultures.* London: Routledge.
Peterson, Richard A., and David G. Berger. [1975] 1990. Cycles in symbol production: the case of popular music. In *On record: Rock, pop and the written word,* ed. S. Frith and A. Goodwin, 140–59. London: Routledge.

Rees, Helen. 2003. The age of consent: Traditional music, intellectual property and changing attitudes. *British Journal of Ethnomusicology* 12, no. 1: 137–71.

Sreberny-Mohammadi, Amabelle. 1996. The global and the local in international communications. In *Mass media and society.* 2nd ed., ed. J. Curran and M. Gurevitch, 177–203. London: Arnold.

Stokes, Martin. 2003. Globalization and the politics of world music. In *The cultural study of music: a critical introduction,* ed. M. Clayton, T. Herbert, and R. Middleton, 297–308. New York: Routledge

Tibet Information Network (TIN). 2000a. *China's great leap west.* London: Tibet Information Network.

———. 2000b. *Different voices: The media in Tibet.* London: Tibet Information Network.

———. 2004. *Unity and discord, music and politics in contemporary Tibet.* London: Tibet Information Network.

———. 2007. Border shootings and travel restrictions. http://www.tibetinfonet.net/content/update/58 (Accessed 31 May 2007).

United Nations Educational, Scientific and Cultural Organization (UNESCO). 1982. *Cultural industries: A challenge for the future.* Paris: UNESCO.

Wallis, Roger, and Krister Malm. 1984. *Big sounds from small peoples: The music industry in small countries.* London: Constable.

———. [1984] 1990. Patterns of change. In *On record: Rock, pop and the written word,* ed. S. Frith and A. Goodwin, 160–80. London and New York: Routledge.

Wang, Shujen. 2003. *Framing piracy: Globalization and film distribution in greater China.* New York: Rowman and Littlefield Publishers.

# Developing a retro brand community: Re-releasing and marketing anti-apartheid protest music in post-apartheid South Africa

Michael Drewett

*Department of Sociology, Rhodes University, Grahamstown, South Africa*

1980s South Africa was a constrained context within which to produce protest music. Apartheid censorship prevented protest music from reaching a mass market. This was an especially dire situation for white protest musicians who (unlike black musicians) were restricted by a small potential audience and also limited by the cultural boycott, precluding the possibility of an international audience. In the post-apartheid era some of these earlier protest recordings have been re-released by independent labels hoping to profit from the recordings but also in search of broader audiences for this important aspect of South Africa's musical heritage. Yet it has been difficult to do more than market to "retro brand communities" of former fans. This paper considers marketing strategies used to promote re-releases of anti-apartheid protest songs, given the peculiarities of the convergence of retro time and space with present spatial dynamics, in a society willing to forget its musical heritage.

The advent of compact discs in the 1980s saw the ascendance of a reissue culture in the United States, Western Europe and elsewhere: as CD sales grew, record companies trawled their vaults in search of gold nuggets that, when re-released, would realise maximum revenue with minimum capital investment and risk (Barfe 2005, 301; Burnett 1996, 45). In many instances, this turned out to be a very lucrative exercise. Certainly, even in South Africa, Western re-releases continue to fill many stacks in music outlets and account for a fair proportion of the country's album sales. Yet, the story is different for many local South African re-releases, particularly music with a protest theme, directed at the apartheid government during the 1970s and '80s.

During the apartheid era, most protest popular music was banned from airplay and sometimes even from retail, so only a marginal audience ever got to hear it (Drewett 2003; Gilder 1983; Kerkhof 1986; Korpe and Reitov 2004; Sony 1991). This was especially true of protest music performed by white musicians, who were confronted with a much more limited market than that available to black musicians (Chapman 1988). In the post-apartheid era, some of these earlier recordings have been re-released by independent labels hoping to make some money from the recordings but also in search of broader audiences for this important aspect of South Africa's musical heritage. Yet, it has been difficult to do more than market to converted former fans wanting to simply replace their vinyl collections, especially when the only old songs commercial radio stations play are the tried-and-tested "golden oldies" that received substantial airplay in the 1980s. By means of a predominantly socio-historical account, this paper considers the peculiarities of the convergence of retro time and space with present spatial dynamics, in a society too willing to forget the past and its musical heritage.

It is argued that marketing apartheid-era protest music as a specific brand for South Africans who were once associated with the protest movement, or who were not but wish to be associated with those ideals, has the potential to create a vibrant "brand community" that will support re-released music albums through its purchase power and word-of-mouth promotion of the music (Muniz and O'Guinn 2001). Given that this community in most part previously existed as an informal brand community during the apartheid era, the present marketing task involves appealing to a scattered brand community whose only ties are to a former era and deleted catalogue. As such they can be seen to constitute a *retro brand community*, one that is still relevant today, given the ethical importance of appropriate political identities in post-apartheid South Africa. Gabriel Biehal and Dipankar Chakravarti (1982, 1986) suggest that consumer choices are based on a combination of memory and external information. If marketing re-released protest music is to be successful, it follows that advertising campaigns need to provide the consumer with information about the product while simultaneously appealing to the consumer's memories of the past, creating a sense of nostalgia for the product as it would have been experienced at the time of its original release. However, the overarching significance of apartheid-era white protest music is not simply about nostalgia, but involves a re-examination of the relevance of former white protest music in the face of contesting understandings of the role of white South Africans in the past and present, not dissimilar to the contestation and re-examination of the relevance of the Bauhaus in Germany and elsewhere in the twenty-first century (see Volkmann and de Cock 2006). Certainly, Mark Hill and Maryon King (2001, 34) argue that memory can assist transformation if it constructs a past that serves the purposes of the present. If consumers can be convinced of the ongoing relevance of apartheid-era protest songs, new life will be breathed into old songs, allowing them the opportunity to be heard by a more widespread audience than ever before.

## The original (apartheid) context: protest songs by white South African popular musicians

In order to explore the difficulties experienced in re-releasing apartheid-era protest songs, this paper begins with a socio-historical consideration of the political and economic context within which these releases originally took place. As indicated, the focus is on protest music released by predominantly white pop/rock bands that, although concerned about social injustices, were nevertheless hoping to reach a broad audience and in the long run have an impact on the collective conscience of the country. In exploring this context, this paper will document three interrelated obstacles to white musicians recording protest music during the apartheid era. These are: first, severe music censorship practiced by government censors and (consequently) record companies; second, the United Nations cultural boycott against South African artists; and third, the conservative practices of the major record companies in South Africa.

### *Formal apartheid music censorship*

The apartheid government established a notoriously elaborate censorship system including a censorship board, broadcast censorship and police surveillance. The first official censorship board was established as a result of the 1963 Publications and Entertainment Act and operated in more or less the same form until the Film and Publications Board replaced it in the post-apartheid era (Merrett 1994). The board was only authorised to pass judgment on publications submitted to it by the police, customs office and members of the public, and in the process, banned well over a hundred music albums and seven-inch singles (Drewett 2004; Jacobsens Publishers 1991). Musicians and record companies were wary of the censorship board because it was always possible that one's recording could be submitted and banned, leading to its withdrawal from retail outlets and consequent serious economic losses (Drewett 2004).

Furthermore, the South African Broadcasting Corporation (SABC) instituted its own censorship via a censorship committee that vetted all material submitted for broadcast. The SABC possessed a virtual monopoly of the South African airwaves, and its decision to ban material from the airwaves thus had dire consequences for any musicians and record companies attempting airplay to promote their musical releases. The SABC's overzealous defence of apartheid and Calvinist ideology gave rise to stringent censorship procedures resulting in the banning of thousands of songs from airplay during the 1960s, '70s and '80s. This degree of censorship had an enormous effect on musicians, especially those releasing controversial material, particularly of a political nature (Drewett 2004; Reitov 1998; Korpe and Reitov 2004).

An additional obstacle for white musicians, resulting from SABC policy, was the SABC's apartheid segregation of the airwaves. In accordance with apartheid policy, each of South Africa's black African cultures had its own SABC radio station (for example, Radio Xhosa, Radio Zulu and so on) on which lyrical content had to match the station's language identity. However, the SABC commercial music radio station (Radio 5) that catered for English and Afrikaans speaking South Africans played mostly foreign Western popular music. It was against such overseas competition that white South African popular musicians had to compete. In the absence of a local quota system (such as in Australia at the same time), the SABC's policy made it extremely difficult for white South African musicians to access broadcast coverage, and in order to have any chance of doing so, it was clear that they needed to tone down any controversial lyrics (see Drewett 2003 and Clegg and Drewett 2006 for more detailed accounts of popular music censorship in South Africa during the apartheid era).

### *The cultural boycott*

The acceptance in December 1968 of the United Nations General Assembly's Resolution 2396 gave rise to a cultural boycott against South Africa. Accordingly, all member states and organisations were asked to cut "cultural, educational and sporting ties with the racist regime" (Willemse 1991, 24). After years of mounting pressure, the boycott finally started to affect musicians in the early 1980s, particularly through the establishment of a "Register of Artists, Actors and Others who have performed in South Africa" (in terms of UN General Assembly Resolution 35/206E of December 1980). Driven in particular by the British Anti-Apartheid Movement, the African National Congress, and the Azanian People's Organisation (AZAPO), the boycott's most severe effects were in preventing South African musicians from performing outside of the country and in preventing overseas musicians from performing in South Africa (Stewart 1986, 4). Although some overseas musicians and record companies refused to market and sell their music in South Africa, most nevertheless did do so. This created a difficult and restricting situation for local South Africans musicians, unable to market their music overseas yet competing with international releases in local retailer outlets and on national airwaves.

The boycott imposed a double-bind of censorship on South African protest musicians. They were restricted by South Africa's severe censorship practices and then, to make matters more difficult, could not promote and market their music overseas. The very rationale of the boycott was to deprive South Africans of "normal" interaction with the outside world, and therefore, one of the intentions of the boycott was to deprive white musicians (and by default black musicians, too, in terms of the "total boycott" strategy) from realising international success.[1] However, this is not to suggest that, in the absence of the cultural boycott, transnational record companies would necessarily have successfully promoted local releases outside of South Africa. Deanna Campbell Robinson, Elizabeth Buck and Marlene Cuthbert reveal that during the 1980s the two dominant transnational major labels operating in Nigeria made no "serious efforts to promote Nigerian musicians internationally despite the fact that most of the national musicians are licensed to them" (1991, 193). This demonstrates that marketplace dynamics need to be considered integrally with the political dynamics of the cultural boycott. It cannot be assumed that major record companies would have marketed all or even more than just a few South African musicians overseas in the absence of the boycott. For this reason, the focus now turns to the record companies themselves.

## The corporate priority of South African major record companies in the 1980s

Robert Burnett (1996, 17) notes that the transnationals' involvement in local contexts is double edged, distributing overseas music and attempting to identify local trends to exploit internationally. In South Africa, it has generally been most lucrative to act as distributors of overseas music, releasing it on the South African market. This "international imperative" of transnational record companies was (and still is) routinely implemented through directives and accompanying marketing materials from international marketing departments (see Negus 1999, 162–72). The focus on international sales is crucial for global record companies wanting to maximize profit, given that "international sales can provide the corporation (and musicians) with extra income for proportionately less additional investment in production costs" (Negus 2001, 25). Certainly, Rob Allingham, Archivist at Gallo, believed this to be the most significant factor in the way the transnationals operated. He argued:

> It was a hell of a lot easier for them to make money out of something that was pre-recorded, pre-packaged. They just got the master shipped over here, they got a nice little press kit that they just cranked up for local consumption. All they really had to do was suss which of these golden pears from America or the UK could be transplanted here, and they could make money out of it. And that definitely diverted their attention away from the tougher business of having to actually create something here. (1998)

Local context was an important factor in the majors' approach. Roger Wallis and Krister Malm (1984, 105–8) argue that the transnationals' pursuit of extra sales of international products varies from time to time according to finance and politics. It certainly is not a foregone conclusion that overseas distribution is lucrative. However, the cultural boycott in South Africa in the 1980s, together with tight copyright controls and a local fascination with Western culture, ensured that it was most profitable for local record companies to market overseas music. The result was that locally produced (particularly) white pop/rock suffered severely, as borne out by Chris Chapman, who noted that by the late 1980s:

> the development of the South African music industry has progressed in leaps and bounds on the black side, while on the white side it has ground to a virtual standstill. … White contemporary

> pop/rock musicians … find themselves playing to a tiny market with minimal rewards and incentives. (1988, 79–80)

Albums usually sold less than one thousand copies, and the most popular seldom sold more than a few thousand copies within the predominantly minority white (and generally English) market. The rewards and incentives for musicians were thus minimal (80). In turn, pressure was placed on musicians in the recording studio to produce radio-friendly (both musically and lyrically) music. Knowing that the market was small, the best way to increase sales was to have music played on the radio, particularly the SABC. For financial reasons, record companies were prepared to follow the formulaic requirements of the SABC and market their music accordingly, rather than attempting to set trends by cultivating a protest musical culture. The temptation to censor lyrics accordingly was therefore immense. This was true of all musicians wanting to promote their music. The constraints upon musicians whose music only appealed to a marginal audience was obviously much more severe. Clearly, those marginal musicians who recorded protest lyrics were very unlikely to ever reach more than an extremely limited audience.

### The (marginal) white anti-apartheid popular music protest scene

Despite the repressive context discussed so far, not all avenues were closed to musicians wanting to record music of a protest nature. There were a few resistant independent record labels that recorded music by some of the musicians singing protest songs. The first of these was Third Ear Music, established by David Marks in the late 1960s. Third Ear Music worked with a variety of musicians and put together a host of folk concerts and recordings of these concerts. Prominent musicians to record with Third Ear Music included Johnny Clegg and Sipho Mchunu (who later formed Juluka) and Roger Lucey. By the early 1980s, Third Ear music was becoming less involved in releasing albums, and as a result, musicians with an alternative message were finding it even more difficult than before to be recorded. It was at this stage that the most significant of apartheid-era independents was established. Shifty Records was started in the early 1980s by musician Lloyd Ross, who thus describes the beginnings of Shifty:

> I was playing in bands, there was a whole lot of music going down that was getting neglected by the industry at large, and I thought something should be done about it. I started collecting gear with a friend of mine, Ivan Kadey, and we put a little studio together in a caravan. The idea was of mobility and hence the name Shifty – it could shift from here to there – and we pretty much achieved that. We went and recorded in quite a few locations in South Africa. (1998)

Importantly, the Shifty approach was to record music neglected by the majors but which was nevertheless important South African music that ought to have been preserved. Ross's approach was to allow the musicians to express themselves as they wanted to, provided they fitted into Shifty's prescribed framework. While Shifty Records and Third Ear Music did submit records to the SABC, these were rarely played, and if so, only the non-political songs received airplay. Both record companies also had albums banned outright by the Directorate of Publications. In the end, Ross said: "It was very frustrating trying to get stuff played on the radio. Eventually I just gave up. I didn't take stuff to radio anymore" (1998).

#### *"Shot Down" – Cherry Faced Lurchers*

To examine in some depth and exemplify the difficulty faced by musicians who released popular protest songs, it is useful to explore one particular protest song that, for a marginal audience, became an anthem of white resistance to apartheid, but that remains scarcely heard by the majority of South Africans. The song is "Shot Down" by the Cherry Faced Lurchers (1985). The band's songwriter and front person, James Phillips, formed various bands during his two-decades-long musical career, but it was with the Cherry Faced Lurchers that he wrote and released his most politically overt and resistant music. The Lurchers' songs were often sardonic, cleverly questioning issues within South African society and expressing sentiments in every day South African English language, easily related to by their audience. Musically, they traversed a counterpoint of slightly loose and clumsy garage-band rhythm and brittle post-punk minimalism. As their patience with the apartheid government waned, their songs became angrier and more direct, but they never lost their clever nuances, never postured simple political rhetoric. Phillips died as the result of a car crash in 1995, but band member Lee Edwards explained the difficulties experienced by the Lurchers in trying to make a commercial success of their music in apartheid South Africa:

> We wanted our music to do well. … What we wanted to achieve was to sell records and have time to work on the music. … It is a hard thing to describe but we were serious about it but there was another side to things where you weren't, because you knew that whatever was recorded wouldn't get airplay. So there was always this feeling of hopelessness – that the powers that be could just say "look your song is not desirable" and you wouldn't get any airplay. … There was no outlet, so you basically had to rely on people that came to see your gigs, you had to rely on the newspapers reprinting press releases. (1998)

And, as was the pattern, overseas outlets were also closed to the band, even though the Cherry Faced Lurchers were strongly anti-apartheid in their stance, in terms of supporting anti-apartheid festivals and in their overt lyrics. On the basis of their political stance, the Lurchers were hoping to perform at the *Culture in Another South Africa* (CASA) anti-apartheid conference in Amsterdam in 1987 but were turned down in favour of black bands like the less politically overt 1950s revivalist African Jazz Pioneers. Edwards was understandably frustrated:

> We naively hoped that something would happen. The one thing that I remember was a shining light for us was when the ANC had this Arts and Culture thing in Amsterdam. And we were on the short list for that. And at the time I felt quite sure that we should, that we would get to go, because of the stuff we were saying, and being fairly unique in the South African music scene, musically. And then we didn't get to go, and to this day I do not understand why bands like the African Jazz Pioneers, nothing personal against them, but I don't understand why they went ahead of us. You know: not having any lyrics and playing stuff that was sort of twenty, thirty years old. (1998)

Many of the protest songs performed and recorded by white South African musicians were appreciated within the political and cultural scenes within which the musicians operated. For example, there was the alternative scene at the Jameson's nightclub in central Johannesburg where the Cherry Faced Lurchers and many other alternative political bands received enthusiastic support when they played there. Given that these scenes were amongst the only places audiences could hear alternative music, and given the bonds that developed between audience members in these semi-illicit gatherings, the audiences inadvertently became what Muniz and O'Guinn (2001) refer to as a "brand community." Fans of alternative music, released by Shifty Records in particular, bonded together in their admiration of Shifty's anti-establishment releases. Furthermore, the community that evolved was "marked by a shared consciousness, rituals and traditions, and a sense of moral responsibility" (Muniz and O'Guinn 2001, 412). In the strictest sense, the alternative music scene did not constitute a brand community, given that devotion was not restricted exclusively to a single commercial brand (such as Shifty Records) but to a marginally broader collective of record companies and musicians, and unlike brand communities, their commitment was not explicitly commercial (Muniz and O'Guinn 2001, 415). However, consumption of the music in one form or another was the primary characteristic of the musical culture. Certainly, a commercial and cultural ethos developed around Shifty Records releases so that the company could legitimately lay claim to having its own fan base, and it was this fan base that Shifty targeted with its offbeat advertising campaigns and promotions.

In 1985, Shifty Records recorded a Cherry Faced Lurchers concert at Jameson's and offered to release it as an album. The band agreed to the release, because, as Edwards explained: "We didn't try to work with the majors at all. I think we always knew they would not be interested in us, and I think we also knew that whatever we were saying, the majors would want to tone down" (1998). The subsequent album (entitled *Live at Jameson's* 1985)[2] achieved cult status amongst the less than 1,000 fans who bought the album and unknown others who illegally copied it. The album received no airplay, and the outstanding resistant track "Shot Down" was specifically refused airplay by the SABC. However, the groundswell of support for "Shot Down" within the alternative music scene grew with its subsequent release on a Shifty Records anti-conscription compilation album called *Forces Favourites* (1985). The song is a guilt-ridden cry of a young white man who, in a moment of chilling self-realisation, laments his role in supporting apartheid, as the following extract demonstrates:

> I'm a white boy who looked at his life
> Gathered in his hands and saw it was
> All due to the sweat of some other
> Man
> That one who got
> Shot down in the streets.

Edwards explained that the song became an "anthem for the left. It was a song that people very strongly identified with. I think there was a lot of sentiment in our stuff that people could relate to" (1998). It so typified the feeling of the white left that Andrew Worsdale chose it as the theme song and title for his full-length feature film *Shot Down* (1986) about white cultural resistance in South Africa. Like the song, the film achieved cult status amongst a marginal South African audience.

The repressive apartheid context, together with Shifty's own lack of resources, especially on a marketing and distribution level, meant that the song only ever gained the status of an anthem for the marginal few who stumbled across the song through live performances or by somehow getting to hear one of the two albums on which it appeared. A similar fate was shared by many other popular music protest songs including Roger Lucey's "Lungile Tabalaza" (1979) and "You only Need Say Nothing" (1979), the Kalahari Surfers' "Don't Dance" (1984), Jennifer Ferguson's "Suburban Hum" (1986), Edi Niederlander's "Bitter Fruit" (1986) and Bright Blue's "The Rising Tide" (1988), just to name a few of the many songs by white musicians denied broadcast and therefore the opportunity to be heard by a national South African audience during the apartheid era.

## Marginal protest music: "popular" or not?

It is clear that most, if not all, of the white musicians who recorded music with a protest element were doing so in part as a commercial activity – whether to make money and/or distribute their music in an attempt to reach as wide an audience as possible. In this sense, their music forms part of the general category of "popular music," given that the commercialisation of popular music is core (although not the sole prerequisite) to any music's status as "popular." David Coplan (1985, 269), Donald Clarke (1995, 6), Johan Fornäs (1995, 102) and Roy Shuker (1998, viii–ix) are amongst those who consider the "popular" in "popular music" in relation to a mass media market. Accordingly, "popular music" is not only a stylistic term but has to do with the commodification of music: that it is performed and/or recorded as a product for a popular market. Yet, the music under discussion here in the most part failed to become popular in a quantitative sense, given that in general it failed to sell to more than a very marginal audience. Accordingly, it is worth considering Sarah Cooper's point that "given the number of records that hit the market each week, it isn't just raw talent that makes a hit. Something else must make it stand apart" (1996, 149). The difference, for Cooper, is a well-managed and imaginative PR campaign, usually including access to radio play and the promotion of the product within the retail set-up. This is crucial; for in the popular music market, "success is determined by indices of the music industry such as radio play and phonogram sales" (Burnett 1996, 37). Yet, the apartheid context of censorship, the cultural boycott and conservative record company practice meant that many songs were barred from airplay, some were barred from retail outlets, and in addition, distributive networks (operated by major record companies with a conservative bias) were not conducive to widespread distribution and availability of local protest music. This is in contrast to the situation in the United States' 1960s counter-cultural context in which the potential markets were much bigger and the music was not censored, allowing record companies to exploit the sales potential of large-scale social movements that developed around civil rights and the Vietnam War. As a result, unlike South Africa, recorded music became central to politics and "generally played a significant role in solidifying activists in the social movements" (Eyerman and Jamison 1998, 116). Douglas Holt (2002) argues that products that undermined societal mores allowed 60s youth culture to pursue rebellious identities by avoiding brands that appeared to embody marketers' engineered prescriptions according to conventional agendas. Record companies could thus profit from creative branding that associated music with the broader counter-cultural movement. As has been noted, in South Africa, the potential to market music in this way existed, but the promotional spaces and potential market were far more restricted.

Clearly, as Martin Cloonan has noted, "if the very essence of popular music is the intention to reach a mass audience, then it follows logically that the censorship of popular music must involve attempts to prevent it from becoming a mass medium" (2003, 19). In other words, censorship and other forms of control, such as play-listing and government broadcast licensing policy, affect the ability of certain music to become popular (in sales terms) in the first place. It follows, therefore, that censored music needs to be regarded as popular, simply in terms of the intention behind the production of the music, together with the potential of that music for commercial success, were it not for the obstacles placed in its way. This contention seems to correspond with Roy Shuker's (1998, viii) point that in any case, some forms of popular music are quite exclusive: for example, thrash metal. It is important, however, to take heed of Campbell Robinson, Buck and Cuthbert's (1991, 12) point that in order for music to be "popular" it does need to be (at the very least) appreciated within the musicians' own communities. This could be a global audience, a national or regional audience, or perhaps even a local scene.

The repressive apartheid context (involving the interrelated factors discussed so far) certainly affected the "popular" status of many protest songs, yet they remained appreciated within the quasi brand communities who supported the bands and the scenes where they performed. In refusing to be silenced, resistant musicians forged a public space, no matter how marginal, in which their music could be heard. This allowed their music to embody a "sense of community, a type of experience and identity pointing beyond the walls of the self" (Eyerman and Jamison 1998, 173). Although this sense of community might have been imagined, it nevertheless had an impact on the musicians' and their audiences' identities, and therefore was able to have lasting impacts on individuals and communities. As will be argued later, the relevance of this sense of community – both as a social and commercial entity – is central to post-apartheid marketing of apartheid-era protest popular music.

In South Africa during the apartheid era, protest songs left behind a valuable legacy that reflected people's lived experiences during that era. Musicians who opposed apartheid in whatever manner left behind different images of South Africans, contesting the inequalities to which they were subjected. The various resistant songs recorded by South Africans survive in individual memories and in marginal collective memories, a term that accurately describes the process in which marginally popular songs are cut short through structural intervention before they have the chance to reach their potential, deprived of the opportunity to be marketed for a wider ("popular" in a strictly quantitative sense) audience. For "alternative" white audiences, protest songs by white popular musicians could be especially related to, given the common obstacles and lived experience of the lives of the musicians and audiences alike. It was frustrating to the members of this alternative brand community that their music was not played on the radio and more well known. Nevertheless, they were able to enjoy the music on a more immediate level, as frustrating and insular as that was.

## The place of apartheid protest music in post-apartheid South Africa

With the official transition to democracy in April 1994, South Africans of all backgrounds celebrated the arrival of a "rainbow nation" in which social differences were celebrated rather than used to keep people apart, and it was claimed that the heritage of different groups would be equally valued. Yet, it soon became evident that resentment towards white oppression during apartheid would taint the majority's view of white South Africans within post-apartheid society. White South Africans who had resisted apartheid became perturbed by a trend towards a rewriting of history that (in a sense) airbrushed them out of the struggle against apartheid. A useful illustration of this process as it relates to white musicians is found in Lee Hirsch's film *Amandla! A Revolution in Four-Part Harmony* (2002). The film omits the role of white musicians from its documentation of music in the struggle against apartheid. Ironically, the film relies heavily on hearsay accounts provided by black musicians such as Hugh Masekela and Miriam Makeba who were in exile for most of the period covered in the film. There was no mention of white musicians such as Roger Lucey, James Phillips, Jennifer Ferguson or even the more internationally successful Johnny Clegg, all of whom tackled the South African state through their music. Hirsch clearly catered for a US audience, many of whom were more likely to have heard of Makeba and Masekela than local musicians performing in South Africa at the time. It was also easiest to package a binary black versus white construct of the struggle against apartheid. Yet, Hirsch's account is reflective of the dominant account of the struggle present within the South African media in the twenty-first century. This trend is especially prevalent on national state-owned radio and television – the two areas of the media on which record companies are most reliant for widespread coverage of new and re-releases. While some record companies nevertheless persevere with music that is inconsistent with the views of the political elite, there are others that, driven primarily by the profit motive, perpetuate the process of commodifying and mythologizing a racial binary view of popular musicians and the anti-apartheid struggle.[3] Many South Africans are happy to forget about the past, while an even larger group, influenced by media messages and commodity fetishism, are indeed settling for the dominant (and easy to comprehend) binary account of apartheid according to which all whites were oppressors and only blacks resisted apartheid.

The most significant aspect of this historical amnesia is that it is quite possible that powerful protest songs such as Roger Lucey's "You Only Need Say Nothing" and the Cherry Faced Lurchers' "Shot Down" will be forgotten, and thus cease to be part of any group's collective memory, no matter how marginal. Indeed, one of the conclusions reached by participants of a South African music censorship seminar hosted by Freemuse in 2001,[4] was that music censorship "affected the collective memory in a negative way," with the result that "the younger generation grows up with no knowledge of the 'hidden music' of the days of apartheid" (Korpe and Reitov 2004, 82). Yet, the struggle to remember is not over. James Phillips's memory was beginning to fade even further from the national musical landscape when Lloyd Ross of Shifty (these days a film director) released a film about Phillips's life ironically entitled *James Phillips: Famous for Not Being Famous* (2004), which documents Philips' mostly unsuccessful struggle to gain recognition as a musician in the face of the obstacles outlined in this paper. This was broadcast on national television and has been released as a DVD. Ross's film not only demonstrates "the struggle of memory against forgetting" (Kundera 1980, 3), but also documents the pride of journalists, fellow musicians and fans as they reflect on what Phillips's music meant to them. This pride emphasises a crucial value of protest music. Regardless of what it means to society at the time of its initial performance and consumption, its long-term value is in forging a sense of community, a collective memory that allows audiences to re-remember their past. As Alice Walker suggests, listening to old freedom or protest songs "show(s) us the way home" (1997, 62), mobilising audiences around sonic memories that can empower them, reminding them of what has been achieved and allowing them to take pride in their allegiance to those resistant sounds. In this sense, white South African protest music can play a similar role to that which reggae music plays for Jamaicans. According to Stephen A. King "reggae music serves to develop and maintain a healthy and positive self-image of 'blackness' while, at the same time, intensifying cohesion and 'groupness' within the movement" (2006, 117).

The contested nature of memory has important implications for marketing. Kathryn Braun, Rhiannin Ellis and Elizabeth Loftus note:

> A consumer's past is constantly being updated to fit one's changing self-knowledge and social contexts. … As time passes there lies a greater likelihood that temporally available information will be used to reconstruct, and perhaps distort, how the experience is remembered. (2002, 3–4)

They argue that marketers can act as a "memory guide" by using autobiographical referencing to affect consumers' memories of their pasts in a particular way. If the self-images established through marketing are positive ones, consumers are more likely to buy into and want to be associated with the product. At a time when, according to the dominant view, "whiteness" is synonymous with support for apartheid and racism more generally, despite the fact that some whites did resist apartheid and many feel committed to a democratic South Africa, there is a need for progressive white South Africans to establish morally positive self-images of "whiteness," not based on racial superiority but on a commitment to South Africa's democratic status.[5] Christopher Ballantine notes that the "recidivist tendency to essentialist typecasting" has become so indiscriminate "that not even anti-apartheid activists have been exempt from its 'blanket insults'" (2004, 128).[6] This negative tendency can in part be countered (as Ballantine argues) through the creation of new popular music that resists premature closure and racial typecasting. However, it is suggested here that this tendency can also be countered by democratic white South Africans listening to, and acknowledging the sentiments of, white anti-apartheid protest music. This process allows for morally positive connections to be drawn, both with the past but also with others who were and/or are similarly drawn to the music. This could provide the beginnings of a more widely experienced collective memory or marginal collective memory. From a marketing perspective this means that memories can be constructively used (Braun, Ellis and Loftus 2002, 18) to promote apartheid-era protest music by means of autobiographical referencing that draws positive associations between consumers and events from the past. How this can be achieved is considered in the ensuing discussion.

## Retro protest or what? Marketing apartheid protest music in a democratic age

The transition to democracy in South Africa saw the end to the cultural boycott and severe apartheid era music censorship. In addition, Gary Baines (1998) argues that the introduction of a local content quota system (of 20% local music on commercial music radio stations) led to a South African music "explosion" in which the record industry began to record and market South African music more seriously than before, partly with the new needs of radio in mind. The government-appointed Independent Broadcast Authority (IBA) proposed legislation implementing a quota system on the basis that South Africa's music industry required protection from foreign music, which had historically dominated the airwaves. At the time, it was estimated that 80% of royalty revenue left South Africa as a result of licensing agreements between South African and international record companies (Baines 1998, 69). Furthermore, the IBA paved the way for a more democratic broadcast policy, by breaking up the SABC monopoly into numerous independent regional radio stations and a plethora of community and student radio stations scattered throughout the country.

Initially, it seemed that the removal of apartheid era barriers might create conditions conducive to the re-release of white protest music from the apartheid era, as part of an attempt to publicise an important strain of South Africa's musical heritage. Musicians, record company representatives and audiences who had supported the alternative protest music scene hoped that hidden "gems" would finally be given the recognition they deserved, not as new hits, but as protest "classics" promoted in acknowledgement of the power of the music and the commitment of the musicians involved. The changed circumstances of the country meant that a new marketing strategy would be needed to promote the music. The music in question was no longer relevant in the same way as previously, given that with the demise of apartheid, the need to protest the system as an existing injustice was no longer necessary. However, as was noted above, the existence of this genre of music acts as an ongoing reminder of those white musicians and audiences who took a stand against apartheid. As such, it remains relevant in the post-apartheid era, an ongoing statement of white South Africans' past and present opposition to social injustice. In order for record companies to maximise events from the past in an effective marketing campaign, they would to some extent need to use autobiographical references to remind South Africans of the role of music in the past and to locate potential consumers within those memories of the past. The effective use of past images could represent aspirations associated with consumers' support for the anti-apartheid struggle and a closely related sense of freedom and unity.

The first record company to seriously explore this possibility was Third Ear Music. The company devised the *Hidden Years Project* as a theme around which to promote the Third Ear Music back catalogue and previously unreleased live performances by resistance musicians during the apartheid era. However, from the outset Third Ear had difficulty promoting its archival music in a manner that corresponded with contemporary radio station play-listing formats. This emphasises the problem of disequilibrium between music industry interests and those of the media on which it is dependent but does not control (Frith 2001, 44), a problem exacerbated for marginal record companies with political agendas. Commercial radio stations throughout the country were opting for the internationally tried-and-tested formula of playing the latest hits and proven classics, in other words playing songs that people know – whether songs that people currently like or ones they used to like and enjoy hearing again. This policy fosters a conservative collective memory, especially in South Africa, where the collective musical memory (especially for white audiences) is of unchallenging politically palatable songs that successfully negotiated the apartheid censorship network. For George Lipsitz, this sort of adult-oriented "oldies" programming amounts to "demographic tyranny" and "cultural conservativism" because nostalgia for a conservative past "can be quite racist and regressive, a way of precluding rather than promoting new possibilities" (Lipsitz 1990, 265). Although Lipsitz has in mind conservative radio stations' preference for adult-oriented pop oldies over more innovative music stemming from the pluralities of the post-industrial US city (such as rap and Latin dance mix), his argument also holds for the South African context where many music stations opt for the safer route of playing previous and existing mainstream "hits," rather than playing a constructive role in promoting a re-remembered past and alternative way forward. Indeed, Jody Berland (1993, 104–5) argues that the very purpose of format radio is to distract the listener from turning off the radio, offering a pleasantly bland soundtrack to our daily routines. The idea that commercial radio offers the listener an uncritical selection of sonic wallpaper with which to circumnavigate their daily routines is borne out by Zayne Derbyshire, Programme Manager for regional South African radio station Algoa FM,[7] who summed up the approach of regional commercial radio stations when he explained: "Our policy is to play the hits, not to break them" (quoted in Scheckter 2006, 162). Like many other regional stations in South Africa, for play-list guidance Algoa FM looks to the US and UK charts as well as South Africa's foremost national music station, 5fm. Yet, 5fm DJ Nicole Fox, points out:

> 5FM is a commercial Top 40 hit radio station. It cannot be everything to everyone and, as such, niche markets may have to be overlooked. … While we may lose some listeners who are firmly fixed in their niches we gain more numbers with people wanting to hear the best of a mix of genres. (quoted in Scheckter 2006, 163)

Although these radio spokespeople refer to new music, their statements also sum up their stations' approaches to older music (often referred to as "golden oldies," "rock classics" and so on). They will rarely play unknown old music. The problem of radio play for niche music has been further exacerbated by the manner in which the issue of broadcast licenses and the practices of most radio stations in post-apartheid South Africa have upheld the ethnic divisions of the apartheid era. The post-apartheid popular music market thus remains strongly segmented into different niche markets broadly divided according to the major race groups as defined by apartheid ideologues. Importantly, Scheckter states that (just as in the late apartheid era) "a niche in the white market is a lot smaller than the black population, and less commercially viable for radio" (2006: 153).

Given that the *Hidden Years* songs had not enjoyed success in the apartheid era (for reasons already outlined), they could only be played on commercial radio if the broadcasters could somehow be persuaded to "break" old songs on contemporary radio. With this in mind, Third Ear announced that its wish was

> not to recreate the past but look forward to the future with hope and pride – this country had a lot to offer (that) was seldom heard in the dark old days! There were musicians who contributed, in no uncertain terms, to the remarkable changes in our country – we have a foundation of experience and talent on which to build so that music and musicians cannot be forgotten. (Third Ear Music 1994, 2)

However, despite campaigning for airplay, Third Ear Music was unsuccessful in its attempts to secure meaningful airplay for its releases. The only airplay achieved was by means of documentaries about the *Hidden Years Project* or interviews with *Hidden Years Project* musicians. These were scattered and few, taking place at odd times without much publicity, so in general, only the unexpecting listener got to hear them. The *Hidden Years Project*'s only success was in attracting foreign and local funding to digitise archival recordings and release some of these recordings on compact disc. One of the most successful of these re-releases was a Roger Lucey compilation including controversial political songs banned by the Directorate of Publications in 1982. Yet, even this release only sold in the hundreds, bought mostly by Roger Lucey fans who wanted to replace old vinyl recordings or who never had his original recordings to begin with (given that one was banned from retail and the other was in any case confiscated from retail outlets by the police). Some of the sales were also the result of Lucey's more recent fame, based on a documentary film about the apartheid police's attempts to end his career because of his controversial music (*Stopping the Music* 2002). In this sense, the re-release was of archival interest to collectors and curators. The *Hidden Years Project* has subsequently been transformed into an archival project of academic interest and is no longer viewed as a viable commercial option, especially given the lack of radio interest in the music on offer. Third Ear has entered into an agreement with the University of KwaZulu-Natal, whereby the archives are turned into an academic resource, open to scholars for postgraduate research. As part of the process, the archives are being digitised and intermittent releases will continue. Third Ear Music relies on its own website (www.3rdearmusic.com) and that of the One World cyber music shop (based in Johannesburg) to market and sell its re-releases. Importantly, the Third Ear website and mailing list have opened a potential marketing opportunity for Third Ear Music. Third Ear Music markets itself as an exclusive brand for people who remember or who have stumbled across the secret hidden years music. The exclusiveness of the website and mailing list has led to the development of a brand community who communicate with each other through Third Ear's own and other mailing lists, where memories and opinions are shared and news of new releases are eagerly awaited. As revealed below, this is a strategy used by other record companies promoting similar music.

The most serious attempt at re-releasing apartheid-era white protest music is by independent record company Fresh Music, owned by former WEA representative, Benjy Mudie. Mudie, a fan of South African English pop and rock music from the late 1960s to the present, has over the past several years launched a series of re-releases on a sub-label known as Retro Fresh. Most of the re-releases have been licensed from the original apartheid-era record companies, including both major record companies and independents, including Shifty Records. Mudie claims that Retro Fresh is a labour of love simply to release the music, yet it clearly has a certain commercial potential, especially as the Retro Fresh catalogue includes not only previously marginal music (such as the Cherry Faced Lurchers' *Live at Jameson's*) but albums that were commercially successful during the apartheid era. Mudie has therefore successfully piggy-backed on the local content quota system by providing radio stations with digitally remastered versions of well-liked South African classics (whose airplay promotes sales of the albums in retails outlets), yet previously unknown musicians and their songs remain unplayed and unheard on radio.

Shifty Records (in their own right) and some of the independents and majors have also re-released music from the apartheid era, with varying success. Yet, in all instances, a formerly censored protest song has yet to be successfully promoted through these re-releases. Fresh Music opted for innovative marketing for its Retro Fresh releases. In general, Fresh Music has followed the successful global marketing strategy of "positioning and imbuing cultural products with social significance to make them attractive to consumers" (Shuker 2001, 45). Fresh Music has particularly marketed its retro releases as trendy purchases for the modern consumer. The company's marketing strategy has included effective use of the internet to promote its releases. Visitors to the Fresh Music website (www.freshmusic.co.za) are able to order releases over the Internet, or alternatively they can do so through South Africa's leading music cyber stores. Fresh Music has also made use of feature stands in independent record shops, where all (or most) of the re-releases are attractively displayed, each compact disc featuring a distinctive and eye-catching Retro Fresh sticker that informs the potential consumer that the album includes features like rare photographs, extra tracks, band bio information, and liner notes. Retro Fresh, although a commercial venture, has thus (like Third Ear Music) realised the value of marketing apartheid-era music as archival material for collectors or otherwise intellectual consumers, many of whom are interested in the music because of its historical significance as much as the music itself.

Fresh Music, by marketing apartheid era releases as Retro Fresh, commissioning fans to write sleeve notes, and inviting consumers to contact the record company with ideas for future re-releases has combined the idea of retro-releases with the concept of a brand community, suggesting that it is possible for retro brand communities to develop around their memories and fondness for products from a bygone era. Through the Internet, these fans get together, communicate and not only feel a close connection to the brand but an even stronger connection to each other based on actual and imagined encounters in the past (Muniz and O'Guinn 2001, 418). For example, sleeve notes that describe in intimate details a live concert and the emotions generated by a particular performance may remind consumers of an actual or similar occasion or even cause consumers to imagine themselves at the event, so the marketing of the product through such descriptions may alter the way consumers remember their own past (Braun, Ellis and Loftus 2002, 2). Marketing nostalgia in this way fulfils both a marketing need for the record company and a personal need for consumers. Braun, Ellis and Loftus note that in any case "a consumer's past is constantly being updated to fit one's changing self-knowledge and social contexts" (2002, 3), so the use of autobiographical referencing in marketing can positively facilitate an already occurring identity construction process. This process operates on what Mark Hill and Jane Cromartie refer to as an active view of memory, according to which we are constantly involved in a process of forgetting past events, given that forgetting involves "a separation between our selves and our former selves, as well as between ourselves and others" (Hill and Cromartie 2004, 87). Accordingly, forgetting can be utilised as part of a marketing strategy to lure people into a sense of nostalgia for a forgotten past. The product is symbolic of the past and as such offers the consumer the possibility to recapture a sense of the self they were at the time of the marketed event and a sense of the community that they were part of. Purchasing the product thus involves a grappling for "oneness" against the pull towards "otherness" brought about by the passing of time and the scattering of the original community. However, if the marketing integrally involves the encouragement of a retro brand community, the product acts as a monument to the past, as an attempt to thwart the ongoing slippage of the present into the past (Hill and Cromartie 2004, 89). Furthermore, the newly (re-)discovered brand communities, through the exchange of memories, facilitate the development of newly constructed identities, suggesting "the simultaneity of memory and of being – the past as contemporaneous with the present that it has been" (Malkin 1999, 56).

Considering the importance of white South Africans' involvement in anti-apartheid activity for their identity in present day South Africa, marketing by means of facilitating and making use of retro brand communities allows present day white South Africans to remember the positive contribution made by white cultural activists in the struggle against apartheid. The retro brand community is integrally dependent on actual brand communities of the past (for example, Shifty Records consumers and audiences at the Jameson's live music venue), imagined members of the original brand communities, and new consumers, who feel an affinity for the retro product and who want to share ideas with other members of the retro brand community. In other words, the retro brand community in part relies on a re-released retro product for its existence, and in part relies on a brand community that has previously existed as an active community but that is now scattered around the globe. A critical component of marketing for a retro brand community involves an attempt to recreate or regroup the former (or retro) brand community, through the use of clever marketing and the use of websites and mailing lists that are seldom directly related to the brands, but that function in order to celebrate the brands.

## Concluding discussion

The marketing strategies used in the re-release of apartheid-era protest songs clearly seem to be caught between (one the one hand) publicising the albums as quaint archival items to be accumulated by collectors, curators and researchers, and (on the other hand) promoting the music for a retro brand community of reminiscent former political bohemians and activists wanting to remember or re-imagine their anti-apartheid pasts. Autobiographical referencing in the form of sleeve notes to describe what it was like "back then" especially emphasises the convergence of retro time and space with present spatial dynamics. The image of a trendy "forty-something" coming home and slipping a newly purchased compact disc into the CD player, and then taking in the sounds of an album s/he last heard scratching on a long-discarded record player (when the apartheid police were still patrolling the townships and the apartheid censors were controlling the airwaves) vividly contrasts the temporal fluidity at play. Even in the post-apartheid present, the listener can be transported by the music that, in Christine Lucia's words "makes 'being there' possible, gives the listener a sense of identification with place that is dependent not on place but on time, since being there in the Heideggarian sense implies a temporal rather than a spatial ontology" (2002, 138). In this moment of temporal displacement, listeners reposition themselves in ways that give rise to new (or perhaps more accurately "renewed") ways of conceptualising themselves. As Simon Frith notes, music in this context is "important for collective identity [because] communities know themselves through their musical memories" (2001, 38). Listening to old protest songs allows audiences to experience recollections that can foster links between present and past identities, an exercise that, given negative racial typecasting (discussed above), takes on a special significance in terms of creatively merging previous identifications (with the resistance music scene) with present circumstances to reinvent senses of "whiteness" in contemporary South Africa. In this process of reinvention, the product is transformed from undesirable contraband during the apartheid era to a celebratory symbol of white resistance in the post-apartheid era.[8] However, the new elite does not actively support this view of white resistance, and thus, it retains an element of contest, although to somewhat different ends. This process of revisiting the past through music would be especially successful if the "space-binding" medium of radio were used to "overcome physical barriers" (Berland 1993, 112), mediating renewed identities to a broad listener base through more innovative play-listing. This broader base of listeners could join with the retro brand community and, through ongoing word-of-mouth recommendations, further promote re-released music.

However, persuasive arguments about cultural heritage and identity politics are unlikely to convince radio station programme managers to change their "golden oldies" policy, and without radio station support, it will continue to be difficult for record companies to successfully market previously marginalized apartheid-era protest songs to a wide audience. "After all," as Simon Reynolds has noted, "if the radio is mostly playing records you already know and like (and therefore probably already own), you are hardly likely to rush out to the record store" (2005, 530). The central obstacle confronting record companies therefore remains similar to that experienced during the apartheid era: an inability to secure broadcast coverage. While in the former era the situation was politically motivated, the present context is largely commercially driven, provided one accepts that catering for the audience's collective amnesia and diluted preferences is a commercial (and not a political) decision.

When considering the implications of broadcast policy for record company marketing strategies, it seems fitting to conclude with Fresh Music's Retro Fresh concept: what is it exactly, that Fresh Music, Third Ear Music, and others are marketing when they release apartheid era protest songs? "Retro Fresh" conjures images of a revitalised, re-released package that breathes new life into old music. However, the record companies in question do not seem to have a clear idea as to how this image of freshness relates to songs that protest issues from a bygone era. They certainly have not successfully communicated any such message to broadcasters and audiences. Yet, the argument in favour of this music is there to be made. A clever advertising campaign could link past resistance to present-day support for democratic values using relevant songs as a musical backdrop. Encouraging the development of retro brand communities around re-released music certainly offers a cautious way forward. Putting marketing money into such campaigns is a risk that could pay off. Yet, the bottom line, even for independent record companies, is profit. Costly advertising campaigns could lead to serious losses. It is safer and potentially more profitable, therefore, to cater for the fringe: market retro releases as effectively as possible, using cost effective but creative "backyard" media strategies with the initial target of covering one's costs, but hoping to make some money with each release. The tactic of encouraging retro brand communities seems to be the most likely of strategies to succeed. However, to date this approach has not achieved very high sales. It seems clear, therefore, that marketing to a small consumer base with limited resources once again leaves the musicians struggling to be heard.

## Notes

1. For a more detailed account of the cultural boycott in South Africa, see Drewett (2006).
2. *Live at Jameson's* in one quintessential moment brought together all the central components of the white anti-apartheid music brand community and related cultural ethic – Shifty Records, the Jameson's venue, James Phillips (as one of the most influential white protest musicians) and a vocal audience whose interaction with the music is clearly captured in the recording. As such, it stands as an iconic reminder of the interweaving of cultural politics and consumption.
3. I am indebted to one of the anonymous referees for suggesting that I include this point in the paper.
4. Freemuse (an abbreviation of Free Musical Expression) is an international human rights and music organisation based in Denmark (see www.freemuse.org).
5. Importantly, in the South African context, such ties have never been strictly along racial lines, and this is more so the case now than ever before.
6. Ballantine's (2004) article "Rethinking 'Whiteness'? Identity, Change and 'White' Popular Music in Post-Apartheid South Africa" provides a detailed account of racial typecasting and slurs

aimed at white South Africans since 1994. He provides an interesting account of the "self-reinvention" of white popular musicians through music in the post-apartheid era.

7. Located in Port Elizabeth in the Nelson Mandela Metropole and catering for the Eastern and Southern Cape regions of South Africa.
8. The transformation of the object from contraband to celebratory item is not dissimilar to the changing representations of homosexuality in film as outlined by Andrew Keating and Damien McLoughlin (2005, 146). Over time, there was a move away from representing homosexuality as threatening, unadjusted and destructive to more positive representations that depict homosexuality as natural and unthreatening.

## References

Allingham, Rob. 1998. Interview by Michael Drewett. Johannesburg, April 17.

*Amandla! A revolution in four-part harmony.* Directed by Lee Hirsch. Supervisory production by Nancy Abrahams. Santa Monica, CA: Artisan Entertainment, 2002.

Baines, Gary. 1998. Catalyst or detonator? Local music quotas and the current South African music "explosion." *Social Dynamics* 24, no. 1: 66–87.

Ballantine, Christopher. 2004. Rethinking "whiteness"? Identity, change and "white" popular music in post-apartheid South Africa. *Popular Music* 23, no. 2: 105–31.

Barfe, Louis. 2005. *Where have all the good times gone? The rise and fall of the record industry.* London: Atlantic Books.

Berland, Jody. 1993. Radio space and industrial time: the case of music formats. In *Rock and popular music: Politics, policies, institutions,* ed. T. Bennett, S. Frith, L. Grossberg, J. Shepherd and G. Turner, 104–18. London: Routledge.

Biehal, Gabriel, and Dipankar Chakravarti. 1982. Information-presentation format and learning goals as determinants of consumers' memory retrieval and choice processes. *Journal of Consumer Research* 8, no. 4: 431–41.

———. 1986. Consumers' use of memory and external information in choice: Macro and micro perspectives. *Journal of Consumer Research* 12, no. 4: 382–405.

Braun, Kathryn, Rhiannon Ellis, and Elizabeth Loftus. 2002. Making my memory: Advertising can change our memories of the past. *Psychology and Marketing* 19, no. 1: 1–23.

Burnett, Robert. 1996. *The global jukebox: The international music industry.* London: Routledge.

Campbell Robinson, Deanna, Elizabeth B. Buck, and Marlene Cuthbert. 1991. *Music at the margins: Popular music and global cultural diversity.* Thousand Oaks, CA: Sage Publications.

Chapman, Chris. 1988. Popular music and the markets of apartheid. *Staffrider* 7, no. 2: 79–83.

Clarke, Donald. 1995. *The rise and fall of popular music.* New York: St. Martin's Press.

Clegg, Johnny, and Michael Drewett. 2006. Why don't you sing about the leaves and the dreams? Reflecting on music censorship in apartheid South Africa. In *Popular music censorship in Africa,* ed. M. Drewett and M. Cloonan, 127–36. London: Ashgate.

Cloonan, Martin. 2003. Call that censorship? Problems of definition. In *Policing pop,* ed. M. Cloonan, and R. Garofalo, 13–29. Philadelphia: Temple University Press.

Cooper, Sarah. 1996. Access some areas: PR in the music industry. In *Girls! Girls! Girls!,* ed. S. Cooper, 148–60. New York: New York University Press.

Coplan, David. 1985. *In township tonight: South Africa's black city music and theatre.* Johannesburg: Ravan Press.

Drewett, Michael. 2003. Music in the struggle to end apartheid: South Africa. In *Policing pop,* ed. M. Cloonan and R. Garofalo, 153–65. Philadelphia: Temple University Press.

———. 2004. *An analysis of the censorship of popular music within the context of cultural struggle in South Africa during the 1980s.* PhD dissertation, Rhodes University.

———. 2006. The cultural boycott against South Africa: A case of defensible censorship? In *Popular music censorship in Africa,* ed. M. Drewett and M. Cloonan, 23–38. London: Ashgate.

Edwards, Lee. 1998. Interview by Michael Drewett. Johannesburg, September 14.

Eyerman, Ron, and Andrew Jamison. 1998. *Music and social movements.* Cambridge: Cambridge University Press.

Fornäs, Johan. 1995. Listen to your voice! Authenticity and reflexivity in karaoke, rock, rap and techno music. In *Popular music – style and identity,* ed. W. Straw, S. Johnson, R. Sullivan, and P. Friedlander, 99–110. Montreal: Centre for Research on Cultural Industries and Institutions.

Frith, Simon. 2001. The popular music industry. In *The Cambridge companion to pop and rock,* ed. S. Frith, W. Straw and J. Street, 26–52. Cambridge: Cambridge University Press.

Gilder, Barry. 1983. Finding new ways to bypass censorship. *Index on censorship* 12, no. 1: 18–22.

Hill, Mark, and Jane Cromartie. 2004. That which is "not": Forgetting … *Consumption, Markets and Culture* 7, no. 1: 69–98.

Hill, Mark, and Maryon King. 2001. Comparative vs. noncomparative advertising: Perspectives on memory. *Journal of Current Issues in Research in Advertising* 23, no. 2: 33–52.

Holt, Douglas. 2002. Why do brands cause trouble? A dialectical theory of consumer culture and branding. *Journal of Consumer Research* 29, no. 1: 70–90.

Jacobsens Publishers. 1991. *Index of objectionable literature.* Pretoria: Jacobsens.

*James Phillips: Famous for Not Being Famous.* Directed by Lloyd Ross. Johannesburg: Shifty Studio, 2004.

Keating, Andrew, and Damien McLoughlin. 2005. Understanding the emergence of markets: A social constructionist perspective on gay economy. *Consumption, Markets and Culture* 8, no. 2: 131–52.

Kerkhof, Ian. 1986. Music and censorship in South Africa. *Rixaka: Cultural Journal of the African National Congress* 2, no. 2: 27–31.

King, Stephen, A. 2006. Protest music as "ego enhancement": Reggae music, the Rastafarian movement and the re-examination of race and identity in Jamaica. In *The resisting muse: Popular music and social protest,* ed. I. Peddie, 105–18. London: Ashgate.

Korpe, Marie, and Ole Reitov. 2004. Not to be broadcasted. In *Sounds of change: Social and political features of music in Africa,* ed. S. Thorsén, 70–86. Stockholm: SIDA.

Kundera, Milan. 1980. *The book of laughter and forgetting.* Harmondsworth: Penguin.

Lucia, Christine. 2002. Abdullah Ibrahim and the uses of memory. *British Journal of Ethnomusicology* 11, no. 2: 125–43.

Malkin, Jeanette. 1999. *Memory-theater and postmodern drama.* Ann Arbor: University of Michigan Press.

Merrett, Christopher. 1994. *A culture of censorship: Secrecy and intellectual repression in South Africa.* Cape Town: David Phillip.

Muniz, Albert M., and Thomas C. O'Guinn. 2001. Brand community. *Journal of Consumer Research* 27, no. 4: 412–32.

Negus, Keith. 1999. *Music genres and corporate cultures.* London: Routledge.

——. 2001. The corporate strategies of the major record companies and the international imperative. In *Global repertoires: Popular music within and beyond the transnational music industry,* ed. A. Gebesmair and A. Smudits, 21–31. London: Ashgate.

Reitov, Ole. 1998. "Only doing my duty: Interview with Cecile Pracher." *Index on Censorship* 27, no. 6: 83–5

Reynolds, Simon. 2005. *Rip it up and start again: Postpunk 1978–1984.* London: Faber and Faber.

Ross, Lloyd. 1998. Interview with Michael Drewett. Johannesburg, April 14.

Scheckter, Jonathan. 2006. *A holistic approach to consumption analysis in the popular music market.* MComm dissertation, Rhodes University.

*Shot Down.* Directed by Andrew Worsdale. Johannesburg: Film Resource Unit, 1986.

Shuker, Roy. 1998. *Key concepts in popular music.* London: Routledge.

———. 2001. *Understanding popular music.* 2nd ed. London: Routledge.

Sony, Warrick. 1991. Strange business: The independent music culture in South Africa. *Staffrider* 9, no. 4: 113–9.

Stewart, Peter. 1986. On the cultural boycott. *Reality* 18, no. 6: 3–5.

*Stopping the Music.* Directed by Douglas Mitchell. Produced by Michael Drewett. Grahamstown: Cutting Grooves, 2002.

Third Ear Music. 1994. Hidden years project proposal. Photocopy of unpublished document.

Volkmann, Christina, and Christian de Cock. 2006. Consuming the Bauhaus. *Consumption, Markets and Culture* 9, no. 2: 129–36.

Wallis, Roger, and Krister Malm. 1984. *Big sounds from small people: The music industry in small countries.* London: Constable.

Willemse, H. 1991. Censorship or strategy. In *The purple shall govern,* ed. D. Smuts, and S. Westcott, 24–25. Cape Town: Oxford University Press.


## Discography


Bright Blue. 1988. The Rising Tide. From *The Rising Tide.* EMI. EMCJ (L) 4063771. Also available on CD: *Every Now and Then: The Best so Far … 1984–2001.* EMI. CDSRBL 286 146. CD.

Cherry Faced Lurchers. 1985. Shot Down. From *Live at Jameson's.* Shifty Records. SHIFT 7. Album with bonus tracks also available on CD: FRESHCD132.

Ferguson, Jennifer. 1986. Suburban Hum. From *Hand Around the Heart.* Shifty Records. SHIFT 23. Album also available on CD: BANGCD 005.

Kalahari Surfers. 1984. Don't dance. From *Own Affairs.* Gross National Product. GNP 333. Also available on CD: *Volume 1. The Eighties.* ReR KS1. And *Forces Favourites* (see Various below).

Lucey, Roger. 1979. Lungile tabalaza. From *The Road is Much Longer*. 3rd Ear Music. Also available on CD*21 Years Down the Road.* 3rd ed. 0034-F CD-R.

Lucey, Roger. 1979. You only need say nothing. From *The Road is Much Longer*. 3rd Ear Music. 3EE 7004. An apartheid-era censored version of this track is available on CD: *21 Years Down the Road.* 3rd ed. 0034-F CD-R.

Niederlander, Edi. 1985. *Ancient Dust.* Mountain Records. MOULP (V) 40. Album also available on CD: MI UK CD 1.

Various. 1985. *Forces Favourites.* Shifty Records. SHIFT 10. (Not available on CD.)

# Music meanings in movies: The case of the crime-plus-jazz genre

Morris B. Holbrook

*Graduate School of Business, Columbia University, New York, NY*

This paper explores the role of film music in creating meanings of concern to those with an interest in consumption, markets, and culture. Specifically, the paper examines ways in which the significance of ambi-diegetic cinemusical moments – that is, music performed on-screen (diegetic) in a manner that advances the dramatic development of plot, character, and other themes (non-diegetic) – enrich our interpretation of three key exemplars from the crime-plus-jazz motion-picture genre: *Pete Kelly's Blues* (1955), *The Cotton Club* (1984), and *Kansas City* (1996). Key homologous parallels and contrasts among these three films touch on various consumption-, markets-, and culture-related themes in general and on the contrast or tension between commerce (crime) and art (jazz) in particular.

## Introduction

This paper proposes that the role of music in general or jazz in particular as a key aspect of meaning in an artistic offering such as a motion picture calls for an interpretive analysis of the music itself – ***not*** merely the lyrics to songs; ***not*** just the non-musical screen personas of the performers; and ***not*** only the extra-musical aspects of costumes, props, or scenery; but ***rather*** the details of the actual musical compositions and performances. This logic pursues the viewpoint offered in previous analyses of symbolic consumption in motion pictures, television programs, novels, and plays (Holbrook and Grayson 1986; Holbrook and Hirschman 1993) insofar as the interpretation of (say) clothing, automobiles, or décor goes beyond the recognition of their roles as costumes, props, or scenery to embrace their special significance and deeper meaning as manifestations of symbolic consumer behaviors that work toward the dramatic development of plot, character, and other themes. In this – like other aspects of props (a Rolex wristwatch or Ferrari automobile), costumes (Prada shoes or a Vuitton handbag), décor (a Victorian living room or a colonial dining area), scenery (a well-manicured lawn or the view of a dingy back alley from a tenement window), and so forth – the music that film characters choose for consumption in the form of playing, singing, listening, and/or dancing sheds light on their personalities, moves the plot forward, and conveys other important dramatic messages. Thus – following earlier cinemusical interpretations (Holbrook 1985, 2003, 2004, 2005a, 2005b, 2005c, 2006, 2007) – the analysis here focuses ***not*** on the role of ***non-diegetic film scores*** (background music or underscoring produced off-screen in ways that advance a film's dramatic development), and ***not*** on the more mundane aspects of ***diegetic source music*** (performances that appear on-screen to support the realism of the narrative action by enhancing the verisimilitude of the mise-en-scène), but ***rather*** on the importance of ***ambi-diegetic film music*** that appears ***on-screen*** (like diegetic music) but that works in significant ways to advance key ***dramatic meanings*** (like non-diegetic music) (Holbrook 2003; cf. Biancorosso 2001; Marks 2000; Rosar 2002).

Describing this interpretive strategy in the abstract makes little progress toward demonstrating its potential applicability. For this reason, the interpretation of ambi-diegetic music in motion pictures will be illustrated by an analysis of cinemusically meaningful on-screen jazz performances in three key films from the crime-plus-jazz genre in general and by an appreciation of how these cinemusical moments illuminate the parallel theme of commerce-versus-art in particular (cf. Holbrook 2005c, 2006; Bradshaw, McDonagh, and Marshall 2006). Specifically, the following interpretive analyses will examine the meanings of cinemusical performances as these illuminate the contrast or conflict between commerce (crime) and art (jazz) in *Pete Kelly's Blues* (1955), *The Cotton Club* (1984), and *Kansas City* (1996).

## The role of film music in the crime-plus-jazz genre

For better or worse, jazz musicians – almost always in need of a night's work and a good day's sleep – often perform at expensive nightclubs, fancy grills, posh watering holes, brassy brasseries, comfortable taverns, dangerous roadside restaurants, boisterous beer halls, dank dives, sleazy bars, and any number of other establishments ranging from the most upscale and elite that money can buy to the most downscale and bedraggled that one might imagine, where folks can go to have a drink, eat some peanuts, chew a steak, and listen to some good music. Most of the people who hang out in such venues are doubtless perfectly decent nine-to-five workers who just want to have a little fun, toss back a couple of shots, and snap their fingers to some hip sounds. But low-life gangsters, hoodlums, and felons also need a place to congregate. And it appears, especially in crime films, that jazz clubs often provide their typical meeting places of choice. For this reason – with a lot of help from the *film-noir* genre, from the movie or television scores of composers like Henry Mancini (the TV series *Peter Gunn* during the late-1950s), and from partially valid stereotypes that just won't die – jazz has become a sure-fire signifier for the premonition of robbery, blackmail, kidnapping, or murder. If the cocktail pianist flats a fifth in his solo on "Honeysuckle Rose," can a fusillade of machine-gun fire be far behind?

Some day, an ambitious musical historian with far more patience and way better funding than the present author will trace this trend from (say) *After the Thin Man* (1936) to *The Pink Panther* (1964) to *Manhattan Murder Mystery* (1993) to *The Score* (2001) to *Inside Man* (2006). But, in the meantime, let us confine our attention to three particularly conspicuous and representative examples of the crime-plus-jazz genre – namely, *Pete Kelly's Blues* (1955), *The Cotton Club* (1984), and *Kansas City* (1996). Taken together, these three films span the last half of the past century and give us some clear insights into the ways in which the crime-plus-jazz motion-picture genre has deployed ambi-diegetic cinemusical meanings involving performances presented on-screen for the purpose of dramatic development.

## Preview: three illustrations of ambi-diegetic cinemusical meanings in the crime-plus-jazz motion-picture genre

In short, the present essay explores how on-screen film music can function ambi-diegetically to advance the dramatic development of a motion picture. We shall consider detailed illustrations based on our cinemusical interpretations of the aforementioned three representative examples from the crime-plus-jazz genre. As a brief overview, consider the following set of parallel homologous comparisons among the three films of interest – to be developed more systematically in the three major sections that follow.

As indicated here, the three films of interest show key similarities and contrasts. More importantly, in their various ways, they reflect the manners in which the ambi-diegetic meanings of on-screen music contribute to a film's dramatic development in the crime-plus-jazz genre. All converge on a key homologous parallel between crime-versus-jazz and commerce-versus-art – namely, crime : jazz :: commerce : art. These points provide the major focus for detailed illustrations in the next three sections.

| | *Pete Kelly's Blues* | *The Cotton Club* | *Kansas City* |
|---|---|---|---|
| Release Date | 1955 | 1984 | 1996 |
| Director | Jack Webb | Francis Ford Coppola | Robert Altman |
| Setting | Speakeasy | Nightclub | Nightclub |
| City | Kansas City | New York | Kansas City |
| Time | 1927 | 1930-ish | 1934 |
| Hero | Pete Kelly | Dixie Dwyer | Lester Young |
| Actor | Jack Webb | Richard Gere | Joshua Redman |
| Instrument | Cornet | Cornet | Tenor sax |
| Dubbing | Dick Cathcart | Richard Gere | NA |
| Synchronization | Excellent | Excellent | Real-Time |
| Heroine | Ivy Conrad | Vera Cicero | Honey O'Hara |
| Actress | Janet Leigh | Diane Lane | Jennifer Jason Leigh |
| Other Musicians | Al Gannaway;<br>Joey Firestone | Duke Ellington;<br>Cab Calloway | Charlie Parker |
| Actors | Lee Marvin;<br>Martin Milner | Zane Mark;<br>Larry Marshall | Albert J. Burnes |
| Dubbed By | Matty Matlock (cl);<br>Nick Fatool (d) | Mark Shane (p);<br>Larry Marshall (v) | NA<br>NA |
| House Band | Matty Matlock (cl)<br>Dick Cathcart (tp)<br>Eddie Miller (ts)<br>Moe Schneider (tb)<br>Ray Sherman (p)<br>George Van Eps (g)<br>Jud De Naut (b)<br>Nick Fatool (d) | Bob Wilber (cl)<br>Lew Soloff (tp)<br>Joe Temperly (bs)<br>Britt Woodman (tb)<br>Mark Shane (p)<br>Mike Peters (g)<br>John Goldsby (b)<br>Chuck Riggs (d) | Don Byron (cl)<br>Nicholas Payton (tp)<br>J. Redman, Craig Handy, James Carter<br>David Murray, and David Newman (ts)<br>Geri Allen and Cyrus Chestnut (p)<br>Russell Malone and Mark Whitfield (g)<br>Ron Carter and Christian McBride (b)<br>Victor Lewis (d) |
| Singing | Peggy Lee<br>Ella Fitzgerald | Lonette McKee | Kevin Mahogany |
| Ambi-Diegetic Jazz | Expresses Emotions;<br>Reflects stresses;<br>Motivates action | Recreates Color barriers;<br>Reflects angst;<br>Shows integrity | Poor on realistic Depiction;<br>Good on dramatic Development |
| Key Parallels | Crime : jazz ::<br>Commerce : art | Crime : jazz ::<br>Commerce : art | Crime : jazz ::<br>Commerce : art |

### *Pete Kelly's Blues (1955)*

*Pete Kelly's Blues* (1955) – starring its director Jack Webb in the role of Pete Kelly, a cornet-playing bandleader whose gig in a 1927 Kansas City speakeasy puts him in conflict with Fran McCarg (Edmond O'Brien), a gangster trying to extort money from the band – comes across as a cinematic disaster until you stop paying attention to its improbable plot, ignore its awkward acting, and regard it instead as a fine vehicle for the presentation of some excellent jazz. At the time he made this film, Webb was riding high on the success of his television show *Dragnet*, on which he played a tough, curt, macho, world-weary cop. So what does he play in *Pete Kelly's Blues*? Of course: a tough, curt, macho, world-weary cornet player.

The only problem is that – in enacting a love story between Kelly and the beautiful Ivy Conrad (Janet Leigh) – Pete's tendency to talk to Ivy in roughly the same manner in which Sergeant Joe Friday addresses the common criminals on *Dragnet* renders the scenes deliciously comic, but with an uneasy feeling that Webb did not intentionally play them for laughs. Further, the crime-related aspects of the story-line go way over the top. When McCarg clumsily imposes his extortion racket on the musicians, the band's drummer Joey Firestone (enacted by the same Martin Milner who later starred as the guitar-playing hero in *Sweet Smell of Success* [1957]) goes bonkers and – very, very foolishly – insults McCarg so flagrantly that the crime boss has no choice but to gun him down like a mallard on the first day of duck-hunting season. This tends to make Kelly angry and disoriented to the point where the bandleader – also very, very foolishly – spends the rest of the movie ducking the romantic advances of Conrad until the preposterous scene at the end in which she traps him in a dance to a schmaltzy hurdy-gurdy in the very same ballroom where, at that very moment, Kelly is in the process of stealing McCarg's personal papers for the purpose of incriminating him and thereby ending his reign of terror. When McCarg and his henchmen burst upon the scene – presumably attracted by the horrendous racket of the noisy calliope – an improbable fusillade of gunfire results in the loathsome hoodlum's demise via a veritable *coup de schmaltz*.

So – as an interpretive strategy – let us ***forget*** the story-line and, instead, ***go for the music***. In this connection, the film opens with a soulful rendition of "Just a Closer Walk with Thee," played by a mournful cornet with gospel-choir accompaniment around the grave at a burial service in New Orleans circa 1915. This dirge segues, in the manner of the old New Orleans funerals, into a happy version of "Oh, Didn't He Ramble" as joyful marching music for the traditional spirited procession back to town. On the way, the cornet of the deceased falls off the hearse wagon, to be kicked around in the mud, pawned, and passed down from hand to hand for a few years until Pete Kelly wins it in a craps game and ultimately learns to play it well enough to become a band leader. All this establishes the link of jazz with its African-American ancestry and sets the stage for the authenticity of Pete Kelly's commitment to his horn – quite consistent with that evinced by (say) Rick Martin (Kirk Douglas) and Bleek Gilliam (Denzel Washington) in such previous and subsequent productions as *Young Man with a Horn* (1950) and *Mo' Better Blues* (1990), respectively (Holbrook 2005c).

As we pick up the story of Pete Kelly, we find the cornetist playing a rousing version of "Smiles" in a small Kansas City speakeasy in 1927. The music in this scene bursts with light-hearted abandon provided by a group of real-life musicians put together by Matty Matlock (clarinet) and featuring Dick Cathcart (trumpet), Eddie Miller (tenor sax), Moe Schneider (trombone), Ray Sherman (piano), George Van Eps (guitar), Jud DeNaut (bass), and Nick Fatool (drums) – essentially the same LA band that recorded together many times during the mid-1950s under the name of The South Rampart Street Paraders. The full contents of five such albums have recently reappeared in a reissue set entitled *Classic Columbia Condon Mob Sessions* (Matty Matlock et al. 2001) and might serve as the gold standard for happy-go-lucky Chicago-styled Dixieland-jazz revivalism at mid-century. Matlock – an under-appreciated jazz giant who spent much time behind the scenes in such aggregations as the Bob Crosby Band – was a master of the New-Orleans-Chicago-Dixie-styled clarinet-obbligato flourishes and knew how to bend himself to perfection around the crisp lead horns of the trumpeters with whom he worked (including, besides Cathcart, the formidable Red Nichols, the impressive Clyde Hurley, and the marvelous Wild Bill Davison).

Interestingly enough, the music from *Pete Kelly's Blues* found its way onto long-playing records in at least three different versions. First, the renditions of tunes from the movie recently reissued on Mosaic (2001) appeared under the name of Matty Matlock and his Jazz Band (1955) on Columbia. The same group – calling itself Pete Kelly's Big Seven, with a narrative by Jack Webb – recorded essentially the same repertoire for RCA Victor (1955). And songs performed in the film by Peggy Lee and Ella Fitzgerald, accompanied by the Matlock band, also showed up on a record album entitled *Songs from Pete Kelly's Blues* released by Decca (1955).

In "Smiles" and in other ensemble pieces featured throughout the film, Jack Webb benefits from this hospitable musical setting with aplomb. Apparently, the actor was a major jazz fan – owner of over 6,000 recordings and an amateur cornet player who diligently practiced the horn. According to Richard Sudhalter's liner notes for Mosaic (Matlock et al. 2001), Webb had worked before with Dick Cathcart in a short-lived radio version of *Pete Kelly's Blues* in mid-1951, and Meeker (1981) reports that Cathcart continued to perform for the 1959 television series based on the film. Undoubtedly, Webb's fondness for the music inspired his directorial and thespian efforts in the movie version of *Pete Kelly's Blues*. Certainly, his aptitude on the horn facilitated the near perfection Webb achieved in synchronizing his cornet miming with the trumpet sounds ghosted by Cathcart. The effect helps to preserve the aura of great jazz – its spontaneity amidst precision – and moves the story forward by revealing the Kelly character as a serious musician with a high level of bandstand charisma.

These personality characteristics qualify Kelly for the amorous advances of Conrad, who invites him to a drunken party where, as the couple dances, an on-screen orchestra plays "I Never Knew" – the tune that turns out to be Ivy's leitmotif – a lovely ballad that captures something of her gentle nature. When Ivy later visits Pete to apologize for her tipsy behavior at the rowdy party, the non-diegetic soundtrack again plays "I Never Knew" as they work their way toward a first passionate kiss. Usually, "I Never Knew" appears in the non-diegetic score – whenever images or thoughts of Ivy come into play – for example, on the aforementioned awful-sounding out-of-tune calliope in a scene at the Everglade Ballroom and, later, via a full orchestral treatment when Ivy proposes marriage in a rather charming way. Again, we hear this non-diegetic leitmotif when Conrad waits for Kelly in her car outside the speakeasy, they argue, she tells him that he wouldn't get married unless he found a girl who looks like a cornet and adds that she is "three valves short," they break off their engagement, and she drives away with the classic line, "Gosh, I'm sorry to see me go." Yet again, the theme appears in the background when Ivy tries to make up with Pete and to renew their relationship at the very moment when he is rushing off in search of McCarg's incriminating documents, too busy to talk with her, and in the mood to dismiss her brusquely. But, as the film approaches its end, we encounter two occasions when the Conrad leitmotif shows up in dramatically important ambi-diegetic form.

First, in the suspenseful scene at McCarg's office, the calliope machine plays "I Never Knew" as a basis for Ivy to ask Pete to dance, under circumstances fraught with imminent danger. The ludicrous sound of the hurdy-gurdy playing the old jazz/pop standard by Ted FioRito (music) and Gus Kahn (words) perfectly complements the wildly improbable nature of this dance episode – in which Conrad just wants to hold Kelly and twirl around in a romantic way while he wrestles with a life-threatening crisis that she knows nothing about. In a sense, the song "I Never Knew" deserves more respect than that. Recall that FioRito wrote the tunes to other such classics as "Toot Toot Tootsie" and "Laugh! Clown! Laugh!" As a lyricist, Kahn created an even longer list of masterpieces like "Dream a Little Dream of Me," "I'll See You in My Dreams," "It Had to Be You," "Liza," "Love Me or Leave Me," "Makin' Whoopee," "My Baby Just Cares For Me," "My Buddy," "The One I Love Belongs to Somebody Else," "Yes, Sir, That's My Baby," and "You Stepped Out of a Dream" – plus "Toot Toot Tootsie" (with FioRito). As one of the best and most widely circulated hits for both songwriters, FioRito and Kahn's "I Never Knew" (1925) has been performed and recorded by an endless succession of musical heroes including Louis Armstrong, Charlie Christian, Nat "King" Cole, John Coltrane, Tommy Dorsey, Duke Ellington, Benny Goodman, Coleman Hawkins, Zoot Sims, Frank Sinatra, Teddy Wilson, and Lester Young – plus Peggy Lee and George Van Eps (both of whom appear in *Pete Kelly's Blues*). In other words, the song has an impressive musical pedigree, is associated with the finest jazz artists, and carries amorous associations from an era evocative of the budding jazz-age romance between Kelly and Conrad.

Hence, in the song's second crucial on-screen appearance, we experience a feeling of triumph when the ambi-diegetic music in the film's last scene turns out to be none other than "I Never Knew" – this time performed by Kelly himself, playing in the old speakeasy to an appreciative audience that includes Conrad. This concluding performance sounds jubilant, recalling the atmosphere surrounding "Smiles" when the movie began, and again at the Everglade Ballroom when things were temporarily going well for the band and for the Kelly-Conrad romance. In that earlier Ballroom scene, a *Dragnet*-type voiceover by Webb tells us that, on its own merits, the Everglade is a pretty drab scene, ***but*** that the good thing about the place is Ivy. And – BAM! – we see and hear the start of a crackling version of … "Smiles." At the end – with an authentic Chicago-style version of "I Never Knew," performed full-tilt by the Matlock band with Jack Webb and the guys doing their convincing miming on-stage – things have returned to normal. McCarg, the wicked crime boss, is dead. Kelly and Conrad have found true love. And all is well – both musically and socially.

But there is more ambi-diegetic jazz of (1) musical note and (2) dramatic substance in *Pete Kelly's Blues*. In the first connection (musical note), Webb the director gives us two wonderful performances by Ella Fitzgerald playing the part of Maggie Johnson, the singer at Fat Annie's, a wayside roadhouse where the musicians meet for their secret rendezvous. In this capacity, Fitzgerald does little to advance the movie's plot line but rather serves to provide a transcendent touch of musical excellence. Indeed, Ella's singing presents us with a remarkable gift that we, as viewers, must take time to appreciate. When we first encounter her at Fat Annie's, Maggie is singing "Hard Hearted Hanah" in a joyfully Fitzgeraldesque rendition backed by a piano-bass-and-drums trio (Don Abney, Joe Mondragon, and Larry Bunker, respectively, on the soundtrack but played by black actors on-screen). Visually, as Maggie, Ella seems stiff. But musically, as herself, she hits those pitch-perfect notes for which she is so justly famous – with all her trademark glissandos and coloratura effects thrown in for good measure – working her way three times to the high note on the concluding phrase, a repeated D-natural on the words "***vamp*** of Sa***van***nah, G … A." The first two times, she reliably nails the D-naturals with her enviably precise vocal instrument. On the third, she leads us to the same moment in the song – at which point we fully expect to hear those two D-naturals one more time – but then lifts her voice up a half-step to produce two shining E-flats (in effect, a downward appoggiatura, from the fourth to the third of the tonic chord). In context, the effect of this little musical surprise – a phrase often found in gospel music and associated with a soul-jazz feeling – is ***electrifying***.

Later, Kelly again visits the roadhouse and finds Maggie in the midst of singing "Pete Kelly's Blues" (with words by Sammy Cahn and music by Ray Heindorf written especially for the film). Until now, this tune has served as the film's principal non-diegetic music – supplying background effects whenever something particularly seedy needs to happen, such as Pete mixing a drink for an already-inebriated guest or arguing heatedly but fruitlessly with a gangster. In Maggie's ambi-diegetic version, we hear the piece for what it was apparently intended to be – a bluesy torch song sung as only Ella could sing it. Thus, Maggie's performance, however irrelevant to the main story-line, carries an important part of the movie's meaning – anchored in the commerce-versus-art theme (paralleling the crime-plus-jazz genre) – namely, that there is great music out there, as performed by someone of Ella Fitzgerald's caliber (art in the form of jazz), to be treasured far beyond the sort of monetary gain that crooks and hoodlums covet as the sordid lucre from their larcenous capers and squalid shake-down schemes (commerce in the form of crime).

In the second connection referred to earlier (dramatic substance), the ambi-diegetic music provided by Peggy Lee – playing the part of Fran McCarg's girlfriend Rose Hopkins (for which she received an Academy Award nomination as best supporting actress) – contrasts vividly in style and function with that provided by Ella Fitzgerald. Specifically, unlike Ella's songs, Peggy's musical performances are crucial to the dramatic development of the film. Something has to get Kelly angry enough to resist McCarg's strong-arm tactics. That "something" turns out to be the way McCarg treats Kelly's friend Rose, whom the film portrays as a talented but frail songbird – deeply miserable in her abusive relationship with the gangster, profoundly wishing that she had settled down with a family when she had the chance, touchingly apologetic when McCarg tries to foist her torch-song talents upon Kelly's band of Dixielanders, and pitiably drowning her resulting sorrows in whiskey. In short, Rose contrasts with Maggie in almost every way imaginable: Rose : Maggie :: Peggy : Ella :: Swing : Blues :: Light : Dark :: Soft : Loud :: Insecure : Solid :: Fragile : Strong :: Cool : Hot :: Inebriated : Sober :: Disturbed : Sane :: Caucasian : African American.

When she performs her "try out" number with Pete's band, Rose sings "He Needs Me" – a song specially composed for the film by Arthur Hamilton and subsequently often recorded by such worthy female singers as Rebecca Kilgore, Cleo Laine, Gloria Lynne, Polly Podewell, Nina Simone, Frances Wayne, and Peggy Lee herself – in a compelling performance that resembles nothing so much as a white distillation of Billie Holiday. In this scene, Rose stands at the edge of the stage – statuesque and virtually immobile, with her left hand resting on the piano and her right arm hanging loosely at her side – delivering the torchy lyrics in a husky but dead-accurate voice, soft and sultry, but with perfect intonation and pellucid enunciation. She is terrific. And she follows this stunning performance by moving to center stage to sing "Sugar" – accompanied by fine obbligatos from Kelly – still standing stoically immobile but doing incredibly expressive things with her eyes and lips and looking as precariously alluring as a beautiful rose (her name) that is about to be hit by a terrible storm (her boyfriend). In subsequent stages of the film, "He Needs Me" serves as non-diegetic music to underscore scenes that portray the degradation of this flowerlike singer.

Clearly, Kelly is impressed by the formidable talents of this tragic songbird, but – more important to the ambi-diegetic role of this music – her musical style and demeanor bring out a protectiveness in him that he has not shown in his other relationships (including that with Ivy). These protective instincts stand their test in a parallel follow-up scene in which Rose – having drowned her sorrows in way too much booze – tries but fails to perform "Somebody

Loves Me" with the band. Predictably, McCarg reacts with characteristic violence and beats her up. Semi-conscious, she falls down the stairs and suffers a head injury that reduces her to the mental capacity of a five-year-old and confines her to a state hospital for the insane.

Following the music rather than the verbal text, we should observe that – when playing drunk during a humiliating performance in front of a loud and hostile crowd – Peggy Lee acts her role as a debilitated lush by slurring and forgetting the words ***but still sings perfectly in tune***! In this connection, notice that the ***only*** time Liza Minnelli sings with good intonation during *New York, New York* (1977) is when she does a soft-pedaled imitation of Peggy Lee. Even in the mental hospital, as a brain-damaged patient, Rose ***still sings in tune*** – this time, a forlornly childish song called "Sing a Rainbow," also written by Arthur Hamilton for this film but not followed up by other singers (with the unfortunate exception of Astrud Gilberto). Here, Rose spends her time playing with a limp rag doll and crooning this sad song about red-yellow-pink-and-green to herself in a demented state of perpetual regression to infancy. This scene, colored so strongly by Peggy Lee's distraught ambi-diegetic singing, furthers the dramatic development by revealing Kelly's decent side and highlighting his protectiveness toward Rose. Indeed, hearing her pathetically sing that forlorn children's song arouses his righteous indignation to the point of taking action against McCarg.

So – to put it mildly – ambi-diegetic cinemusical meanings play a key role in *Pete Kelly's Blues*. In innumerable cases, on-screen performances of jazz pieces and songs sung by singers ranging from competent (Janet Leigh) to accomplished (Peggy Lee) to shimmering (Ella Fitzgerald) perform one or another function in advancing the development of plot, character, or thematic material – Ivy as a bit dipsy but lovable, Rose as a tragic motivation for retribution, and Maggie as a vivid contrast to Rose. Further, much of the jazz in *Pete Kelly's Blues* enjoys the sort of ***in-between*** status celebrated by Kassabian (2001) – in the sense that it often begins as diegetic/non-diegetic music and then reappears as non-diegetic/diegetic music – for example, in the mixed (non)diegetic scoring of such tunes as "I Never Knew," "He Needs Me," and "Pete Kelly's Blues." However, one especially deft use of this transitional device appears to deserve special comment.

Specifically, early in the film, the Kelly band makes a record of the old Donaldson-and-Lyman chestnut "(What Can I Say) After I Say I'm Sorry?" – featuring a nice clarinet solo, taking the tune at an unusually slow tempo, and playing it for all its potential poignancy. This diegetic performance presages the imminent departure of the group's clarinetist Al Gannaway (Lee Marvin), who has been scared off by the intrusion of gangsters into their formerly carefree existence. As Gannaway says goodbye to Kelly outside the studio, we hear the replay of "What Can I Say?" from the recording session inside. The two exchange some references to the Jean Goldkette Orchestra – where Al hopes to find a job and where (we know) the trumpet chair is currently occupied by Bix Beiderbecke, the then-reigning white *enfant terrible* of the cornet. And then, as the band's newly waxed recording of "What Can I Say?" continues in the background, it's "Goodbye, Al."

Later, Gannaway returns, full of rage at how Kelly has caved in to McCarg's shake-down scam. He asks Pete to return the mouthpiece that he once gave the cornetist, as a symbol of friendship, after taking it from a deceased bugler in World War I. The two exchange angry words, Pete knocks Al down and throws the mouthpiece into the dirt beside him, and again, Gannaway leaves, this time on a bitter note. But Kelly redeems himself by following Al in his car and asking his old friend to climb inside for a ride. Repentant, Al returns the symbolic mouthpiece. Everybody smiles. In the background, while this reconciliation unfolds, we hear a performance of the formerly diegetic but now non-diegetic "(What Can I Say) After I Say I'm Sorry?"

### *The Cotton Club* (1984)

Directed by Francis Ford Coppola and starring Richard Gere as the cornetist Dixie Dwyer, *The Cotton Club* (1984) might be characterized as a variation on *Pete Kelly's Blues* (1955) with the addition of numerous songs by Duke Ellington, a great deal of dancing, and an extra half-hour of tedium. In a nutshell, Dixie Dwyer (Richard Gere) recapitulates the role of Pete Kelly (Jack Webb) as a jazz-loving cornet player who gets embroiled in the evil machinations of the Prohibition-Era Mafioso types. Specifically, an especially nasty gangster named Dutch Schultz (James Remar) takes a "liking" to Dwyer because Dwyer saved Dutch's life in a barroom bomb attack. Dutch honors this social debt by employing Dwyer's brother Vincent (Nicholas Cage) and by hiring Dwyer to escort his mistress Vera Cicero (Diane Lane), with whom Dwyer has already had a brief romantic fling and toward whom he feels a strong sexual attraction. Much of the film's action hinges on the hoodlum-related activities of brother Vincent and the temptations presented to Dwyer in trying to keep his nose clean while accompanying the alluring Vera to her rendezvous with Dutch. Ultimately, both Vincent and Dutch meet violent ends, while Dwyer and Vera find a way to (re)unite.

Meanwhile, a subsidiary plot develops (accounting for much of the extra half-hour) in which Sandman Williams (Gregory Hines) working on-and-off with his (real life) brother Clay Williams (Maurice Hines) wins (1) a dancing job at the Cotton Club and (2) the affections of a silver-tonsiled Cotton Club performer named Lila Rose Oliver (Lonette McKee), who is light-skinned and can pass for white or, more importantly, for a jazz singer somewhat in the mold of Lena Horne, thereby affording some of the film's few distinguished musical moments. In an apparently sincere effort to recreate the ambience and musical style of the Cotton Club circa 1930 – a famous locale in Harlem where Duke Ellington performed with his so-called "jungle" orchestra from 1927 to 1932 and where black performers provided the scintillating shows but were not permitted to participate as members of the audience – Coppola populates his film with appearances by Diane Venora as Gloria Swanson, Gregory Rozakis as Charlie Chaplin, Vincent Jerosa as James Cagney, Rosalind Harris as Fanny Brice, and Zane Mark as Duke Ellington. Further, he indulges the tormented efforts by Larry Marshall to recreate the preenings of Cab Calloway on "Minnie the Moocher" – that dreary song with the annoying refrain about "Hi-Di-Hi-Di-Hi-Di-Hi … Ho-Di-Ho-Di-Ho-Di-Ho" – which, surely, might serve as a standard of comparison for the depths of bottom-feeding to which the most obnoxiously commercial, obsequiously pandering, offensively lowbrow music is capable of sinking.

But, beyond these celebrity touches that conspire to add so much needless weight to this production-heavy musical extravaganza, the film offers a great deal of diegetic music that – while enhancing the realism of the mise-en-scène – must prove somewhat controversial in the present context. With impressive accuracy as far as the real-life Cotton Club in the late-1920s and early-1930s is concerned, the film features a very large amount of material provided by a bunch of crackerjack studio musicians reproducing the sounds of the early Duke Ellington Orchestra. For example, the film's soundtrack album *The Cotton Club* (Various 1984) – produced by the movie's musical supervisor John Barry and displaying not (say) a saxophone but (rather) a machine gun on its cover – includes many tunes strongly associated with the Duke, masterfully transcribed and arranged for the film by Bob Wilber (with a little help from people like Sy Johnson, David Berger, Randy Sandke, and Al Woodbury): "The Mooche," "Cotton Club Stomp #1 and #2," "Drop Me Off in Harlem," "Creole Love Call," "Ring Dem Bells," "East St. Louis Toodle-O," "Mood Indigo," "Wall Street Wail," "Slippery Horn," and "High Life." In these recreations, Wilber benefits from the technically proficient contributions of such ace musicians as, among others,

Joe Temperly and Frank Wess (saxophones), Marky Markowitz and Lew Soloff (trumpets), Dan Barrett and Britt Woodman (trombones), Mark Shane (piano), and Chuck Riggs and Dave Samuels (percussion). Together, these studio virtuosi do a masterful job of recreating the famous Ellington sound. But, there's the rub.

Specifically, *The Cotton Club* borrows extensively from the period-relevant Ellington oeuvre to give us a film score saturated with a heavy dose of Duke's "jungle" music from the late-1920s. Then, as later, Duke was a colorist given to exercising his penchant for interesting musical textures or even outlandish sound effects. Thus, from the "jungle music" days in the 1920s until the end in the 1970s, the Ellington Orchestra specialized in a number of always colorful but sometimes grating sonic aberrations produced by trombones with plunger mutes (e.g., "Tricky" Sam Nanton); trumpets with wa-wa effects ("Bubber" Miley or "Cootie" Williams); squealing high-stratosphere brass pyrotechnics ("Cat" Anderson); syrupy, gushing, almost rancid-sounding alto saxophones (Johnny Hodges); and screeching violins (Ray Nance). Leonard Feather manages to put a positive spin on these extraneous intrusions:

> Early Ellington orchestral characteristics included the use of what he originally called "jungle style" effects, through the use of plunger mutes. ... Much of the success of the band ... was attributed to Ellington's unique selection of tonal colors, through orchestral voicings that could never be duplicated because the individual timbre of each man in the orchestra was itself essential to the overall effect. (1960, 191)

In other words, Ellington managed to incorporate a variety of strange sounds into his orchestral fabric. Some call it a "unique selection of tonal colors." Others would call it "noise" – no more pleasing to the ears than (say) a baby's incessant wailing or an unattended car alarm. Thus, even Feather must admit that "Cat" Anderson "spoiled many of his performances with high note effects and poor musical taste" (101) and that Ray Nance "has been known primarily as a comedy personality" with "an excessive accent on grotesque visual mannerisms" (347).

*The Cotton Club* also features Duke Ellington's famed aura of exaggerated flamboyance and bravura sophistication. Duke, the handsome stud, the natty dresser, the savvy bon vivant who regaled his audiences with affected speech mannerisms and with constant reassurances – repeated to the point of irritation – that he, each soloist, and indeed every member of his large aggregation "Love You Madly." True, all this put Duke in an orbit known – to paraphrase his own words – as "beyond category." But it also invited an emphasis on crowd-pleasing showmanship at the expense of art that comes through loud and clear in *The Cotton Club*. The minute we see the figure of Duke Ellington (Zane Mark) dressed in white tie and tails, looking like he is about to explode with self-satisfaction, we know that we will soon be entertained to within an inch of our lives. Indeed, in a spectacular display of the tension between commerce and art, this portentous prophesy provides the major premise for much of *The Cotton Club*.

In this motion picture – often in ways that do not appear to contribute significant meaning to the film's dramatic development – hoofers hoof, tappers tap, and singers, sometimes with screeching incompetence, mercilessly sing. In the latter connection, consider especially the agonized faux-operatic excrescences of Pricilla Baskerville on "Creole Love Call," the noisome delivery by Dave Brown of "Ring Dem Bells," and the trying effusiveness of Gregory Hines on "Copper Colored Gal." However, it is the dancing in *The Cotton Club* that really gets bogged down. The chorus-line numbers – choreographed by someone named Joyce Brown, who is buried in the credits – consist mostly of thick-legged beauties strutting their stuff, lovely to look at individually but painful to watch collectively as they shuffle around the stage in quasi-disarray. Even worse are the tap routines featuring the Williams Brothers (Gregory and Maurice Hines). Indeed, the tap dancing in *The Cotton Club* falls far below the standard expected from a film purporting to capture the great tradition of tapsters harking back to the likes of Bill "Bojangles" Robinson, the Berry Brothers, Sammy Davis and Family, or the nonpareil Nicholas Brothers (on whom the Hines characters appear to be loosely based). In an essentially African-American mode of artistic expression, even such whiter-than-white tapsters as Gene Kelly and Fred Astaire managed to master the one basic requisite of this art form – namely, that the tapping sounds the dancers make with their feet must correspond to the rhythmic cadence of the music to which they are dancing. This basic requisite might seem pretty obvious. But Maurice and Gregory (who passed away in 2003) just don't get it. Thus, the Hines style of tapping involves flicking your feet in a manner that makes clicks totally unrelated to the rhythm of the music to which you are dancing, no beat-reinforcing taps, no flurries of syncopated clicking sounds, just random noises made by feet flailing with arms waving in oblivious excess. Losing contestants on Ted Mack's *Amateur Hour* – back in the days when people took tap dancing seriously – did a better job of synchronizing their tapping with the musical pulse (right before they lost to a seven-year-old ventriloquist or a three-foot-tall baton twirler).

As partial recompense for the painful experience of watching the Cotton Club chorus line dance out of step and the Williams team tap out of rhythm, the film does offer one nice moment of musical fallout from the romantic relationship that develops between Sandman Williams and the light-skinned Lila Oliver when we find Lila singing in an all-white nightclub owned by the evil Dutch Schultz. In this strained setting – "passing" for white in an atmosphere clouded by corruption and potentially riddled with bullets – Lila rares back and lets us have the magnificent "Ill Wind," written for a Cotton Club *Parade* show in 1934 by Ted Koehler (words) and Harold Arlen (music), who had composed "Stormy Weather" for the same venue in the previous year. The latter song – quite similar in feeling and very close in harmonic structure to the former – is indelibly associated with Lena Horne, who memorably performed the piece in the film *Stormy Weather* (1943) and who also recorded "Ill Wind" at about the same time. Just in case we miss this association, the source music for *The Cotton Club* includes a snatch from "Stormy Weather" in the ambi-diegetic performance – a direct quote, near the end, by trumpeter Lew Soloff in the back-up band – by which time, we cannot help but notice that Lila bears a striking resemblance to the young Lena. Hence, "Ill Wind" serves as a perfect vehicle for her ambi-diegetic torch-song delivery – all the more because, in its explicit angst-ridden lyrics and its plentiful implicit musical associations with at least one other world-weary song, it sums up the emotional destructiveness and physical danger of the gangster-dominated scene in which Sandman and Lila seek to nurture a budding romance – thereby developing both Lila's character and relevant aspects of the dramatic setting.

But the aspect of *The Cotton Club* that emerges as its only plausible commendation lies ***not*** in the spectacular diegetic musical extravaganzas described earlier but ***rather*** in the quietly confident and little-celebrated way in which Richard Gere ***plays his own cornet solos***. Historically, matinee idols have sometimes met with mixed success when trying to bring their musical talents to fruition on the silver screen. Recall, for example, Jimmy Stewart's wobbly-voiced rendition of Cole Porter's "Easy To Love" in *Born To Dance* (1936). Or the misplaced method acting of Marlon Brando in *Guys and Dolls* (1955) – proving beyond doubt that "the method" cannot help a person carry a tune. Or even the otherwise magnificent Fred Astaire – just about any time he opened his mouth to sing in a relentlessly off-key croak. But Richard Gere is something else!

Apparently, recalling Jack Webb, Gere played the trumpet in a band during his high-school years and retains enough technique to enable him to learn some simplified horn solos written out note-for-note in a Bix-like style by the acclaimed mainstream jazz artist Warren Vaché (the back of whose head, playing cornet as a stand-in for Gere, appears in one brief musical scene). Ultimately, Gere's cornet playing is the only taste of humanized reality in the whole film and is therefore much to be savored. Specifically, this ambi-diegetic jazz reveals the character of Dwyer as at least serious about something (his music) and as a person of enough integrity (artistic commitment) to make us care what happens to him (a passable career as both musician and screen actor in gangster movies) and to help us believe that he deserves the love of an appealing woman such as Vera. If Dwyer did not play the cornet so attractively, we would be hard-pressed to find any persuasive reason to like him at all. Hence, as an instantiation of the art-versus-commerce theme, his ambi-diegetic cinemusical performances contribute meaningfully to the dramatic development of the film.

Unfortunately, however, these performances are few and far between. Inexplicably, they make no appearance whatsoever on the aforementioned soundtrack album. However, a careful viewing of *The Cotton Club* suggests at least one occasion on which the cornet work by Gere as Dwyer deserves careful notice and more than a little admiration. Specifically, in a scene where Dutch meets with his fellow mobsters while Dwyer and Vera wait impatiently in utter boredom, the gangster suddenly asks Dwyer to play that piece by Bix Beiderbecke. Dwyer responds by tossing off Beiderbecke's cornet solo from "Singin' the Blues" – the legendary performance that Bix (cornet) recorded with, among others, Frank Trumbauer (C-melody sax), Miff Mole (trombone), Jimmy Dorsey (clarinet), and Eddie Lang (guitar) on 4 February 1927. The importance of this improvisation emerges in the liner notes provided by producer George Avakian for *The Bix Beiderbecke Story* (n.d.):

> *Singin' the Blues* … is usually considered one of the three most celebrated solos in jazz history (the other two being King Oliver's cornet choruses on *Dippermouth Blues*, and Johnny Dodds' rendition of the original Alphonse Picou clarinet solo in *High Society*). It is a solo of intense, brooding beauty, carefully built up to a typical tumbling break in the middle, with a surprise explosion after it. There was hardly a contemporary white musician of jazz pretensions who didn't learn it by heart. Fletcher Henderson paid the ultimate tribute by recording it twice in a version for his whole brass section, and in the thirties Will Osborne and Adrian Rollini both waxed similar arrangements for full orchestra.

The present author knows the Beiderbecke solo by heart because – when he was a boy – his father used to play it verbatim on the piano. Years later, when searching for an apartment on New York's Upper West Side to be occupied by a visiting colleague, the author answered an anonymous ad in the *New York Times* for a sublet up on Riverside Drive and, when he got there, discovered that the whole place was filled with the most exquisite Oriental rugs. The owner had died, and his son gave a tour of the beautiful apartment with great courtesy and patience. At the end of this encounter, the son of the deceased mentioned that he used to be in the music industry but had taken a leave of absence to manage his Armenian father's rug-import business. He said he had been a record producer. When asked what sort of music he had recorded, he began, "Well, have you ever heard of Erroll Garner?" The author realized at once that he had struck pay dirt. The son's name, it turned out, was none other than … George Avakian. Such a nice man, so dedicated to this music. Besides his expertise on the subject of Beiderbecke and contributions to the priceless Bix reissues, Avakian was a tireless producer for such artists as Duke Ellington, Louis Armstrong, Benny Goodman, Dave Brubeck, Paul Desmond, Miles Davis, Sonny Rollins, J. J. Johnson, Erroll Garner, Art Blakey, Keith Jarrett, Charles Lloyd, and Bill Evans. We might wonder what

George Avakian – now in his late-eighties – thinks of Richard Gere's musical performances in *The Cotton Club*. Most likely, he approves.

### *Kansas City* (1996)

In approaching Robert Altman's *Kansas City* (1996), let us interpret this film from an angle consistent with our focus on the meaning of ambi-diegetic jazz – namely, as a continuation of the crime-plus-jazz genre in general, with implications for the commerce-versus-art theme in particular. This interpretation places *Kansas City* (1996) in the direct line of descent from *Pete Kelly's Blues* (1955) through *The Cotton Club* (1984) to the more recent cinematic scene. As suggested by the three-fold homologies developed as a table of parallel comparisons in the introduction, the problem is that *Kansas City* pursues the familiar themes without the help of any real music-performing hero. Indeed, instead of a horn-playing protagonist such as Pete Kelly (Jack Webb) or Dixie Dwyer (Richard Gere) to occupy the film's central core, the always-quirky Altman gives us a gun-toting anti-heroine.

This anti-heroine appears in the form of Blondie O'Hara (Jennifer Jason Leigh), whose major pre-occupation is to rescue her ne'er-do-well husband Johnny O'Hara (Dermot Mulroney) from the evil clutches of the gangster boss Seldom Seen (Harry Belafonte), who hangs out with all the other local Bad Boys at the Hey-Hey Club, where an exceedingly impressive roster of major jazz talent plays full-time 'round-the-clock jazz on a 24/7/365 basis in a kind of perpetual musical nirvana, more or less oblivious to the vile corruption that surrounds them on all sides. That corruption includes the violent detainment of Johnny, who has infuriated Seldom by mugging one of Seldom's out-of-town gambling customers. Betraying a grotesque degree of ***customer orientation*** and spouting caricatured rhetoric that sounds like a reading from the textbook for ***Marketing 101***, Seldom and his henchmen evince the link between commerce and crime while giving Johnny a very hard time – asking difficult questions, with typical Altmanesque irony, such as whether he likes the movies. Not really, it appears.

By contrast, Blondie loves motion pictures, idolizes movie stars, and has learned most of what she knows about both styling her peroxide-tortured hair and being a gun moll from watching old Jean Harlow films such as *Hold Your Man* (1933), which she brags she has seen six times. Desperate to free Johnny, she launches an elaborately convoluted scheme based on kidnapping one of her sister's manicure clients – Carolyn Stilton (Miranda Richardson), the wealthy but pharmacologically challenged wife of an unloving presidential advisor to FDR named Henry Stilton (Michael Murphy) – in order to force Henry to help get Johnny released. Predictably, the upshot of all this – after two hours of agonizing – is that Carolyn and Blondie have become sympathetic friends, but in a misbegotten recapitulation of Clark Gable's and Jean Harlow's misadventures in *Hold Your Man*, Johnny and Blondie are both … deceased.

This febrile, disjointed, gangster-laden story hovers like a lead balloon over the surface of the ambi-diegetic jazz that limns the atmosphere of the seedy Hey-Hey Club, where much of the action takes place. Miscreants obsessed with filthy lucre and other ill-gotten monetary gain come here to lie, to cheat, to steal, and to kill each other, while the musicians – Altman seems to say – just behave like the true artists they are (the ones with whom Altman identifies and hopes that we also identify). The guys in the band more or less ignore all the crime-related violence and mayhem, playing their music with total dedication and an air of detachment bordering on indifference to the degradation and vice that surround them. It makes sense to view this scenario as supporting the Altmanesque subtext that a jazz musician (read the true artist with creative integrity or the film director with a flair for spontaneity) must ignore the greed and corruption that run rampant through the interrelated worlds of business and crime (read the commercial pressures of the music industry or the profit motive of Hollywood). Better to remain detached, to do your own thing, and to create inspired improvisations than to become embroiled in the evils of commodification.

In this connection, the illustrious house band at the Hey-Hey Club includes, among others, Don Byron (clarinet); Nicholas Payton (trumpet); Joshua Redman, Craig Handy, James Carter, David Murray, and David "Fathead" Newman (saxophones); Geri Allen and Cyrus Chestnut (piano); Russell Malone and Mark Whitfield (guitar); Ron Carter and Christian McBride (bass); and Victor Lewis (drums). These musicians – all highly respected jazz masters, plus others too numerous to list here – play with total aplomb. The mood characterizing this scene is captured to telling effect by Oliver Stapleton's somber cinematography – all in hues of black, brown, gray, and other brooding colors. The club patrons wear the right clothing, adopt the right postures, and signify their approval with loud vocal encouragement.

The legitimacy of this scene benefits from the fact that the cinemusical performances are filmed in real time – that is, we see the jazz musicians captured on film ***while they are actually playing***, a stupendously worthwhile innovation in jazz filmology that harks back to the work of Bertrand Tavernier in *Round Midnight* (1986). Indeed, so good is the real-time ambi-diegetic music in *Kansas City* (1996) that Altman issued a 75-minute companion release entitled *Robert Altman's Jazz '34: Remembrances of Kansas City Swing* (1997), comprising full-length versions of tunes represented only by excerpts in the film. *Jazz '34* makes no pretense to dramatic content but ranks as one of the finest cinemusical presentations of jazz ever offered.

At many junctures in *Kansas City*, the on-screen presence of a musical group – jamming away on familiar tunes like "Indiana," "I Surrender Dear," and "Lullaby of the Leaves"; swinging "Blues in the Dark," "St. Louis Blues," and "Harvard Blues"; or playing simple head arrangements of well-known Kansas City standards such as "Moten Swing," "Tickle Toe," and "Froggy Bottom" – adds an aura of authenticity to a mise-en-scène that depends heavily on Altman's use of diegetic jazz with the KC flavor. A problem arises, however, in that most of these musicians – generally in their twenties or thirties in 1996 and born thirty or forty years after the heyday of the music they are called upon to play – do not sound very much like their KC role models. Rather, they mostly sound like exactly what they are – namely, young modernists trying to emulate a relaxed, bluesy sort of style from days of yore. The Kansas City feeling is there, found in such details as Mark Whitfield's Freddie-Green-styled comping on guitar and the smoothly chugging rhythm section with Geri Allen (piano), Christian McBride (bass), and Victor Lewis (drums) that this chording supports – approximating, as it does, the famous Green-Basie-Page-Jones sound associated with the "Count" Basie Band. But the harmonic language that characterized the historical guys from Basieland is totally transformed. The note selections of a Joshua Redman (as Lester Young), a Craig Handy (as Coleman Hawkins), or a James Carter (as Ben Webster) deviate sharply from anything that would ever have entered the head of the real Pres, Bean, or Ben. Young's ardent lyricism, Hawkins' busy arpeggios, and Webster's breathy throatiness – all quite old-fashioned by today's standards – are nowhere to be found. Instead, we hear three well-trained guys who sound as if they went to school on the Wayne Shorter transcriptions and the Jamey Aebersold play-along recordings – which, mostly, they did.

The real question that we should ask ourselves is whether the manifest musical incongruities just described really matter. On this issue, we might anticipate a continuum of opinions ranging between two divergent extremes, each of which deserves exploration. Let us call these polar perspectives the ***anti-Altman*** and the ***pro-Altman*** positions, respectively.

The ***anti-Altman position*** places a high positive value on the role of ***diegetic*** music in the ***realistic depiction*** of the mise-en-scène. This ***realism-oriented perspective*** would argue along the following lines.

(1) In order to achieve realistic depiction, a film must depict realistically.
(2) To depict realistically, the film must use props, costumes, décor, scenery, settings, and other aspects of consumption symbolism appropriate to the time and place in which the action occurs.
(3) Conversely, the appearance of consumption symbolism that is inappropriate to the time and place of the action tends to detract from the film's realistic depiction. For example, in the 1934 world of *Kansas City*, it would be inappropriately unrealistic to have Blondie drive a Chrysler PT Cruiser, to have Johnny wear a Tommy Hilfiger sweatshirt, to have Carolyn addicted to Prozac, or to have Henry plan his trip to Washington on a Treo Smartphone.
(4) By the same logic, realistic depiction requires that a film's diegetic music match the time and place in which the action occurs. Musicians playing at the Hey-Hey Club in Kansas City circa 1934 should look, sound, and behave as much like Lester Young, Coleman Hawkins, Ben Webster, "Hot Lips" Page, Jo Jones, Walter Page, "Count" Basie, Jay McShann, Mary Lou Williams, and the rest as humanly possible. Lester should hold his horn at a 90-degree angle, should play with spare melodic lyricism, should wear a porkpie hat and a thin moustache, and should utter phrases like "I feel a draft" or "I've got eyes" or "Lady Ben" or one of his other patented expressions.
(5) *Kansas City* gets the porkpie-hat part more or less right; but, in general, Lester Young (Joshua Redman), Coleman Hawkins (Craig Handy), Ben Webster (James Carter), Herschel Evans (David Murray), and the others come across as contemporary jazz players dressing up for a movie. In one scene, a saxophonist (James Carter as Ben Webster) plays a squealing passage that Ornette Coleman might have been proud of and then gives the others a look that comes more out of a Hip-Hop than a Hey-Hey sensibility. In another, Cyrus Chestnut delivers a mock version of stride piano with a harmonic structure so far past Bill Basie that it sounds more like something from Bela Bartok. Similarly, Geri Allen captures the piano style of Mary Lou Williams about as much as Jackson Pollack resembles Rembrandt. Meanwhile, Victor Lewis on drums recalls Jo Jones far less than "Philly" Joe Jones. Elsewhere, Ron Carter plays a pizzicato bass solo on "Solitude" (Altman's favorite song since his housekeeper introduced him to Duke Ellington back in the 1930s) in a manner not heard prior to the 1950s and with a tone not found in jazz until his own post-Scott-Lafaro playing with Miles Davis in the 1960s and beyond. Both he and Christian McBride on bass produce sustained low notes as different from the thumpy sound of (say) Walter Page as it is possible to imagine. And if Kevin Mahogany bears any resemblance to Jimmy Rushing on "I Left My Baby" – other than a tendency to be somewhat rotund – then this similarity remains a well-kept secret that *Kansas City* will do nothing to betray (especially given that Mahogany sings from behind the bar in the manner of Joe Turner).
(6) So every time we hear these musicians play – that is, often and for long periods throughout the entire film – we cannot help but think … ***anachronism***.
(7) In this sense, we may conclude that Altman's choice of diegetic jazz clashes with the film's objectives of realistic depiction.

***But***, in response to this anti-Altman argument, the ***pro-Altman position*** places a high positive value on the role of ***ambi-diegetic*** jazz in the ***dramatic development*** of plot, character, and other themes. This contrasting ***drama-oriented perspective*** would argue as follows.

(1) In order to achieve dramatic development, a film must develop dramatically.
(2) To develop dramatically, the film must use props, costumes, décor, scenery, settings, and other aspects of consumption symbolism that resonate with the emotions, identifications, and associations of leading characters, plot lines, and emerging themes.
(3) Conversely, the appearance of consumption symbolism that is inappropriate to the characters' emotions, plot-related identifications, or thematic associations tends to detract from the film's dramatic development. For example, in the sin-infested, crime-ridden, danger-filled world of *Kansas City*, it would be dramatically inappropriate to have Blondie drive a convertible sports coupe, to have Johnny wear tennis clothes, to have Carolyn drink beer, or to have Henry travel to Washington in a pickup truck.
(4) By the same logic, dramatic development requires that ambi-diegetic cinemusical meanings match the emotional tone, plot-related identifications, and thematic associations of the characters and events around which the action occurs. Musicians playing at the Hey-Hey Club in Kansas City should look, sound, and behave like guys at the periphery of a world embroiled in crime that they seek to escape by means of immersion in jazz.

In this connection, consider the following description of KC during the 1930s taken from a Website called "Club Kaycee," sponsored by The University of Missouri – Kansas City (www.umkc.edu/orgs/kcjazz/jazzspot/0venue.htm):

> During the 1920s and '30s, Kansas City was known as the "Paris of the Plains." Old Kaycee was the commercial and entertainment center for points North, West and South. … Political Boss Tom Pendergast made good-times and apparent prosperity possible. … Under the control of the Pendergast Machine, Kansas City was a wide open town and prohibition had little effect on "business as usual." Major industries included bootlegging, gambling, and prostitution. … Edward Morrow advised his readers in the *Omaha World Herald*, "If you want to see some sin, forget about Paris and go to Kansas City. … Kansas City probably has the greatest sin industry in the world." … Many of the city's clubs never closed. According to Milton Morris, owner of the Hey Hay Club [note the different spelling, disguised a bit in the film], it was customary to christen new clubs by giving a cab driver five bucks and the key to the front door of the club with instructions to drive as far as he could and throw away the key. Five dollars would send a cab a long way in those days. Club owners never closed their doors.

The evocation of this scene found in Altman's mise-en-scène for the Hey-Hey Club – which seems to be something of a composite of the real-life Hey-Hay, Cherry Blossom, and Reno Clubs – appears dramatically true to the emotions, identifications, and associations of importance. Specifically, the musicians drift in and out – talking, drinking, and even sleeping, but obviously coming to play. They take turns and trade choruses on the bandstand. For the most part, they maintain a laid-back KC-based rhythmic feeling in their performances. In the words of Gabbard, "the musicians … play in their own, more extroverted styles while trying to suggest the 'flavor' of their predecessors' playing" (2000, 145). And, most importantly, the jazz artists provide the counterpart to the "sin industry" so rampant elsewhere in the film – the point of contrast that spells out the alternative lifestyle to which those of an Altmanesque persuasion are called – namely, immersion in your own creative integrity though the world around you may be going to hell in a hand basket. Here, the parallels with

Altman-in-Hollywood suggest a strong and important art-versus-commerce subtext. Elsewhere, as revealed especially in the droll cynicism of *The Player* (1992), Altman finds the crass commercialism of the movie industry positively lethal. In reviewing *The Player*, Roger Ebert noted the "cold sardonic glee" with which Altman made this satiric "movie about today's Hollywood":

> This is material Altman knows from the inside and the outside. … Hollywood cast him into the outer darkness in the 1980s, when his eclectic vision didn't fit with movies made from marketing studies. … here is a movie that uses Hollywood as a metaphor for the avarice of the 1980s. (1992)

(5) *Kansas City* in general and its ambi-diegetic cinemusical meanings in particular get not only the porkpie-hat part pretty much right, but also a lot of the other emotions, identifications, and associations that surround the jazz community on the edge of a politically and ethically corrupt turmoil. In this film, the jazz musicians have no lines to recite. They do not interact with the criminals, do not dirty their hands with political involvements, and do not get involved with the gambling, drug dealing, prostitution, kidnapping, larceny, or murders that flank them on all sides. They just sit there and play their instruments – a feat requiring an almost superhuman dedication to their art and a prodigious ability to focus on the creative process despite the most harrowing distractions from all directions at once. To repeat, this situation significantly parallels the artistic struggles of Robert Altman in Hollywood.

Some sense of the fidelity with which Altman has captured these aspects of the KC jazz scene comes to light in the following description offered by Russell:

> Kansas City saxophonists in particular were a formidable lot. One night in 1934 at a club called the Cherry Blossom the leading saxophonist in jazz, Coleman Hawkins, had been challenged by a trio of Kansas City men – Lester Young, Herschel Evans, and Ben Webster, all unknown at the time – in a session that wore on until late the next day and left Hawkins battered and defeated. … Places with names like the Reno and Sunset, the Cherry Blossom, Subway, Hi-Hat, … and the Hey-Hay Club … had live music. The music began early in the evening and … continued around the clock. (1973, 30) … A *remarkable feature* of music in Kansas City was that *nobody told the musicians what to play or how to play it*. Jazzmen were *free to create* as the spirit moved them. … The gangsters who ran the clubs did not interfere. As the result of favoring conditions – steady work, isolation, a concentration of talent, and *almost total lack of commercial pressures* – Kansas City had developed a jazz style of its own. (32, italics added).

Once we abstract our way past the differences in musical style between the 1930s KC musicians and the young guys deployed in the ambi-diegetic jazz of *Kansas City*, it becomes clear that Altman has done a superb job of conveying the key thematic elements portrayed in the preceding quotation from Russell (1973) – namely, a fiercely competitive level of musicianship, an active club scene where the music never stops, a surrounding atmosphere of crime and corruption, and the ***freedom*** of the musicians to pursue ***maximum creativity*** unhindered by interference from the gangsters or by commercial pressures that might impede their ***artistic integrity***.

(6) So every time we hear these musicians play – that is, often and for long periods throughout the entire film – we must focus on the relevance of this ambi-diegetic jazz to the evocation of the film's major characters, plot lines, and thematic ideas. In this connection (cf. Gabbard 2000), a particularly effective use of ambi-diegetic jazz

appears in the scene featuring musicians at the Hey-Hey Club in which we witness a titanic tenor-saxophone battle between Coleman Hawkins (Craig Handy) and Lester Young (Joshua Redman). This frenetic musical ***cutting contest*** contrasts with the juxtaposed scene in which some of Seldom's henchmen drive a traitor named "Blue" Green (Martin Martin) to a distant and deserted location where, as the tenor battle concludes at 4:10 a.m. and as the two competing musicians shake hands triumphantly, the gangsters viciously knife "Blue" to death and leave him to the dogs. This disturbing demonstration of violently ***homicidal cutting*** contrasts with the parallel musical confrontation to telling effect. Here, we see a vivid opposition between the forces of rapacious criminality (evil commercialism) and the voices of pure jazz (artistic integrity). And lest we miss the point, the unfolding drama of the relevant homology is driven home by the ***cinematic cutting*** via which Altman presents both sides of the juxtaposition simultaneously. In short, we observe ***cutting*** from ***three vantage points*** that, in effect, compose a revelatory sort of ***dialectic*** consisting of a ***thesis*** ("cutting" via a sublime saxophone battle); an ***antithesis*** ("cutting" via a murder by stabbing); and a ***synthesis*** ("cutting" via a cinematic montage). Thus, in Altman's foreboding use of ambi-diegetic jazz to presage the counterposed forces of evil about to unfold, the on-screen music does its job of providing contrasting emotions, identifications, and associations to perfection. The fact that Joshua Redman and Craig Handy sound more like each other than like either Lester Young or Coleman Hawkins becomes irrelevant. The important set of homologies has far more to do with the vivid contrast between Joshua-and-Craig trading choruses as opposed to murderers stabbing "Blue" Green. The relevant dialectical tension and resolution provide a deep sense of … ***synthesis*** (cf. Gabbard 2000).

(7) In this sense, we may conclude that Altman's choice of ambi-diegetic jazz fulfills the film's objectives of dramatic development. Along similar lines, another astute use of on-screen jazz pursues the "in between" aspect of what Gabbard refers to as "shifts between diegetic and extradiegetic registers" (2000, 146). Specifically, in the scene where Blondie and Carolyn first begin to form a sympathetic bond, we hear piano music that soon turns out to emanate from Geri Allen playing the role of Mary Lou Williams at the Hey-Hey Club.

According to Gabbard:

> Surprising the audience by showing them that Geri Allen/Mary Lou Williams has been playing behind the first moment of bonding between the two female leads is typical of how Altman … rethought the conventional practice of cinema sound in … *Kansas City*. (147)

In another passage from Russell, we find the following highly relevant account of the peripheral role played by Charlie Parker – the immortal "Bird" – on the Kansas City jazz scene circa 1934:

> Charlie Parker was very much a product of this vigorous grassroots musical culture. … His father was … a singer and dancer. Charlie's mother, Addie Boyley, was a local girl whom the entertainer had married in her seventeenth year. (1973, 32) … Between 1928 and 1939 … Charlie Parker underwent a metamorphosis from an unexceptional schoolboy studying at Crispus Attucks grammar school to one of the geniuses of American music. (33)

This aspect of Bird's background, it turns out, becomes a central metaphor in Altman's film – one that we notice only gradually and only if we pay very careful attention (cf. Gabbard 1996).

An early scene in *Kansas City* shows a young girl – 14-year-old Pearl Cummings (Ajia Mignon Johnson) – arriving at the train station where she expects to be met by some well-intentioned but incompetent white society ladies who have charitably brought her there for purposes of giving birth to her illegitimate baby but who have managed to be late for meeting the train. Returning from a trip with his high-school marching band – alto saxophone in hand – a youthful Charlie Parker (Albert J. Burnes) finds Pearl sitting in the white section of the waiting-room seats, warns her that this is forbidden, and then – with common sense and protectiveness far beyond his years – takes her with him to the mezzanine of the Hey-Hey Club where, still holding his horn in case we have missed the point, Charlie proceeds to act as a sort of Greek Chorus by explaining to Pearl, as well as to us viewers, the significance and identities of the musicians performing on the stage below in general and of Lester Young in particular.

Meanwhile, when Blondie kidnaps Carolyn, she takes the wealthy politician's wife to the Western Union office for purposes of sending a telegram calling him back from his trip to Washington, DC. There, we encounter the cleaning lady doing her evening chores. However improbably, this cleaning lady turns out to be Addie Parker (Jeff Feringa) – Charlie's mother (who actually did have a job with Western Union in real life). But this is typical Altman – a director for whom all roads, no matter how disparate, tend always to lead toward convergence in the end. In this connection, recall (say) *Nashville* (1975) or *Short Cuts* (1993). In a similar spirit of convergence, the telegraph-office scene gives Blondie a chance to ask Addie how her son Charlie is doing with his music. It turns out that Charlie Parker is doing just fine, thank you. Meanwhile, via his protectiveness toward Pearl, Charlie is busy revealing himself to be one of the two estimable characters (not counting the ambi-diegetic musicians) to be found in the film – the other, in her own warped way, being Blondie (in one of Jennifer Jason Leigh's most surpassingly quirky roles).

Ultimately, it is really Parker through whose eyes we see much of the film unfolding. He sits up there in the balcony while the musicians play their ambi-diegetic jazz and, also, while the gangsters carry Blondie screaming from the Hey-Hey Club. There he sits while all the musical beauty and criminal ugliness transpire. He of all people in the film appreciates the deep opposition between crime (commercial greed gone amuck) and jazz (artistic integrity held aloft). And, of course, he also seems to represent the sensibilities of the director Robert Altman (cf. Gabbard 2000, 151).

In this connection, notice that – like Charlie Parker – Robert Altman came from Kansas City. Like Parker in the film, Altman himself was 14-years-old when Parker, as leader of Jay McShann's saxophone section, left town. It takes little imagination to envision Robert Altman, at age fourteen, sitting in the balcony and watching the heroic Charlie Parker perform in the same manner that Charlie Parker in Robert Altman's film sits and watches his own avowed hero Lester Young.

So, in the last analysis, maybe this film ***does*** have a real music-performing hero after all. Maybe its true cinemusical hero is Lester Young – through the eyes of Charlie Parker – via the sensibilities of Robert Altman. Charlie Parker was born in Kansas City on 29 August 1920. Robert Altman was born in Kansas City on 20 February 1925. But Bird has been dead for fifty years. Fortunately, Altman survived until 2006 to tell the tale.

## Conclusion

The foregoing interpretations begin with a table of homologous parallels among three major crime-plus-jazz films. The specific analyses of each film suggest that all three lend themselves to an understanding based on the contrast or conflict between commerce (as represented by the selfish, greedy, and/or tainted aspects of crime) and art (as represented by the creative, honest, pure aspects of jazz). Though this subtext remains mostly implicit – below the surface level – in all three motion pictures, it appears clearly to those willing to unfold the meanings implicit in the juxtaposition of crime and jazz that colors all three films and that speaks volumes about the underlying tension between commerce and art. Commerce – as mirrored by the persistently self-interested and resolutely evil activities of common criminals – comes across as inherently evil or at least highly suspicious. Art – by contrast, as mirrored by the bravely self-sacrificing and stubbornly courageous jazz performances of the true music-for-music's-sake heroes – emerges as a force that shines forth as a source of sweetness and light. Apparently, in the face of crime, *film noir* has a potential bright side. And its name is jazz.

## References

*After the Thin Man.* Directed by W.S. Van Dyke. Burbank, CA: Warner Home Video, 1936.

Biancorosso, Giorgio. 2001. Beginning credits and beyond: Music and the cinematic imagination. *ECHO* 3, no. 1. http://www.humnet.ucla.edu/echo/volume3-issue1/biancorosso/biancorosso.html.

*Born to Dance.* Directed by Roy Del Ruth. Burbank, CA: Warner Home Video, 1936.

Bradshaw, Alan, Pierre McDonagh, and David Marshall. 2006. Response to "Art versus commerce as a macromarketing theme." *Journal of Macromarketing* 26, no. 1: 81–3.

*Cotton Club.* Directed by Francis Ford Coppola. Santa Monica, CA: MGM Home Entertainment, 1984.

Ebert, Roger. 1992. The player. *Chicago Sun Times,* April 24. http://rogerebert.suntimes.com.

Feather, Leonard. 1960. *The new edition of the encyclopedia of jazz.* New York: Bonanza Books.

Gabbard, Krin. 1996. *Jammin' at the margins: Jazz and the American cinema.* Chicago: University of Chicago Press.

———. 2000. Kansas City dreamin: Robert Altman's jazz history lesson. In *Music and Cinema,* ed. J. Buhler, C. Flinn, and D. Neumeyer, 142–57. Westport, CT: Wesleyan University Press.

*Guys and Dolls.* Directed by Joseph L. Mankiewicz. Santa Monica, CA: MGM Home Video, 1955.

Holbrook, Morris B. 1985. The consumer researcher visits Radio City: Dancing in the dark. In *Advances in consumer research,* vol. 12, ed. E.C. Hirschman and M.B. Holbrook, 28–31. Provo, UT: Association for Consumer Research.

———. 2003. A book-review essay on the role of ambi-diegetic film music in the product design of Hollywood movies: Macromarketing in La-La-Land. *Consumption, Markets & Culture* 6, no. 3: 207–30.

———. 2004. Ambi-diegetic music in films as a product-design and placement strategy: The sweet smell of success. *Marketing Theory* 4, no. 3: 171–85.

———. 2005a. The ambi-diegesis of "My Funny Valentine." In *Pop fiction – the song in cinema,* ed. Steve Lannin and Matthew Caley, 48–62. Portland, OR: Intellect.

———. 2005b. Ambi-diegetic music in the movies: The Crosby duets in *High Society*. *Consumption, Markets and Culture* 8, no. 2: 153–82.

———. 2005c. Art versus commerce as a macromarketing theme in three films from the young-man-with-a-horn genre. *Journal of Macromarketing* 25, no. 1: 22–31.

———. 2006. Reply to Bradshaw, McDonagh, and Marshall: Turn off the bubble machine. *Journal of Macromarketing* 26, no. 1: 84–7.

———. 2007. When bad things happen to great musicians: The role of ambi-diegetic jazz in three tragedepictions of artistic genius on the silver screen. *Jazz Research Journal.* 1, no. 1: 99–128.

Holbrook, Morris B., and Mark W. Grayson. 1986. The semiology of cinematic consumption: Symbolic consumer behavior in *Out of Africa. Journal of Consumer Research* 13, no. 3: 374–81.

Holbrook, Morris B., and Elizabeth C. Hirschman. 1993. *The semiotics of consumption: interpreting symbolic consumer behavior in popular culture and works of art.* Berlin and New York: Mouton De Gruyter.

*Hold Your Man.* Directed by Sam Wood. Burbank, CA: MGM/Warner Home Video, 1933.

*Inside Man.* Directed by Spike Lee. Hollywood, CA: Universal Studios, 2006.

*Kansas City*. Directed by Robert Altman. Los Angeles, CA: New Line Home Video, 1996.
Kassabian, Anahid. 2001. *Hearing film: Tracking identifications in contemporary Hollywood film music.* New York: Routledge.
*Manhattan Murder Mystery*. Directed by Woody Allen. Culver City, CA: Sony Pictures, 1993.
Marks, Martin. 2000. Music, drama, Warner Brothers: the case of *Casablanca* and *The Maltese Falcon.* In *Music and cinema,* ed. J. Buhler, C. Flinn, and D. Neumeyer, 161–86. Hanover, NH: Wesleyan University Press.
Meeker, David. 1981. *Jazz in the movies.* New York: Da Capo Press.
*Mo' Better Blues.* 1990. Directed by Spike Lee. Hollywood, CA: Universal Studios, 1990.
*Nashville.* Directed by Robert Altman. Hollywood, CA: Paramount, 1975.
*New York, New York.* Directed by Martin Scorsese. Beverly Hills, CA: United Artists, CBS/Fox Video, 1977.
*Pete Kelly's Blues.* Directed by Jack Webb. Burbank, CA: Warner Home Video, 1955.
*Player.* Directed by Robert Altman. Lyme, CT: New Line Home Video, 1992.
*Robert Altman's Jazz '34: Remembrances of Kansas City Swing.* Directed by Robert Altman. Los Angeles, CA: Rhapsody Films, 1997.
Rosar, William H. 2002. Film music – what's in a name? *Journal of Film Music* 1, no. 1: 1–18.
*Round Midnight.* Directed by Bertrand Tavernier. Burbank, CA: Warner Brothers, 1986.
Russell, Ross. 1973. *Bird lives! The high life and hard times of Charlie (Yardbird) Parker.* New York: Charterhouse.
*Short Cuts.* Directed by Robert Altman. Los Angeles, CA: New Line Home Video, 1993.
*Stormy Weather.* Directed by Andrew L. Stone. Beverly Hills, CA: 20th Century Fox, 1943.
*Sweet Smell of Success.* Directed by Alexander MacKendrick. Culver City, CA: MGM/UA Home Video, 1957.
*The Pink Panther.* Directed by Blake Edwards. Los Angeles, CA: MGM Home Entertainment, 1964.
*The Score.* Directed by Frank Oz. Hollywood, CA: Paramount Pictures, 2001.
*Young Man with a Horn.* Directed by Michael Curtiz. Burbank, CA: Warner Home Video, 1950.

## Discography

Lee, Peggy and Ella Fitzgerald. *Songs from Pete Kelly's Blues.* Decca 8166, 1955, reissued as Decca MVCJ-19197, 1999.
Mancini, Henry. *The Music From Peter Gunn.* BMG 7446599610 2, 1999.
———. *More Music From Peter Gunn.* RCA Victor 74321 29857 2, 1995.
Matlock, Matty, Dick Cathcart, Moe Schneider, Eddie Miller, Ray Sherman, George Van Eps, Jud DeNaut, Nick Fatool, and others. *Classic Columbia Condon Mob Sessions.* Mosaic MD8-206, 2001.
Matlock, Matty and his Jazz Band. *Pete Kelly's Blues.* Columbia CL 690, 1955, partially reissued as Mosaic MD8-206, 2001.
Pete Kelly's Big Seven (Matty Matlock, Dick Cathcart, Moe Schneider, Eddie Miller, Nick Fatool, George Van Eps, Ray Sherman, Jud DeNaut). *Pete Kelly's Blues.* Nar. Jack Webb. RCA Victor, 1955, reissued as BMG DRC12081 CCM-055-2, 1998.
*The Bix Beiderbecke Story* (Bix Beiderbecke). Prod. George Avakian. Columbia CL 845, n.d.
Various. *The Cotton Club: Original Motion Picture Soundtrack.* Prod. John Barry. Geffen GEFD-24062, 1984.

# Towards a critical understanding of music, emotion and self-identity

David Hesmondhalgh

*Institute of Communications Studies, University of Leeds, UK*

The article begins by outlining a dominant conception of these relations in sociologically-informed analysis of music, which sees music primarily as a positive resource for active self-making. My argument is that this conception rests on a problematic notion of the self and also on an overly optimistic understanding of music, which implicitly sees music as highly independent of negative social and historical processes. I then attempt to construct a) a more adequately critical conception of personal identity in modern societies; and b) a more balanced appraisal of music-society relations. I suggest two ways in which relations between self, music and society may not always be quite so positive or as healthy as the dominant conception suggests: 1) Music is now bound up with the incorporation of authenticity and creativity into capitalism, and with intensified consumption habits. 2) Emotional self-realisation through music is now linked to status competition. Interviews are analysed.

Music provides a particularly interesting example of modern relations between consumption and self-identity. Many people report that music plays a very important role in their lives. This role does not appear to have diminished with industrialisation, commodification, and the mass consumption of music; if anything, it has grown. The continuing and perhaps growing importance of music in everyday life may be based on two contrasting but co-existing dimensions of musical experience in modern societies. The first is that music often feels intensely and emotionally linked to the private self. As one leading music sociologist has put it, music is a set of cultural practices that have come to be intricately bound up with the realm of the personal and the subjective (Martin 1995, 2). The second is that music is often the basis for collective public experiences, whether in live performance, or simply by virtue of the fact that thousands and sometimes millions of people can come to own the same recordings. These features are not necessarily contradictory; in fact, they may support and reinforce each other. Our excitement or sadness can be intensified through the sense that such emotions in response to a particular piece of music are shared, or even *potentially* shared. This feeling can be especially strong at a live performance, but it is just as possible when experiencing music individually, when we might, however semi-consciously and fleetingly, imagine others – a particular person or untold thousands – being able to share that response. (This is one of the pleasures of pop music and also perhaps a reason why many people are suspicious of it.)

Music, then, represents a remarkable meeting point of the private and public realms, providing encounters of self-identity (this is who I am; this is who I'm not) with collective identity (this is who we are; this is who we're not). Of course all cultural products have this potential – films, television programmes, even shoes and cars. Yet music's often-noted link to the emotions arguably makes it an especially powerful site for such encounters. Whether music really is more strongly connected to the emotions than other cultural forms, the fact that it is widely assumed to be so is itself significant. For we now live in societies where the private self has never been, in sociologist Eva Illouz's words, "so publicly performed and [so] harnessed to the values of the economic and public spheres" (2007, 4). It is no longer possible to sustain the idea that the private sphere offers some kind of opposition to, or protection from, a world of public power, with the former understood as "warm" and intimate and the latter as a "cold," rational, administrative domain. No doubt, many people cope with the demands of their working lives by telling themselves that their family offers a "haven in a heartless world" (Lasch 1977). But in reality, those realms we think of as "personal" – our inner selves and our relationships with families, lovers and close friends – are hugely affected by the world beyond them. This may be more so now than ever, as powerful commercial and state institutions in advanced industrial countries increasingly require autonomy, creativity and emotional roundedness in their employees and citizens – an issue I investigate below. This means that music, with its real or projected connections with the emotions and with self-realisation, may itself be increasingly politicised.

This article therefore explores how we might understand the relationships between music, emotion, selfhood and public identity. My goal is primarily theory building, but I also draw on some empirical work.[1] I begin by claiming that there is *a dominant conception of music, emotion and personal identity* in sociologically informed analyses of music, and I show this by examining work by three leading analysts. This dominant conception sees music primarily as *a positive resource for active self-making*. My argument is that this conception rests on a problematic notion of the self and also on an overly optimistic understanding of music, which implicitly sees music as somehow independent of negative social and historical processes. I then draw on other theorists to attempt to construct (1) a more adequately critical conception of personal identity in modern societies and (2) a more balanced appraisal of music-society relations. In particular, I suggest two ways in which relations between self, music and society may not always be quite so positive or as healthy as the dominant conception suggests. The first is that music, with its strong links to the emotions and to values of personal authenticity, may well have become bound up with the incorporation of emotional self-realisation, authenticity and creativity into capitalism, and with intensified consumption habits, processes that some writers plausibly claim may be having damaging effects on the psychological health of male individuals. These possibilities are explored via the analysis of an interview with a man who has a particularly strong attachment to musical consumption. The second is that such emotional self-realisation is linked to status competition, in particular over the degree to which individuals are "emotionally sensitive" and over involvement in hedonistic collective activity. Again I examine interview material to explore these possibilities. In the conclusion, I draw out some implications of the piece for the study of musical consumption, and for cultural consumption in general. I also briefly distinguish my perspective from two other critical perspectives that a hasty reading might confuse with my own, those influenced by Adorno and Foucault.

## The dominant conception: music as a positive resource for self-identity

In recent studies of musical consumption, a particular view of the relationship between music, emotion and self-identity has come to prevail. I want to show this by discussing three important contributions by sociologically informed commentators. I begin with anthropologist Ruth Finnegan's (2003) survey of a range of ethnomusicological research. Finnegan argues that more attention needs to be paid to emotion in music. But, she is clear that the emphasis should not be on "trying to penetrate and pin down hidden internal states" but rather "on the manner, variably practiced and conceptualized in different contexts, in which people are personally involved in their musical engagements" (188). Finnegan emphasises the sheer range of emotions at work in musical performance and practice:

> It is not so much self-conscious internalized "feelings" – though in some cultural settings that is indeed one element – as the contextualized manner of people's musical engagements: joyfully, fearfully, attentively, reflectively, proudly; in a spirit of exaltation or energy or irritation; in sorrowful, celebratory or nostalgic mood; with boredom (that too!), with dance, with tranquillity. (188)

Finnegan then summarises her view of how music itself figures in people's emotional lives: "Whether in deeply intense fashion or more light-touch action, music provides a human resource through which people can enact their lives with inextricably entwined feeling, thought and imagination" (2003, 188).

Music, then, is seen as a *resource*, and one at the disposal of humans conceived in a particular way: creative, active, imbued with agency, diverse, and performative (in the interactionist sense, rather than in the way in which the post-structuralist writer Judith Butler [1993] uses the term).

A second account of music and identity relevant to my concerns in this article is by Simon Frith in his book *Performing Rites* (1996). The overall aim of that book is to provide a sociologically informed aesthetics of popular music. The book climaxes with an eloquent account of the power of popular music, which is a summation of this aesthetics. Underlying this account is the idea that music has a particular and special ability to offer a route towards self-creation through fantasy. Music

> seems to make possible a new kind of self-recognition, to free us from everyday routines, from the social expectations with which we are encumbered. ... Music constructs our sense of identity through the experiences it offers of the body, time, and sociability, experiences which enable us to place ourselves in imaginative cultural narratives. (Frith 1996, 275)[2]

This is linked to a very constructionist conception of the self, which seems to be derived from symbolic interactionism, mediated here through the emphasis in cultural studies on the centrality of symbolic forms in modern social processes: "Identity comes from the outside, not the inside; it is something we put or try on, not something we reveal or discover" (275). I shall return to this conception of the self in due course, but the main point I wish to make is that here, as in Finnegan's account, there is a strong sense of music as a resource that allows people to enrich their lives.

The third contribution is that of Tia DeNora. In two insightful, readable, and stimulating books, *Music in Everyday Life* (2000) and *After Adorno: Rethinking Music Sociology* (2003), DeNora has made an extremely important contribution to the sociology of music. As explained above, it is her account of music, emotion and the self that I am particularly concerned with, and so her chapters entitled "Music as a technology of self" (DeNora 2000, 46–74) and "How does music 'channel' emotions?" (DeNora 2003, 83–117) are most relevant here. Self-identity is understood as a production of the continuing activity of individuals, rather as a fixed inner essence, as in older conceptions of personality. The title of the first of these chapters recalls Foucault's use of the term "technologies of the self" (Foucault 2000), but in fact, DeNora's approach to subjectivity is very un-Foucauldian and owes more to interactionism, pragmatism and Anthony Giddens's conception of modern self-identity as based upon reflexivity (DeNora 2000, 46; Giddens 1991). Drawing on interviews and ethnography, DeNora aims to show music

> in action as a device for ordering the self as an agent, and as an object known and accountable to oneself and others… Music is a material that actors use to elaborate, to fill out and fill in, to themselves and to others, modes of aesthetic agency and, with it, subjective stances and identities. (2000, 73–4)

Again, as with Finnegan and Frith, there is a strong sense of music as a resource to be used. This is applied explicitly to emotions: "music is a resource for modulating and structuring the parameters of aesthetic agency – feeling, motivation, desire, comportment, action style, energy" (De Nora 2000, 53). This should not be understood as the expression by music of "some internal emotional state"; rather, "music is part of the reflexive constitution of that state" (57). DeNora calls this kind of reflexive activity "emotion work" (2003, 96; 2000, 53). And as with Finnegan (including the latter's classic study of *The Hidden Musicians* – Finnegan [1989]) and Frith, the attitude is overwhelmingly positive. Time and again, for DeNora, music is found to be enriching experience, adding to agency and enhancing dimensions of people's everyday lives. It can be used for attaining and maintaining states of feeling, for aiding concentration, and more generally for retrieving memories and therefore "remembering/constructing who one is" (DeNora 2000, 63). This is demonstrated using a set of interviews and ethnographic observations with subjects who appear to be overwhelmingly white, middle-class, educated women.

It is perhaps worth briefly relating this dominant tendency in the study of musical consumption and experience[3] to other research that may be more familiar to readers of this journal. Reviewing 20 years of articles in *The Journal of Consumer Research*, Eric J. Arnould and Craig J. Thompson identify a number of features of what they call consumer culture theory (CCT), "a family of theoretical perspectives that address the dynamic relationships between consumer actions, the marketplace, and cultural meanings" (2005, 868). There are overlaps between the dominant conception outlined above and key features of this CCT tradition. As Arnould and Thompson put it:

> CCT research has emphasized the productive aspect of consumption. [It] explores how consumers actively rework and transform symbolic meanings encoded in advertisements, brands, retail settings, or material goods to manifest their particular personal and social circumstances and further their identity and lifestyle goals. … From this perspective, the marketplace provides consumers with an expansive and heterogeneous palette of resources from which to construct individual and collective identities. (871)

Here too, then, the emphasis is on the active and reflexive agency of consumers – though there is more stress than in the dominant conception of music consumption and self-identity, discussed above, on the market origins of the cultural products that provide consumers with their resources (Frith's work is a major exception to this – see Frith [1981]).[4] In media sociology, too, this emphasis on the active nature of consumption has been strongly manifest. In some respects, for example, DeNora's approach recalls the uses and gratifications tradition in communications research, with its emphasis on how audiences "use" media products to fulfil certain personal needs (for example, Herta Herzog [1941] on the way women gain "emotional release" from daytime radio serials). In other respects, it has much in common with the "uncritical cultural populism" (McGuigan 1992) of audience research in Anglophone media and cultural studies in the 1980s and 1990s, when a focus on "active audiences" was the basis of what one writer has called a "consumptionist orthodoxy" within those academic fields (Born 1993).

## Beyond the dominant model: problems of self-realisation in modern societies

I now want to question the positive conception of music, and some assumptions about the self, underlying the accounts of music, emotion and self-identity discussed above. I do not doubt that people mobilise music in the various positive ways outlined by these writers. As I explore elsewhere (Hesmondhalgh 2007), there are many positive, emancipatory aspects to people's relationships to music in modern societies. Yet, the dominant conception (music as a positive resource for self-identity) seems to me to downplay various ways in which music may become implicated in some less pleasant and even disturbing features of modern life. The dominant conception rightly emphasises the social nature of music and of self-identity, but if music is as imbricated with social processes as the dominant conception suggests, then it is hard to see how people's engagements with music can be so consistently positive in their effects, when we live in societies that are marked by inequality, exploitation and suffering. While it is true that people have been miserable and mistreated in all human societies, it is also the case that, as numerous sociologists have taught us, including Georg Simmel and C. Wright Mills, private lives, personal biographies and mental states should not be detached from history. Can music really be so autonomous that it floats free of social forces? And, turning to self-identity, might not people's projects of self-creation (to use DeNora's term) or self-recognition (to use Frith's), *and therefore their uses of music as part of these projects*, have some more difficult and troubling dimensions than emerges in the dominant conception?

There is a psychological dimension to this that I cannot develop in this article but which I want to signal here. The dominant conception underestimates the psychic difficulties that individuals face in constructing a coherent and healthy self-identity. It is true to say that humans can act on their environment and upon their selves, but they surely do so in ways that are limited not only by social and historical factors (such as poverty, deprivation, lack of education or training) but also by their own personal biographies. One need not be a full-on Freudian to recognise that damaging experiences in early life can place severe constraints on what it is possible to do in later life – including the way we interact with music and how we might use it to shape our selves.

In this article, however, it is the way in which emotions and self-identity become bound up in problematic aspects of modern societies that I want to explore, and then apply to music. A seminal contribution was by Arlie Hochschild (1983), who analysed workers' experiences of service employment. These jobs appeared comfortable and rewarding, but for Hochschild, involved new and distinctive forms of control and alienation, whereby workers were being required to internalise at the deepest level the emotional responses required *to look as though they love their jobs*. Her most striking example was the way that flight attendants are trained to smile by airlines that promote their service on the basis that "our smiles are not painted on." One implication of Hochschild's study was that the emotional self-management made possible by new forms of self-identity in capitalist modernity could be appropriated in dubious ways by powerful interests. If this is true, then this suggests that the use of music to achieve emotional self-management – analysed by DeNora and others – may not always be healthy either.[5]

My main interest here, though, is on the historical dimensions of the appropriation of goals of self-realisation and autonomy by powerful interests. The German social theorist Axel Honneth has argued that increasingly, in the twentieth century, "members of Western societies were compelled, urged or encouraged, for the sake of their own future, to place their very selves at the centre of their own life-planning and practice" (2004, 469). As a result, individual self-realisation becomes linked to "institutionalized expectations" and "transmuted into a support of the system's legitimacy" (Honneth 2004, 467). Honneth does not sufficiently specify what this might mean in his suggestive article, but a more thorough sociological account, compatible with Honneth's, is provided by Luc Boltanski and Eve Chiapello in their tour-de-force *The New Spirit of Capitalism* (2005). Boltanski and Chiapello differentiate two principal ways in which capitalist societies have been criticised – social critique and artistic critique. Social critique emphasises poverty, inequality, the opportunism and egoism of private interests, and the destruction of social bonds brought about by capitalism. Artistic critique, with its roots in bohemianism and romanticism, instead stresses capitalism as a source of disenchantment and inauthenticity, and the limits it places on freedom, autonomy and creativity (Boltanski and Chiapello 2005, 35–8). Boltanski and Chiapello trace how, faced with a crisis of legitimacy and motivation in the late 1960s, under pressure from both the social and artistic critiques (coming together in the events of 1968 in France and across much of the world) capitalist institutions responded by validating the artistic critique, especially critical demands for autonomy in working life. Measures aimed at providing security for workers were replaced by measures aimed at relaxing hierarchical control and allowing people to fulfil their individual potential (Boltanski and Chiapello 2005, 190). The result is a society based on a "connexionist" model where the self is an individual enterprise, and where transitory relationships and commitments are considered more legitimate than stable ones because rapidly changing one's connections can supposedly lead to personal growth and greater self-realisation. In this connexionist society, individuals are increasingly expected to take responsibility for themselves, even though those selves are borne down upon by all kinds of social pressures. Honneth and Boltanski and Chiapello all write about the potentially damaging effects of that pressure on individuals. However consciously sceptical individuals may be, "the ideal of self-realization is experienced … subliminally … as posing demands upon the manner in which one's subjectivity is to be formed," as Honneth puts it (2004, 467). The result, Honneth claims, drawing on a variety of sources, is a rise in the levels of depression in society – though depression is not necessarily to be understood in clinical terms here. It may involve a combination of "symptoms of inner emptiness, of feeling oneself to be superfluous" with "hectic and enervating activities" (478). Boltanski and Chiapello (2005, 420–4), meanwhile, place greater stress on anxiety and anomie, citing statistics on the rising numbers of suicides.

These writers, then, show how the autonomous self-realisation implicitly celebrated by the dominant conception, has come to be linked to power. All this has a direct relevance to cultural consumption – and indeed to musical consumption. For Honneth, a key basis of "organised self-realisation" was that individuals in the twentieth century increasingly felt compelled "to seek an intensification of one's own feeling of being alive in the consumption of cultural products" (2004). This derives from a protestant undercurrent in which an "uncommon state of emotional excitement was taken to be a sign of God's goodness and grace" (478). This co-existed with the protestant work ethic – and did not necessarily contradict it. For Honneth, drawing on the historian Colin Campbell, this undercurrent eventually becomes the basis for "a massive investment in intensity-enhancing consumer goods" (478). Daniel Bell's thesis that modern individualistic hedonism contradicts the functional demands of capitalism, leading to crisis, has not been borne out. Rather, for Honneth, it has only strengthened capitalism. The presence of shorter and more fragile bonds between people (powerfully analysed by Sennett [1998], among others), and the tendency for leisure to be seen as a key means of self-definition, do not radically conflict with the needs of the capitalist economy. Indeed, according to Honneth, these facets of modern societies have become a productive force in their own right, in that they fuel cultural consumption.

Similarly, for Boltanski and Chiapello, in the new connexionist society that has arisen in the wake of capitalism's appropriation of the artistic critique, "People's aspirations to mobility, to multiply their activities, to greater opportunities for being and doing, emerge as a virtually boundless reservoir of ideas for conceiving new products and services to bring to the market" (2005, 437). Innovation is strongly connected to this need for liberation, including transport and automation, but it now includes devices that allow people to be active while mobile. For Boltanski and Chiapello, intriguingly given our present concerns, music is the archetypal form of such contradictory freedoms.[6]

However, there is another way in which music is connected to these developments, which neither Honneth's article (2004) nor Boltanski and Chiapello (2005) comment upon. This is music's own active role in fuelling capitalism's incorporation of autonomy – in Boltanski and Chiapello's terms, its centrality to the artistic critique. The most prominent musical genres of the last century – jazz, rock, soul and hip-hop – have all been strongly tied up with romantic notions of personal autonomy. Rock in particular accompanied the kind of historical changes tracked by Boltanski and Chiapello, producing a culture that was centred on values of rebellious creativity, but that in retrospect, was assimilated very quickly to values of commercialism. The mainstream rock music of the 1980s and 1990s, with its often unchallenging celebrations of mobility and unfettered individuality, can be seen to conform closely to Boltanski and Chiapello's connexionist world.[7] When dozens of nostalgic rock documentaries look back to the glory years of rock rebellion, they provide a comfortable picture of bohemianism for older viewers now immersed in a very different kind of autonomy.

Such critical perspectives on consumption and self-identity are missing from the dominant conception which sees music as a positive resource for self-making. Admittedly, however, these are large-scale sociological-historical claims. A great challenge is to apply them to the individual lives of people, without doing violence to the specificity of those lives, or to the undoubted truth that people do have some freedom to shape their own cultural practices. While the fundamental aim of this article is primarily to question the *theoretical* assumptions regarding emotion and self-identity underlying studies of musical consumption, in the next section, I reflect on these issues using empirical case studies, in the manner of DeNora's micro-sociological analyses, but examined from a perspective influenced by the critical and historical accounts outlined above.

## Case study 1: a collector

As we have seen, both Honneth and Boltanski and Chiapello point to ways in which the quest for personal meaning and self-realisation in capitalist modernity helps to fuel consumption, and also to how "organised self-realisation" (partly through consumption but also through the development of more formally autonomous types of labour) seems to be resulting in greater society-wide levels of anxiety and depression. It is interesting in this context to consider those people who seem to place a particularly strong emphasis on self-realisation through musical consumption, if only as a limit case, while recognising their atypicality.

For example, one of our interviewees Paul, a 40-year-old hairdresser, was interviewed in a room lined with hundreds of CDs and records. His main loves were rock, R&B, soul and reggae, but his collection included other material too. What united them was music that was in some way "challenging" (the Rolling Stones, Neil Young and Prince were his favourites). He had contempt for music that was "empty," with "no real feeling." At the salon where he worked, Paul was well known for being a musical aficionado, and his conversations with customers often centred on music. However, Paul's collecting was a source of real tension in his relationship with his wife. In Paul's presence, his wife Helen told the interviewer that she found his record collecting and his playing of loud music obtrusive and irritating. She expressed anger concerning the sheer amount of money Paul spent on music and music equipment. And in the salon where he worked, Paul could be very dominant in asserting his views about what kind of music should be played. Paul's relationship to music seemed a defiant statement about his independence – both within the family and within society. He acknowledged that his desire to buy music constantly, to accrue amounts of music that he could not possibly play more than once or twice, was irrational, but he revelled in that irrationality.

Paul's love of music, then, provided an important part of his identity. Whether his pleasure in music might be understood via DeNora's concept of reflexive "emotional work" (see DeNora 2000, 53–8), however, is another matter. Or at least there were uncomfortable aspects to his relationship with music, of a kind that barely seems to appear in the dominant conception of music and self-identity. Active and positive self-making may have been involved here, but there were some other, more ambivalent aspects also involved.

It might be objected that Paul's "problems" here have nothing to do with music, that music was simply a vehicle through which he and his wife found a reason to express their ambivalence towards each other. If music had not been there, one might say, they would have found other ways to quarrel with each other. But this is to see music as passive, as dead matter with no consequence, rather as active material that has an effect upon the world, when combined with human agency. It is surely more interesting to ask: What is it that made music the basis of this disagreement? Why music and *not* something else? And here, it is important I think that Paul was drawn to rebellious, individualistic music and expressed disdain for music he considered conformist. Somehow the notion of music as (at its best) intensely and genuinely expressive comes to stand for Paul as a defence against what he portrays as the emptiness of much of the rest of the world. This attitude, it seems, may indeed help him in certain situations in his life (after all, music undoubtedly has positive uses and I am not denying that), but it is also likely to lead to some psychological trouble too – of a kind that the dominant conception does not recognise. In Paul's case, the quest for personal authenticity through music becomes so important that it almost seems to fill his house, in spite of the objections of his partner. Yet, this authenticity is somehow transferred onto the collection, and music can sometimes seem elusive compared with the solidity of these ordered and alphabetised commodities.

It is also useful in this context to consider the gendered nature of record collecting – and arguably collecting more broadly. It is not fair to try to interpret Paul's motivations on the basis of a short interview, but it seems reasonable to think that at the very least, the obsessive pursuit of completeness and order exhibited by collectors such as Paul might also be an example of disavowal, in that huge amounts of time and effort and emotion are devoted to categorisation and knowledge, rather than to music as a source of "emotional work" (in DeNora's sense). In fact, almost inevitably, most of the records and CDs in Paul's vast collection went unplayed, and he admitted to having difficulty in discussing his emotional engagement with music. There are strongly gendered dimensions to such disavowal; boys in modern societies can be strongly discouraged from open displays of emotion. But, combined with dynamics of social power that are somewhat underplayed in the dominant conception, this can lead to exclusions. As Will Straw (1997, 15) has incisively discussed, the "nerdish homosociality" of record collectors, while relatively harmless compared with more blatant displays of masculinist power in popular music cultures, is as fundamental to the unequal gender politics of pop as any phallic guitar strutting.

## Status competition through music

I turn now to another problematic aspect of music-self-society relations downplayed by the dominant model of music consumption, where music is seen as a positive resource for forging self-identity. This is the way that the use of music for self-realisation, self-management or self-recognition can be subject to aspects of competitive individualism that tend to be prevalent throughout modern societies. The work of Pierre Bourdieu is relevant here. Where writers from various disciplines and traditions (including "consumer culture theory" and media studies of "active audiences" – see above) see an abundance of creative agency in contemporary cultural consumption, Bourdieu's (1984) *Distinction* is well known for stressing its darker, competitive aspects. In fact, Bourdieu singles out music from all other forms of culture in terms of its power to act as a marker of class differentiation.[8] And this is bound up, for Bourdieu, with a number of factors: the way in which music is particularly associated with "interiority," an emphasis on the value of "listening" in modern societies – including in psychoanalysis (which Bourdieu distrusted), and the socially imputed purity of music, its tendency to slip towards negation of the world.

There have been responses to Bourdieu from sociologists of music (Frith 1996; Hennion 2003; see also Hesmondhalgh 2006 on Bourdieu's assumptions about popular culture as manifest in his studies of cultural production). In my view, in terms of the concerns of this article, Bourdieu is too cynical about the role of aesthetic experience, and this may in part derive from his excessively sociological analysis, which is also curiously lacking in any consideration of the emotions when it comes to cultural consumption. Nevertheless, Bourdieu helps us to see that cultural consumption cannot be so easily separated from the competitive individualism of modern societies as writers such as Finnegan, DeNora and Frith imply.

In his article, "On status competition and emotion management," the Dutch historical sociologist Cas Wouters (1991) offers a perspective on modern competitive individualism that in my view is more useful for considering music consumption in relation to emotion and self-identity than Bourdieu's work. Wouters traces how in some respects it has become increasingly difficult for powerful groups to show superiority through traditional means such as "birth," displays of wealth and physical violence. Instead, displays of efforts to experiment with new lifestyles and tastes become increasingly important in the everyday lives of many people in advanced industrial societies, *and so too does an awareness and knowledge of emotions*. In some circles and some situations, we might say, being a sensitive emotional individual is a key marker of superiority. Such superiority needs at its best (its most superior) to come naturally – and this means, for Wouters, that much of the work involved is done in secret in order to conceal from others the effort needed to articulate oneself as an authentic individual. Wouters does not say in this article how the dynamics he observes may take different forms in different social spaces – for example, among different social classes. Nevertheless, I think that there is something suggestive here for the study of music. Music can be part of status battles to show one's openness to a variety of lifestyle pleasures and one's superior emotional range. After all, as we saw at the beginning of this article, music has come to be linked, perhaps more than any other cultural form, with the emotional dimensions of our selves.

Competitive individualism is also a relevant frame for examining how people talk about music's capacity to intensify sociality, celebrated in much of the literature (Filmer 2003). Whether in the dance club, at a funeral, or on a radio show inviting its audience to look back nostalgically on past times, music offers the emotional intensity craved by modern consumerism (recalling Honneth's account, above). This can be about sadness, catharsis and self-awareness; but it can also be about fun, pleasure and sociality. In a hedonistic society of the kind hypothesised by Honneth, then, music may actually be attached even more strongly than other socio-cultural forms to a certain *duty to have pleasure.*[9] By this, I refer to the way modern individuals compete over who is having the most fun, who is gaining most from life. To use modern language, anyone who is not living it large is a loser.

I suggest, then, that there are two ways in which music might be the basis of status battles in modern society: in terms of the emotional sensitivity of its consumers, and in terms of its basis for hedonistic pleasures. To investigate these issues, I now turn again to interview material.

### Case study 2: competition over sensitivity and pleasure

We asked our interviewees to play us records that brought back strong memories through music, and to discuss them. John, a 27-year-old teacher living in Cumbria, played us a club version of a track by Garlic called "Not Over Yet" (remixed by Paul Oakenfold).

> When I first heard it, it was played in a club in Liverpool, right at the end of the night. It's actually called "It's Not Over Yet" and the music sort of went out and everybody thought it was time to go home, and then this came on. … And I just thought great, it's not over yet.

Here, music serves, for reasons that DeNora (2000, 66–8) discusses eloquently in *Music as Everyday Life*, as a repository for memory. It is because music, like clothing or smells, is part of "the material and aesthetic environment" in which it is experienced that the past comes alive when certain music is heard. DeNora, as ever, uses vibrantly positive language to describe this. The creation of musical "moments" are "due in part to the alchemy of respondents' perceived or sensed 'rightness' or resonance between the situation, the social relationship, the setting, the music, and themselves as emerging aesthetic agents" (De Nora 2000, 67).

I reiterate my view that music can have these positive dimensions. But a more balanced sociology of music needs to recognise that music will also be tied to problematic aspects of the self, perhaps especially in societies like ours. There is a methodological issue here in examining interview material. People's memories are unreliable – they may recall happy times through music that were in fact riddled with ambivalence. They may even unconsciously present themselves as having lives (past or present) that are more rounded and dynamic than they really are. Such tricks of memory can be helpful: in bad times, a certain memory – invoked by music or not – may give people hope that the future might be good again, as the past once was. But it may also romanticise or sentimentalise relationships that were in fact deeply difficult and painful. And music is perhaps especially prone to such romanticisation or sentimentalisation because of the special way in which it evokes that intensity of feeling and of collective hedonism that we are encouraged to feel is a mark of being a successful person in capitalist modernity (see above).

In fact, it transpired that this was the last time that this young man went clubbing with his friends. John was by the time of the interview living in rural Cumbria. John indicated elsewhere in his interview that this was not an easy place for him to be, and there was a poignancy to this choice of record: why choose a record explicitly associated with collective fun with friends in the city, when living in this rather isolated environment? We should not rule out the possibility that his choice of this particular musical memory is both an example of how music can positively provide some comfort in recollections made from a different position in one's life, but that it also might be a way in which an interviewee presents herself or himself as having a more rounded and satisfying life than is actually the case. Perhaps

John chose a clubbing record to say "I am someone who has friends, who knows how to have fun in the big city." This is not music's "fault" and there is nothing "wrong" with John doing this, but it means that to see music as a positive resource in self-making may not tell the whole story. Or, to put it another way, there are more ways to read John's responses than via the lens of music as a positive resource for self-identity.

Let me now analyse further interview material, in terms of competitive individualism over "emotional sensitivity." Here I want to outline some different ways in which middle-class people are able to present themselves to interviewers as rounded, musically sensitive individuals. I want to take just three different examples: James, a retired university lecturer; Ian, a social worker; and Lauren, a church minister. In all three cases, I discuss how these people have successfully incorporated a critique of snobbery or exclusion into their accounts, in order to present themselves as open-minded and sensitive people. (And this is one of the things that makes Wouters a more appropriate lens through which to view this material than Bourdieu).

First, James, a retired university lecturer in metallurgy, talked about a favourite Mozart piece (K563): "It's called a divertimento which suggests something light but it's actually a most profound piece of chamber music, fully the equal of any of his string quartets and of course they are as lovely as anything in the world." There are echoes here of some of Bourdieu's respondents in *Distinction* (for example, the case study of the "truly classical" university teacher: see Bourdieu 1984, 288–90). But James was doing more than just displaying his cultural capital – he was also making an implicit set of claims about his emotional sensitivity to music and the way it fitted into his relations with others. In talking about music he does not like, James was extremely careful to qualify his comments ("I mean it's always it's all right for you, it's easy for you to talk, you've had a silver spoon in your mouth all your life"). He also differentiated himself from a "cold," technical or intellectual approach to loving music, embodied in the figure of a piano teacher he knew from church (and this anecdote was followed immediately by "I like her very much as a person"):

> I think she probably thinks I'm a frivolous old devil but she teaches a lot of the youngsters and [...] every now and then she puts on little concerts of her protégés in church after the Sunday service with proceeds to a charity or something like that. And I remember going up to her once after a concert which I had been very impressed by and amongst other things I said – meaning it entirely as a compliment to her – "Well, [...] you have achieved something because your pupils obviously enjoy making music." She looked at me and she almost spat and said, "Music isn't about enjoyment it's about understanding."

What better way of illustrating one's own capacity for enjoyment, for pleasure, than by invoking the figure of someone who is devoted entirely to an insensitive notion of musical understanding?

Second, Ian, a business studies lecturer from London, was one of a number of respondents who emphasised how his tastes had expanded over time, and who was therefore able to put together a personal narrative based on a growing aesthetic consciousness. Ian emphasised his growing omnivorousness ("I've always been interested in literature and music I would say, I've always been interested in most things really, and I suppose what you would call current affairs and what's going on in the world and that kind of thing"). The thread through his expanding musical tastes, beginning with rock ("It was actually more in my mid to late teens that I got into music, you know like we used to listen to John Peel late at night and heard stuff like Captain Beefheart and Kevin Coyne and the Soft Machine"), and expanding into contemporary music, was the idea of "weird" sounds. Ian set this against the "blandness" of "boring" music, across a wide range of musical genres, from soft rock ("When I was in Mozambique, there was a guy who was particularly into *Hotel California* by the Eagles, which I absolutely hated and despised") to traditional rock and roll ("I just found it utterly boring, utterly tedious" – as opposed to the "magic" of blues artists like Robert Johnson) to Mozart ("There was a bit of Mozart on the radio and I was saying how fucking boring it sounded, and how tedious Mozart was"). But Ian displayed his musical – and emotional – openness by showing that he was able to find value in unlikely places, indicating a growing sensitivity that comes with age:

> His ex-partner was really into the Pet Shop Boys and we had this argument about the Pet Shop Boys, he was telling me how they actually have really good well-put-together pop songs – which actually I can hear. You know stuff I would have really hated in the past, I've had my ears opened to, bits of George Michael you know.

Finally, Lauren, an American woman in her forties, had lived in an English city for 25 years and was working as an ordained minister at a local church. Lauren expressed her sadness and anger at the legacy of imperialism via music ("It saddens me no end when I hear Indian and African Victorian hymns, I think 'where's their music, where's their culture?'") and, when asked to play us a piece of music that she had recently enjoyed, chose a track called "Oh Robin" from an album called *Music for a Harmonious World*. This featured singers from England singing in collaboration with singers from South Africa. What Lauren valued was how the music "allowed each other's genres to be there, the English people are singing English style music, the Africans singing African music and the way it moves together is just stunning." This is not just an aesthetic experience, Lauren is saying, it is also ethical, tied to concerns about imperialism and oppression.

Now all these interviewees are involved in using music to construct self-identity. All of them do so sincerely. All of them eschew snobbery by opposing symbols of high culture (the cold, technical piano player; Mozart, hailed as a genius, is in fact "boring"; the Victorians who could not accept otherness). The problem is that in our class-divided society, these people are actually engaged in a new form of status battle, which has replaced the "sense of distinction" analysed by Bourdieu (1984). Important contributions to the sociology of consumption have drawn attention to some of these changing dynamics, including how omnivorousness has replaced snobbery as the goal of "highbrow" taste.[10] Here, I am trying to capture changing dynamics that are specific to music. My claim is that in-depth analysis of qualitative interviews can lead to very different conclusions about music, emotion and self-identity from those drawn by the dominant conception.

A further point is worth noting briefly. It is difficult to imagine working-class subjects being able to tell such convincing stories of self-realisation through music. Rather, our working-class interviewees tended to be flummoxed by attempts to articulate what they like in music. This means that relying on interviews with middle-class subjects in examining musical self-identity in music – as DeNora does – is likely to lead to an incomplete sociology of music.

### Concluding comments

What are the implications of these arguments for the analysis of musical consumption? The main implication is that studies of musical consumption need to be much more cautious in the models of subjectivity they operate. In DeNora's work, for example, there is a considerable and mostly welcome emphasis on the interrelations of music, self and society. But her notion that individuals are capable of somehow producing their own subjectivity via music is problematic. It not only downplays the limits and constraints on the self-making that derive from psychological limitations, but it also posits a model of social self-making that downplays or even ignores negative social processes. The positive way in which the dominant conception understands people's uses of music needs to be complemented. Apparently positive notions of authenticity and autonomy have been incorporated into powerful ideologies – not fully, but at least partially.

There are implications, too, for the study of cultural consumption. Consumer culture theory, for example, as outlined by Arnould and Thompson (2005), shows some striking similarities with what I am here calling the dominant conception of music, emotion and self-identity. It emphasises the active reworking by consumers of meanings encoded in consumer products and the use by these consumers of cultural resources to "produce" their own identities. Similarly, there is a huge amount of work in media studies that purports to show the same dynamics at work among media consumers. But if my criticisms of the dominant conception are correct, then this suggests that consumer culture theory and media sociology also need to be much more cautious in applying these ideas to contemporary consumption and self-identity.

I want to make it clear that my approach here is not an Adornian one. It may superficially seem to have something in common with Adorno's approach to music, in that it stresses the inter-relatedness of music and certain aspects of social power. And it is true that no one has applied a historical understanding of subjectivity so relentlessly to musical culture as a whole than did Adorno. His writings on music have been criticised by many for being historicist, for being insufficiently attuned to the active role of individuals in constructing meaning, and for his speculative drawing of inferences about society from the analysis of particular social phenomena or merely from artistic works. Bigger problems for me are his idealistic requirement that art should aspire to impossible levels of autonomy and dialectic, his failure to recognise adequately the ambivalence and complexity in both "high culture" and "popular culture," and linked to this, his seeming contempt for everyday cultural consumption in modern societies. A significant challenge for critical analysts, then, is to produce a historically informed but *non-Adornian* account of music-related subjectivity. My aim here is to contribute to such a project, and not to revive Adornian criticism (see Born [1993] for important reflections on these issues).

Nor is my approach here a Foucauldian one. Foucault developed a notion of subjectivity that has been hugely influential and that provides an alternative to the interactionist and pragmatist notion of the self that dominates much sociology and that lies at the heart of the dominant conception of music, self and society criticised in this article. Foucault's notion of subjectivity places much more emphasis on power and constraint. It sees the self as constituted in power and discourse, and the job of the critical analyst is to reveal how the self came to be thought of in the ways that it generally is in modern societies. Foucauldians would generally share my suspicion of the notion of active self-making from cultural resources – but from a different standpoint. For Foucault's notion of the self (for example, Foucault 2000) has little or no room for the discussion of emotions, of experience, or any notion of interiority. These are all elements that I think are important to an adequate sociological notion of music consumption in relation to self-identity (for a helpful survey of these issues, comparing different theoretical conceptions of self-identity, see Elliott 2008).

Music, like other cultural forms, provides opportunities for people to make connections with each other, to enrich their inner lives, and even in some cases, to enhance a sense of community. Some people are lucky enough to be able to exploit these opportunities to the full. But because of a number of socio-historical factors discussed in this article, and also for psychological reasons that I have not been able to explore fully here, music's power to enable self-making is constrained, limited and damaged. An adequate sociology of musical consumption needs to recognise this political complexity.

## Notes

1. The empirical material used in this article is drawn from fieldwork interviews carried out with a range of English and Welsh people about their musical practices, tastes and values in 2002–4. Forty-two semi-structured interviews were conducted by a team of seven interviewers – myself, Stephanie Adams, Lorna Ashcroft, Surinder Guru, Jackie Malone, Dave Morris and Ian Robinson – funded by The Open University's National Everyday Cultures Programme. Recruitment aimed at a balance of social classes, a roughly equal mix of men and women, and a reasonable spread of age groups, from those in their 20s to those in their 70s. Five interviews were with "non-white" subjects. My thanks to Tony Bennett and Elizabeth Silva, who directed the programme; to the other interviewers, especially Stephanie Adams; and to those interviewed.
2. I wonder if there are pointers towards a more complex view in Frith's words. After all, this is presented as one kind of self-recognition, and the "seems" here hints at an awareness of the limits of such imaginative self-making.
3. For further critical discussion of cognate studies of musical consumption, including those derived from theories of neotribalism, see Hesmondhalgh (2005).
4. Arnould and Thompson briefly note the presence of a more critical strand of CCT work, which sees identities as aligned in some cases "with the structural imperatives of a consumer-driven global economy" (2005, 871–2).
5. DeNora refers explicitly to Hochschild's studies (2003, 96; 2000, 53), including her concept of "emotional work," yet she does not register Hochschild's critical orientation or her contrastive concept of "emotional labour."
6. The ambivalent qualities of consumer uses of mobile music devices are well captured by Michael Bull (2005), in ways that have implications for the dominant conception. For Bull, users employ iPods and so on to reclaim urban space, but they do so by privatising it.
7. The best accounts of this aspect of rock culture are by Simon Frith (1981) and Keir Keightley (2001).
8. "Nothing more clearly affirms one's 'class,' nothing more infallibly classifies, than tastes in music" (Bourdieu 1984, 19). The contrast with the dominant conception of music consumption is worth noting, along with its opposition to wider views, including leading musicologist Nicholas Cook who asserts that "music is an essentially democratic art" (1990, 2).
9. Bourdieu discusses "pleasure as a duty" in discussing the emerging cultural habits of "the new petite bourgeoisie" (1984, 367). Also relevant here is Featherstone's notion of "calculating hedonism" (1991).
10. A seminal example is Peterson and Kern (1996). However, see Warde, Martens and Olsen (1999) for a helpful survey and critique of some of this American empirical work on the sociology of consumption.

## References

Arnould, Eric J., and Craig J. Thompson. 2005. Consumer culture theory (CCT): Twenty years of research. *Journal of Consumer Research* 31, no. 4: 868–82.

Boltanski, Luc, and Eve Chiapello. 2005. *The new spirit of capitalism.* Trans. Gregory Elliott. London: Verso.

Born, Georgina. 1993. Against negation, for a politics of cultural production: Adorno, aesthetics, the social. *Screen* 34, no. 3: 223–42.

Bourdieu, Pierre. 1984. *Distinction.* Trans. Richard Nice. London: Routledge.

Bull, Michael. 2005. No dead air: The iPod and the culture of mobile listening. *Leisure Studies* 24, no. 4: 343–55.

Butler, Judith. 1993. *Bodies that matter.* London and New York: Routledge.

Cook, Nicholas. 1990. *Music, imagination and culture.* Oxford: Clarendon Press.

De Nora, Tia. 2000. *Music in everyday life.* Cambridge: Cambridge University Press.

———. 2003. *After Adorno: rethinking music sociology.* Cambridge: Cambridge University Press.
Elliott, Anthony. 2008. *Concepts of the self.* Cambridge: Polity.
Featherstone, Mike. 1991. *Consumer culture and postmodernism.* London: Sage.
Filmer, Paul. 2003. Songtime: Sound culture, rhythm and sociality. In *The auditory culture reader,* ed. M. Bull and L. Back, 91–116. Oxford: Berg.
Finnegan, Ruth. 1989. *The hidden musicians.* Cambridge: Cambridge University Press.
———. 2003. Music, experience and the anthropology of emotion. In *The cultural study of music,* ed. M. Clayton, T. Herbert and R. Middleton, 181–92. London: Routledge.
Foucault, Michel. 2000. Technologies of the self. In *Ethics: Subjectivity and truth,* 16–49. Vol. 1 of *Essential works of Foucault, 1954–1984*. London: Penguin.
Frith, Simon. 1981. *Sound effects.* London: Constable.
———. 1996. *Performing rites.* Oxford: Oxford University Press.
Giddens, Anthony. 1991. *Modernity and self-identity.* Cambridge: Polity.
Hennion, Antoine. 2003. Music and mediation: Toward a new sociology of music. In *The cultural study of music,* ed. M. Clayton, T. Herbert and R. Middleton, 80–91. London: Routledge.
Herzog, Herta. 1941. On borrowed experience. *Studies in Philosophy and Social Science* 9: 65–95.
Hesmondhalgh, David. 2005. Subcultures, scenes or tribes? None of the above. *Journal of Youth Studies* 8, no. 1: 21–40
———. 2006. Bourdieu, the media and cultural production. *Media, Culture and Society* 28, no. 2: 211–32.
———. 2007. Aesthetics and audiences: Talking about good and bad music. *European Journal of Cultural Studies* 10, no. 4: 507–27.
Hochschild, Arlie. 1983. *The managed heart: Commercialization of human feeling.* Berkeley: University of California Press.
Honneth, Axel. 2004. Organized self-realization: Some paradoxes of individualization. *European Journal of Social Theory* 7, no. 4: 463–78.
Illouz, Eva. 2007. *Cold intimacies: The making of emotional capitalism.* Cambridge: Polity.
Keightley, Keir. 2001. Reconsidering rock. In *The Cambridge companion to pop and rock,* ed. S. Frith, W. Straw and J. Street, 109–42. Cambridge: Cambridge University Press.
Lasch, Christopher. 1977. *Haven in a heartless world.* New York: Basic Books.
Martin, Peter J. 1995. *Sounds and society.* Manchester: Manchester University Press.
McGuigan, Jim. 1992. *Cultural populism.* London: Routledge.
Peterson, Richard A., and Richard Kern. 1996. Changing highbrow taste: From snob to omnivore. *American Sociological Review* 61, no. 5: 900–7.
Sennett, Richard. 1998. *The corrosion of character: The personal consequences of work in the new capitalism.* New York: Norton.
Straw, Will. 1997. Sizing up record collections: Gender and connoisseurship in rock music culture. In *Sexing the groove: Popular music and gender,* ed. S. Whiteley, 3–16. London: Routledge.
Warde, Alan, Lydia Martens, and Wendy Olsen. 1999. Consumption and the problem of variety: Cultural omnivorousness, social distinction and dining out. *Sociology* 33, no. 1: 105–27.
Wouters, Cas. 1991. On status competition and emotion management. *Journal of Social History* 24, no. 4: 699–717.

# Index

Page numbers in **Bold** represent Figures

Routledge
Taylor & Francis Group

# Culture, Theory and Critique

**EDITORIAL BOARD:**
**Greg Hainge**, *University of Queensland, Australia*
**Richard King**, *University of Nottingham, UK*
**Mark Millington**, *University of Nottingham, UK*
**Mireille Rosello**, *University of Amsterdam, The Netherlands*
**Jon Simons**, *Indiana University, USA*
**Lisa Walsh**, *University of Nottingham, UK*

***Culture, Theory and Critique*** is a refereed, interdisciplinary journal for the transformation and development of critical theories in the humanities and social sciences. It aims to critique and reconstruct theories by interfacing them with one another and by relocating them in new sites and conjunctures. ***Culture, Theory and Critique'*** approach to theoretical refinement and innovation is one of interaction and hybridisation via recontextualisation and transculturation. The reconceptualisation of critical theories is achieved by:

- assessing how well theories emerging from particular spatial, cultural, geographical and historical contexts travel and translate into new conjunctures.
- confronting theories with their limitations or aporias through immanent critique.
- applying theories to cultural, literary, social and political phenomena in order to test them against their respective fields of concern and to generate critical feedback.
- interfacing theories from different intellectual, disciplinary and institutional settings.

Given its interdisciplinary character, ***Culture, Theory and Critique*** will appeal to anyone working at the interface between disciplines such as gender studies, cultural studies, critical geography, historiography, literary theory and criticism, film studies, philosophy, postcolonialism, social and political theory and visual culture.

**SUBSCRIPTION RATES**
2008- *Volume* 49 (*2 issues per year*)
Print ISSN 1473-5784
Online ISSN 1473-5776
Institutional rate (print and online): US$310; £189; €248
Institutional rate (online access only): US$294; £179; €235
Personal rate (print only): US$94; £58; €75

---

**informa**world

A world of specialist information for the academic, professional and business communities. To find out more go to: **www.informaworld.com**

eupdates
Taylor & Francis Group

Register your email address at **www.informaworld.com/eupdates** to receive information on books, journals and other news within your areas of interest.

**For further information, please contact Customer Services at either of the following:**
**T&F Informa UK Ltd, Sheepen Place, Colchester, Essex, CO3 3LP, UK**
**Tel: +44 (0) 20 7017 5544 Fax: 44 (0) 20 7017 5198**
**Email: tf.enquiries@informa.com**
**Taylor & Francis Inc, 325 Chestnut Street, Philadelphia, PA 19106, USA**
**Tel: +1 800 354 1420 (toll-free calls from within the US)**
**or +1 215 625 8900 (calls from overseas) Fax: +1 215 625 2940**
**Email: customerservice@taylorandfrancis.com**

**View an online sample issue at:**
**www.informaworld.com/rctc**

Routledge
Taylor & Francis Group

# Rethinking Marxism

**A Journal of Economics, Culture and Society**

**Please visit the Rethinking Marxism website at http://rethinkingmarxism.org/cms/**

**EDITOR:**
**David F. Ruccio,** *University of Notre Dame, USA*

The aim of ***Rethinking Marxism*** is to stimulate interest in and debate over the explanatory power and social consequences of Marxian economic, cultural, and social analysis. To that end, we publish studies that seek to discuss, elaborate, and/or extend Marxian theory. Our concerns include theoretical and philosophical (methodological and epistemological) matters as well as more concrete empirical analyses-all work that leads to the further development of distinctively Marxian discourses. We encourage contributions from people in many disciplines and from a wide range of perspectives. We are also interested in expanding the diversity of styles for producing and presenting Marxian discourses.

We are interested in promoting Marxian approaches to social theory because we believe that they can and should play an important role in developing strategies for radical social change-in particular, for an end to class exploitation and the various forms of political, cultural, and psychological oppression (including oppression on the basis of race, gender, and sexual orientation). We especially welcome research that explores these and related issues from Marxian perspectives.

**SUBSCRIPTION RATES**
2008 - *Volume* 20 (*4 issues per year*)
Print ISSN 0893-5696
Online ISSN 1475-8059
Institutional rate (print and online): US$363; £218; €290
Institutional rate (online access only): US$344; £207; €275
Personal rate (print only): US$90; £52; €72

---

**informa**world

A world of specialist information for the academic, professional and business communities. To find out more go to: **www.informaworld.com**

eupdates
Taylor & Francis Group

Register your email address at **www.informaworld.com/eupdates** to receive information on books, journals and other news within your areas of interest.

**For further information, please contact Customer Services at either of the following:**
**T&F Informa UK Ltd, Sheepen Place, Colchester, Essex, CO3 3LP, UK**
**Tel: +44 (0) 20 7017 5544 Fax: 44 (0) 20 7017 5198**
**Email: tf.enquiries@informa.com**
**Taylor & Francis Inc, 325 Chestnut Street, Philadelphia, PA 19106, USA**
**Tel: +1 800 354 1420 (toll-free calls from within the US)**
**or +1 215 625 8900 (calls from overseas) Fax: +1 215 625 2940**
**Email: customerservice@taylorandfrancis.com**

**View an online sample issue at:**
**www.informaworld.com/rrmx**

Routledge
Taylor & Francis Group

# Myth & Symbol

**EDITOR:**
**Rochelle Sadowsky,** *University of South Africa, South Africa*

***Myth & Symbol*** publishes original scientific articles pertaining to the study of myth and symbol. It is specifically devoted to a long-neglected, but rapidly developing, domain of research in the humanities dealing with mythological language and symbolic behaviour. The journal strives to be an open forum for the discussion of myth and the implications of myth in contemporary society by means of peer reviewed research articles, critical reviews, historical explorations, theoretical discussions and book reviews. The journal aims to become the platform for original interdisciplinary research in the field of the study of myth in all its aspects.

Co-published with UNISA

UNISA university of south africa PRESS

**SUBSCRIPTION RATES**
Volume 5, 2008, 2 issues per year
Print ISSN 1022-3827
Online ISSN 1753-5972
Institutional rate (print and online): US$200; £102; €160
Institutional rate (online access only): US$190; £96; €152
Personal rate (print only): US$74; £38; €59

---

**informa**world — A world of specialist information for the academic, professional and business communities. To find out more go to: **www.informaworld.com**

eupdates Taylor & Francis Group — Register your email address at **www.informaworld.com/eupdates** to receive information on books, journals and other news within your areas of interest.

**For further information, please contact Customer Services at either of the following:**
**T&F Informa UK Ltd, Sheepen Place, Colchester, Essex, CO3 3LP, UK**
**Tel: 020 7017 5544 Fax: 020 7017 5198**
**Email: tf.enquiries@informa.com. Website: www.tandf.co.uk/journals**
**Taylor & Francis Inc, 325 Chestnut Street, 8th Floor, Philadelphia, PA 19106, USA**
**Tel: +1 800 354 1420 (toll-free calls from within the US)**
**or +1 215 625 8900 (calls from overseas) Fax: +1 215 625 2940**
**Email: info@taylorandfrancis.com. Website: www.taylorandfrancis.com**

**When ordering, please quote: XJ07001A**

**www.informaworld.com/rmas**